Contemporary Issues Series

Immigration: New Directions for the Future

A Critical Analysis of the Federal Government's Role in Changing Immigration Policy

Scott Deatherage
Assistant Professor, Communication Studies, and Director of Forensics
Northwestern University, Evanston, Illinois

National Textbook Company
a division of *NTC Publishing Group* • Lincolnwood, Illinois USA

Published by National Textbook Company, a division of NTC Publishing Group.
© 1994 by NTC Publishing Group, 4255 West Touhy Avenue,
Lincolnwood (Chicago), Illinois 60646–1975 U.S.A.
Manufactured in the United States of America.

4 5 6 7 8 9 0 VP 9 8 7 6 5 4 3 2 1

Contents

Introduction

Last year alone, the Immigration and Naturalization Service approved nearly 700,000 applications made by aliens seeking permanent legal residence in the United States. In the same year, the I.N.S. apprehended another 1.5 million persons seeking illegal entry at the border. Estimates range as to the number of illegal immigrants who go undetected; some figures put the number as high as one million per year. A host of factors drive immigration, legal and illegal, into the United States. Some people come to escape economic hardship, while others want asylum from political repression.

Whatever the instigating factor, as these statistics demonstrate, the 1994–1995 national high school debate topic is both timely and debatable. The issues that it addresses are fraught with controversy and should remain important topics on the public policy agenda for years to come. While the resolution has numerous and varied components, a few are likely to dominate competitive debating, particularly at the outset of the season: This volume excerpts seminal works in these areas so as to provide readers with a solid grounding in these central issues.

In 1990 President Bush signed into law the Immigration Act, Public Law No. 101-649. The law represents the most broad ranging changes in immigration ever attempted. The Immigration Act of 1990, which has its roots in congressional initiatives beginning in 1979, is as controversial as it is complex. The Act makes both quantitative and qualitative changes in the make-up of American immigration. The Act increases the number of acceptable immigrants, making its primary focus the reunification of families who have been separated in previous migrations. The family based provisions of the Act have been particularly controversial, partially because its provisions are difficult to judge and implement. The family reunification grounding of American immigration law has always been open to charges of fraud and abuse, but these 1990 Amendments have intensified that debate.

The 1990 Act also makes some substantial changes in the responsibility scheme for businesses who might have illegal immigrants in their employ. The law aims to better coordinate immigration visas with the needs of business and industry by establishing a hierarchy of preferred skills and professions, but much of the responsibility for enforcing the employment based provisions of the statute resides with employers. The terms of the act make employers liable for failure to perform certain procedures aimed at determining the eligibility status of resident aliens.

Miguel Lawson and Marianne Grin have written a comprehensive treatment of the Immigration Act of 1990 in the *Harvard International Law Journal.* While their work is largely normative, not evaluative, it nonetheless is an essential beginning for any debater looking to understand the nuances of the 1990 Act. In it, they discuss in detail the family based and business based provisions of the law, along with its diversity provisions, themselves a matter of substantial controversy.

The impact of the employment related provisions of the Immigration Act of 1990 are perhaps the most contentious of issues arising from the Act's passage. An excellent analysis of the economic impact of the new Act is Stephen Moore's "Immigration Policy: Open Minds on Open Borders." Moore's analysis is somewhat different from the conventional business related criticisms of the Immigration Act. Rather than focusing on the investigative and reporting burdens of the Act, Moore develops a sophisticated defense of the economic benefits of the admissions hierarchy employed in the legislation. His analysis concludes that "immigration is America's greatest comparative advantage in the world."

The aforementioned family reunification issues are taken up in an evaluative context in a January 1993 article written by the Staff of the National Immigration Law Center. While the authors recognize some of the implementation difficulties anticipated with the passage of the Immigration Act of 1990, they conclude that subsequent I.N.S. steps eased the Act's original difficulties and have made family reunification a realistic objective.

On the subject of diversity provisions, the 1990 Immigration Act has generated substantial debate in both legal and public policy literature. One of the most interesting treatments of the diversity moves of the 1990 Act can be found in Joan Pisarchik's "Rawlsian Analysis of the Immigration Act of 1990." Published in the *Georgetown Immigration Law Journal,* the work is particularly significant considering the recent trend in contemporary debate toward a greater understanding of the ethical systems undergirding public policy choices. Writing from a legal ethic perspective, Pisarchik argues that American immigration law is largely speaking pragmatic, not moral. Her critique of the 1990 Act is scathing in its criticism that the diversity provisions only serve to perpetuate preconceived biases that admit aliens largely on the basis of American economic and political need, rather than on that of moral necessity. In a world where economic resources are limited, American immigration policy, she argues, promotes inequality in the name of economic good. Pisarchik's analysis is one sided; her critique leaves little room for the virtues of economic pragmatism. Despite its one sided nature, however, the piece is essential reading for any debater looking to master the moral and ethical issues underpinning the immigration debate.

Both the ethical and pragmatic implications of immigration policy are played out in terms of a number of particular groups and issues. Three that are certain to be significant topics in competitive debates are women, AIDS carriers and Haitians. Each of these groups are the subject of significant writing and public debate, and each pose unique angles of controversy for the topic.

One fundamental problem that Congress addressed in the 1990 Immigration Act is the various means by which 'immigrant' can be defined. The controversy surrounding various views of immigrant status impacts not only the family and diversity provision of the Act, but in fact reaches to every issue in American immigration policy. William Roebuck's analysis of this definitional question, particularly as it relates to the employment based provisions of the Immigration Act of 1990, is particularly informative. Ultimately, Roebuck's argument is that the employment based provisions of the Act comprise the most significant changes in immigration law in the history of the republic. His work outlines they key definitional and employment based issues that are sure to be considered for the duration of the debate season.

The controversy surrounding the refugee status of women internationally calls into question the fundamental question, what constitutes political persecution for purposes of defining the parameters of immigration eligibility and status? In some cultures, women have historically been treated as second class citizens. Their roles vary from culture to culture, and few if any cultures have sufficient egalitarian traditions so as to have avoided scrutiny regarding their treatment of women.

One essential writing on gender issues in Linda Cipriani's 1993 article, "Gender and Persecution." In it, Cipriani conducts an extensive review of the relationship between gender issues and refugee status around the globe. She tackles the issue in an international law context, evaluating the responsibilities of international parties in the context of United Nations oversight. She concludes that existing protections for women are insufficient, and that the international community, led by the United States, should go further to protect the fundamental rights of women. While her analysis extends beyond American policy, it clearly implicates American responsibilities and necessarily rejects regulatory schemes that limit the ability of women as victims of social, political and culture persecution from attaining asylum.

The appearance of AIDS has complicated American immigration policy substantially. American policy presently excludes HIV carriers, the antibody which precedes AIDS. The clear cut political ground on this issue makes AIDS the hottest issue on this debate resolution. Fully one-third of debates will in some way cross the issue. The reading in this volume, Juan Osuna's "The Exclusion from the United States of Aliens Infected with the AIDS Virus," is an excellent treatus on the legal and political issues that undergird the status quo's prohibition. He concludes that the future status of HIV positive asylum seekers will be determined not by existing statutory authority alone, but by the politics of future presidential administrations and the jurisprudence of federal courts. Indeed, one such court has already found conflict between the congressional ban and the liberty and due process clauses of the United States Constitution.

Integrally tied to, but broader than, the AIDS issue are the questions surrounding the status and treatment of Haitian refugees, would-be political asylum seekers from America's tiny Caribbean neighbor. After a 1990 military coup, political refugees, fearful of repression for their support of the popularly elected Aristide, fled Haiti in overwhelming numbers. Haitian boat people, as they have come to be known, threatened to overwhelm the shores of their Caribbean neighbors, and threatened to create a serious crisis in South Florida.

The United States Coast Guard has, since May of 1992, made a practice of turning back Haitian refugees without hearing. Judging that refugees are economic and not political, thus not eligible for asylum, the I.N.S. instigated a blanket policy to return the refugees when their inflow reached crisis proportions. The United States Supreme Court is on record as supporting the policy; hence the issue has become both a political and constitutional issue. One of the most comprehensive treatments to date on the issue is Thomas Jones' article in the *Dickinson Journal of International Law,* "Haitian Refugee Center, Inc. v. James Baker, III: The Dred Scott Case of Immigration Law." Jones is ultimately critical of present policy, concluding that both the I.N.S. and the Supreme Court erred in their judgment to bar the refugees without hearing. Without question, Haitian refugees are the outstanding example of a group at the center of American immigration policy. Because of their high visibility, the determination of how they are treated will ultimately have a major impact on the status of American immigration and immigration policy for years to come.

More generally, refugee status is the central issue which American immigration policy must address in the 1990s and beyond. In the post cold war world, with nationalism emerging as the dominant organizing principle driving statism, and with its role as the foremost challenge to existing world order, political, economic and cultural refugees will grow exponentially in number and source. Some will seek asylum in the United States, most will find it elsewhere. But the role of American immigration policy in shaping international norms about refugee treatment can not be understated. An outstanding exploration of that relationship can be found in Gil Loescher's 1994 work, "The International Refugee Regime: Stretched to the Limit?" It is essential reading for any student seeking to understand the role of American immigration policy in the New World Order.

The future of American immigration policy is in a state of flux. Despite recent revisions to the law, substantial controversy remains. The issues to be debated are complex and critical. The conclusions offered by Austin Fragomen and Priscilla Clapp in the final excerpts of this volume demonstrate the importance and difficulty of the issues which lie ahead. They conclude, among other things, that failure to refocus attention to the major causes of refugee flow will leave the United States with limited future options and will leave us lurking from crisis to crisis in the years to come.

The Immigration Act of 1990
Pub. L. No. 101-649, 104 Stat. 4978

Miguel Lawson
Marianne Grin

On November 29, 1990 President Bush signed the Immigration Act of 1990 ("the 1990 Act"), the most extensive reform of U.S. immigration law in sixty-six years. The 1990 Act, which went into effect on October 1, 1991, revises and expands the traditional bases of legal immigration to the United States. It also establishes a new, controversial "diversity" program to increase the number of immigrants from countries adversely affected by the Immigration and Nationality Act Amendments of 1965. The 1990 Act represents the culmination of a decade-long reform process that began with the Select Commission on Immigration and Refugee Policy in 1979. Yet, similar to previous attempts at immigration reform, the goals of the 1990 Act may be difficult to carry into practice.

The Immigration Act of 1990 touches almost every aspect of U.S. immigration law. Quantitatively, the Act increases legal permanent immigration to the United States by over thirty-five percent and allows up to 700,000 immigrants to be admitted to the United States yearly. It augments family-sponsored immigration to 465,000 a year and, after September 30, 1994, to 480,000 a year, reaffirming that family reunification is still the first priority of U.S. immigration policy. It more than doubles the number of employment visas granted to skilled workers and their families, increasing it from 54,000 to 140,000 a year.

Qualitatively, the Act changes the array of skills and ethic backgrounds of the immigrants coming to the United States. The Act uses immigration as a policy tool to address the economic needs of the United States, such as labor shortages in certain professional areas. It institutes a "diversity" program to make permanent residency in the United States available to citizens of the countries that were largely excluded under the pre-1990 Act immigration laws.

The main objective of the new law is to revise the numerical limits and preference system regulating permanent legal immigration. Thus, the 1990 Act introduces an overall "pierceable" cap on world-wide immigration and replaces the 20,000 per country limit with a flexible calculation that restricts

Harvard International Law Journal, Volume 33 (1992:255–76).

admissions from any one country to approximately 25,000 persons. No single state may receive more than seven percent (or a dependent area more than two percent) of all family and employment-based visas combined.

The 1990 Act establishes ceilings on the non-refugee admissions of immigrants to the United States and provides for three general categories of immigrants: (1) family-sponsored immigrants, (2) employment-based immigrants, and (3) diversity immigrants. The first category, family-based immigration, remains the primary focus of U.S. immigration policy. The total number of family-based visas is 465,000 for fiscal years (FY) 1992 through 1994 and 480,000 for FY 1995 and beyond. Family-based immigration visas are divided among two categories: immediate relatives and non-immediate family preferences.

Except for the overall limit on the number of family-based visas, there is no annual limit on the immigration to the United States of immediate relatives of U.S. citizens under either the old or the new law. All those who meet the qualifications of the requisite "immediate" relation qualify for entry. The 1990 Act expands the definition of "immediate" relative to include unmarried children under twenty-one, parents (if the U.S. citizen is over twenty-one), and spouses, including spouses of deceased U.S. citizens, provided the couple had been married for at least two years prior to the death of the U.S. spouse.

The number of immediate relative visas issued in a given year is simply deducted from the yearly family-based total. An increase in the number of such visas in one year will decrease the amount available for non-immediate family members the following year. To assure that immediate relatives do not "swallow up" all of the visas in the family-based category, the 1990 Act reserves an annual minimum of 226,000 visas for family preference immigrants. These 226,000 family preference visas are allocated in the following manner to four subcategories: (1) unmarried sons and daughters of U.S. citizens—23,400; (2) spouses and unmarried sons and daughters of permanent resident aliens—114,200; (3) married sons and daughters of U.S. citizens—23,400; (4) brothers and sisters of adult U.S. citizens—65,000. An additional category was enacted for the benefit of spouses and children of aliens newly legalized under Immigration Reform and Control Act of 1986.

It is unclear whether the 1990 Act will result in dramatic reductions of petition backlogs in all of the family preference categories. The Visa Office of the Department of State does not foresee substantial advances in family-based preferences for FY 1992. There is hope that the increase in available visas for the second preference (spouses and unmarried sons and daughters of permanent residents), especially for Mexico, will reduce the waiting list and spill over in the backlogged lower preferences. Specialists indicate, however, that the situation in the family preference category will probably change very little.

In addition to modifying the preference structure and the number of visas available for each family-based preference, the 1990 Act attempts to correct the shortcomings of some of the immigration enactments of the 1980s. Section 701 of the 1990 Act, for example, makes substantial revisions in the 1986 Immigration Marriage Fraud Act ("IMFA"). Amending the 1952 Immigration and Nationality Act ("INA"), the IMFA deters fraud by imposing for immigration-related marriage fraud, criminal penalties of up to five years of confinement or $250,000 in fines. Section 2 of the IMFA adds a new section 216 to the INA that imposes a two-year waiting period in the form of a conditional residency requirement on alien spouses who apply for permanent residency on the basis of their marriage to a U.S citizen or permanent resident alien. If the alien spouse wishes to obtain permanent residency, the two spouses must file a joint petition for a change of status and undergo an interview conducted by the INS in order to ascertain that the "qualifying marriage" was not entered into "for the purpose of procuring an alien's entry as an immigrant;" that the marriage was still valid; and that the U.S. spouse received no payment, other than to cover the expenses, to file the petition on behalf of the alien spouse. Under the old law the requirement of a joint petition could be waived only if the alien spouse showed that "extreme hardship" would result if he or she were deported or that the alien spouse was not at fault for failing to file a joint petition, if the marriage was terminated for good cause.

The 1990 Act dispenses with the good cause requirement and adds a new waiver specifically designed for battered spouses and abused children. The Act allows them to obtain permanent residency as a sole petitioner when a joint petition is unavailable or difficult to get because the citizen or resident alien spouse has physically or mentally abused the immigrant spouse and refuses to agree to a joint petition. The purpose of the provision is to "assure that . . . neither the spouse nor child [is] entrapped in the abusive relationship by the threat of losing [his] legal resident status." The rule has been attacked, however, for its inadequate provisions for confidentiality, and its definition of abuse has been criticized as too restrictive.

One issue that was hotly debated during the drafting of the reforms was whether to grant immediate relative status to spouses and minor children of permanent resident aliens, thus eliminating the second preference. The House version of the legislation, sponsored by Representative Bruce Morrison (D-Conn.), proposed such a grant. Those in favor of this proposal emphasized the possible constitutional right of a permanent resident to live with his or her family, and the data that indicate that prolonged separation encourages illegal immigration. Those against granting immediate relative recognition to spouses and minor children of permanent residents or to other relatives emphasized the "visa multiplier" effect that might occur should such recognition be granted, and claimed that, in general, the economic costs of increased immigration are too high. Economic costs were viewed from both a protectionist and an environmentalist perspective. Senator Alan K. Simpson (R-Wyo.), sponsor of the 1989 Senate bill, argued strongly in favor of eliminating unlimited visas for immediate relatives and for increasing employment-based immigration as a means of serving the national interest by getting the "highest quality" immigrants. Despite arguments to the contrary, however, most data indicate that new immigrants have had slight or no impact on the employment prospects of U.S. citizens. "The conventional economic wisdom pitting American poor against the immigrant poor is crumbling. So too will the conventional wisdom pitting labor against the outsiders." U.S. Government and other studies also lead to the conclusion that the United States does not need to prescreen its immigrants, as "both Census Bureau and Labor Department data confirm that legal immigrants quickly earn as much or more than native-born workers of the same age, work more and tend to be better educated and better trained, are more likely to start new businesses, and contribute far more in taxes than they collect in social benefits."

In addition to the changes it made in family-based immigration, the 1990 Act also significantly revised the law regarding employment-based immigration. Prior to the 1990 Act, 54,000 employment-based immigrants entered the United States annually in two of the six immigrant-visa preferences: the third preference for professionals and persons of exceptional ability and the sixth preference for skilled and unskilled workers. Since the worker's spouse, children, and family members were included in the 54,000 available employment-based visas, the actual number of workers who entered the United States was far less than 54,000. Third and sixth preference immigrants had to be sponsored by an employer who was required to file a labor certification in order to prove that the immigrant would not displace a U.S. worker. The entire application process was time-consuming, and the backlogs for employment-based visas were estimated to be one and a half years for third preference immigrants and three and a half years for sixth preference immigrants.

In drafting the 1990 Act, Congress believed that employment-based immigration must increase substantially and that the admissions procedures for such immigrants must be streamlined. Congress was "convinced that immigration can and should be incorporated into an overall strategy that promotes the creation of the type of workforce needed in an increasingly competitive global economy without adversely impacting on the wages and working conditions of American workers." The 1990 Act attempts to achieve these goals by replacing the third and sixth preferences with five new categories and by increasing the total number of employment-based visas.

As of October 1, 1991, section 121 of the 1990 Act allows 140,000 employment-based immigrants to enter the United States each year, almost tripling the previous level. The new law divides the 140,000 visas among five groups: (1) priority workers; (2) professionals holding advanced degrees and aliens of exceptional ability; (3) skilled workers, professionals holding bachelor's degrees, and other workers; (4) certain special immigrants; and (5) investors.

The first employment-based preference, available to priority workers, is allotted 40,000 visas annually and is divided into three subcategories: (1) aliens with extraordinary ability; (2) outstanding professors and researchers; and (3) certain executives and managers of multinational corporations. All three groups share equal access to the pool of visas, and all are exempt from the labor certification process. The subcategory that is likely to be most utilized in the priority worker preference is that reserved for multinational executives and managers who have been employed for at least one of the three preceding years by the overseas affiliate, subsidiary, or branch of a petitioning U.S. company for which the alien must be coming to work in a managerial or executive capacity. Individuals are expected to have to wait only a few months for a visa, rather than the four years that was the case under the old law.

The second employment-based preference, that reserved for professionals holding advanced degrees and aliens of exceptional ability, is allotted 40,000 visas annually, plus any visas which are not used from the priority worker category. Aliens with advanced degrees or exceptional ability in the sciences, arts, or business are eligible for visas under this preference. Both a job offer and labor certificate are required for immigrants with advanced degrees. If aliens with exceptional ability satisfy the Labor Department's Schedule A, Group II regulations, they will be exempt from the labor certification process.

The third employment-based preference, available to skilled workers, professionals, and other workers, is allotted 40,000 visas annually, plus any unused visas from the first two employment-based preferences. Skilled workers capable of performing a job which requires at least two years of training or experience and professionals with a bachelor's degree are entitled to 30,000 visas. Other workers, or unskilled workers, capable of performing jobs requiring less than two years training or experience are limited to 10,000 visas annually. "This drastic reduction in visas available to unskilled workers, a class of aliens already experiencing long waiting periods, . . . reflects Congress's desire for only skilled immigrants."

The fourth employment-based preference is allotted 10,000 visas for certain special immigrants. Although the old law did not impose a limit on the number of special immigrants entering the United States, the allotment of 10,000 visas may be sufficient to avoid any backlogs, since only 5000 persons enter the United States as special immigrants each year. This, in part, depends on the number of special immigrants who enter under the three new provisions added by the 1990 Act: religious workers, employees at the U.S. consulate in Hong Kong, and aliens dependent on a juvenile court.

The fifth employment-based preference is allotted 10,000 visas each year for foreign investors who invest between $500,000 and $3 million in an enterprise that provides employment for at least ten full-time U.S. workers.

This employment-creation preference is unprecedented in U.S. immigration law, although Congress has attempted to pass a bill incorporating a provision for investors since the early 1980s. The 1990 Act sets a threshold amount of $1 million for most investments. However, to encourage investment in "targeted employment areas," the 1990 Act provides 3000 visas for which the Attorney General may lower the minimum investment to $500,000. Conversely, if an alien invests in a high employment area, the Attorney General may increase the minimum investment to $3 million. While the language of the statute specifies that aliens must enter the United States "for the purpose of engaging in a new commercial enterprise which the alien has established," INS-proposed regulations implementing the employment-based preferences provide that a new enterprise could be established through the purchase of an existing business if sufficient changes are made in the organization and operation of the business. In addition, an investment which expands an existing business is permissible if the investment creates a 140% increase in the business's net worth or number of employees.

In order to deter fraudulent applications for employment-creation visas, the 1990 Act makes the grant of permanent residence to immigrant investors conditional for two years. The INS can terminate the permanent residence status of an alien investor during this conditional period if it finds that the enterprise was created to evade U.S. immigration laws, the enterprise was not established, the required capital was not invested, or the alien did not sustain the enterprise. The 1990 Act also imposes a duty on the immigrant investor to file a petition with the INS before the two-year conditional period expires, requesting that the conditional status be removed. Failure to file this petition will terminate the investor's status. An alien investor who knowingly establishes a commercial enterprise to evade U.S. immigration laws can be jailed for up to five years and fined $250,000.

In addition to increasing the number of employment-based visas, the 1990 Act establishes a diversity program to increase the number of immigrants from "adversely affected" and "underrepresented" countries—in other words, countries that are not well-represented in the ranks of immigrants to the United States. Until 1965 the United States utilized a national origins quota system to limit the number of immigrants from certain countries. This system favored immigration from Europe. However, since 1965, the majority of immigrants have come from Asia and Latin America. This change in the mix of immigrants was an unintended consequence of the Immigration and Nationality Act Amendments of 1965 which repealed the national-origins quota system in effect since the 1920s.

In response to this imbalance, Congress enacted section 314 of the Immigration Reform and Control Act of 1986 which allotted 5000 extra visas for fiscal years 1987 and 1988 to citizens of thirty-six countries that had been "adversely affected" by the 1965 Act. Over one million people applied for visas under this "NP-5" program; natives of Ireland were the big winners. In 1988, Congress extended the NP-5 program for two more years, increased to 15,000 the yearly allotment of visas for fiscal years 1989 and 1990, and enacted another temporary lottery program in order to provide more visas to underrepresented countries. Known as the "OP-1" program, this temporary lottery awarded 10,000 additional visas a year in fiscal years 1990 and 1991.

In the spirit of the above provisions, the 1990 Act promotes diversity in four ways. First, section 131 creates a permanent diversity program beginning in fiscal year 1994. Fifty-five thousand visas will be available annually to natives of foreign states from which immigration was lower than 50,000 during the preceding five years. In order to be eligible, an alien must possess a high school diploma or its equivalent or two years of experience or training. Petitions must be received within a limited time period at a designated post office in Washington, D.C., and only one petition may be filed by each petitioner. Selection is random, and eligibility for a visa expires at the end of the fiscal year in which the alien was selected.

The 1990 Act divides the world into high-admission and low-admission regions and states for the purpose of distributing the permanent diversity visas. While a single state cannot receive more than seven percent, or 3850 of the total visas per year, any unused visas in a particular region may be allocated to other regions in the same fiscal year.

Section 132 of the Immigration Act of 1990 promotes diversity in a second way by creating a transitional program which provides 40,000 visas for fiscal years 1992 through 1994 to the natives of thirty-four countries adversely affected by the 1965 amendments. Congress patterned the transitional diversity program, known as the "AA-1" program, after the NP-5 program created by the Immigration Reform and Control Act of 1986. However, unlike the NP-5 program, aliens who apply for the AA-1 program must have a firm commitment of employment in the United States for at least one year following admission. This requirement will benefit undocumented aliens already residing in the United States. Significantly, Irish immigrants must receive at least forty percent, or 16,000 of the available visas annually. For this reason, the AA-1 program has been described as the "Irish lottery." The AA-1 program is properly termed a lottery because immigrant visas will be distributed to eligible aliens in the chronological order in which they are received by a post office in Merrifield, Virginia. Unlike the permanent diversity program, multiple applications may be submitted.

Section 133 of the 1990 Act promotes diversity in a third way by providing visas in fiscal year 1991 for qualified applicants of the NP-5 program who had been notified of their selection for a visa before May 1, 1990, but for whom visas were not available. Finally, section 134 of the 1990 Act promotes diversity in a fourth way by providing 1000 visas annually through fiscal year 1993 for certain displaced Tibetans residing in India or Nepal.

In passing the 1990 Act, Congress intended to assist the U.S. economy by substantially increasing employment-based immigration, to streamline admission procedures, to promote the diversity of nationalities within the immigrant streams, and to reduce current family-preference backlogs. It is unclear whether the 1990 Act will accomplish these potentially conflicting goals.

In order to reduce the family-preference backlogs, Congress increased the number of visas available to family-based immigrants and reaffirmed family-based immigration as the main basis of U.S. immigration policy. Since the majority of immigrants who have entered the country since 1965 have come from Latin America and Asia, emphasis on family reunification will continue to principally benefit immigrants from these regions and may offset the increase in the number of immigrants from adversely affected and underrepresented countries. While new European and African immigrants admitted under the diversity program will be able to petition for their relatives under the family-based provisions of the 1990 Act, this process will inevitably be very slow and might not increase the diversity of nationalities within the immigrant stream as much as Congress envisioned.

Some commentators argue that the diversity provisions of the 1990 Act restore a modified version of the national origins quota system repealed in 1965. During the first four years after the Act goes into effect, the principal beneficiaries of these provisions will be the natives of Ireland who are guaranteed at least forty percent, or 16,000, of the 40,000 available visas under the AA-1, transitional diversity program. Commentators argue that the diversity program derogates from the principle of universal equal treatment established by the 1965 Act and legitimizes ethnocentric disquiet of some at the "browning of America." Criticism of such social engineering may lead to a congressional repeal of the program.

While Congress intended to improve the economy by "opening the front door" to more skilled workers, critics claim that given the complexity and fluidity of the U.S. economy, congressional efforts to "fine-tune the economy through the skills-based component of [U.S.] immigration policy are unlikely to succeed. . . . Workers imported to the United States in connection with a particular employer, job, or industry often move on, a mobility that the government probably cannot and should not prevent." In addition, although some economists argue that immigration confers a net economic gain upon the United States, other research reveals that "welfare costs of immigration have been growing over time," which may tend to decrease any net gain. Furthermore, "[w]elfare dependency will increase if the economy worsens and if the composition of the immigrant flow continues no change in the direction of more young mothers and children."

In any case, the problem with the U.S. economy is probably not a labor shortage *per se,* but a mismatch between education or skills and needs of the labor market. Congress decided to increase skills-based immigration because it found that it was "unlikely that enough U.S. workers [would] be trained quickly enough to meet legitimate employment needs. . . ." However, increasing skills-based immigrants may "ease pressures to invest in education and training for U.S. workers." If this occurs, immigration policy will be "in conflict with other national priorities . . . by interfering with our resolve as a nation to bring into the economic mainstream some of these who are not now there: minority, youth, the disabled, the disadvantaged, older Americans."

Section 810 of the 1990 Act attempts to prevent such an interference with U.S. educational priorities by creating an estimated $50 million education and training fund, ten percent of which will be utilized to fund college scholarships for needy students enrolled in courses leading to a degree in mathematics or the sciences. While it is unclear whether this fund will have any discernible impact on the gap between skills and employment needs, "[i]t would be myopic . . . for employers, educators, and policy makers to allow short-term migratory patterns to divert them from long-term efforts to develop native skills."

Furthermore, it could be argued that "by focusing exclusively on business needs [in formulating the employment-based preference], Congress has failed to recognize the increasing demand for unskilled workers within the U.S. workforce." According to U.S. Representative Morella (R-Md.), limiting the number of visas available to unskilled workers to 10,000 annually will "exacerbate[ ] already existing shortages of child care, home care, elder care, and other basic skilled workers." Representative Morella predicted that 19,000 visas were needed annually to meet the current demand for unskilled workers. As more women enter the workforce, the demand for unskilled workers will further increase and drive up the cost of these services.

The executive branch has cautioned that the provisions of the 1990 Act will take time to develop. It took approximately five years for the implications of the 1965 Act to become fully understood, for the basic questions of interpretation to be settled, and for the administrators of the law and the interested public to adjust to the new system. Accordingly, Congress prepared for unanticipated consequences of the 1990 Act by creating the Commission on Legal Immigration Reform, which shall submit annual analyses of the social, economic, environmental, and demographic impact of the 1990 Act. According to Senator Kennedy (D-Mass.), a principal sponsor of the legislation, "under the regular review procedures, no number, no level, and no category of immigration will be permitted to become frozen into law, unchanged from decade-to-decade, as has been the case with past legislation." These review procedures should assure that the 1990 Act remains responsive to the constantly changing needs of U.S. immigration policy.

Editor's Note: This article has been edited for publication.

Immigration Policy
Open Minds on Open Borders
Stephen Moore

Give us your energetic, your rich, your talented . . .

Thirty years ago Alfred Sklar escaped to the United States from Cuba—one of the thousands of refugees fleeing Fidel Castro's communist government. Today, Sklar is one of America's leading high-tech entrepreneurs in Silicon Valley. As the founder and director of research at Phoenix Laser Systems, Sklar is recognized as the central brain of a pioneering effort to perfect laser and surgical technologies that could cure several forms of blindness and ultimately revolutionize optical surgery.

"We're going for a clean sweep of eye laser surgical procedures," he boasts. "We're looking to replace all other optical equipment." Others back up this bold claim. The renowned physicist Edward Teller has praised such new laser technology breakthroughs as "potentially more significant" than nuclear fusion. Recently *The Wall Street Journal* echoed this sanguine assessment by writing that Phoenix lasers is "challenging the [optical industry] with radically different machines that could prove cheaper, safer, and more accurate than more common laser approaches."

Sklar's success story in America is inspiring, yes. But by no means is it unusual. He is just one of tens of thousands of immigrants who are helping to secure America's global leadership in high-technology industries. In the 1980s, thousands of firms in America's high-tech corridors—from Route 128 in Massachusetts to Silicon Valley in California—turned to immigrants as a source of talent and brainpower, a factor that many say has helped to maintain the United States' competitive role in developing cutting-edge computer, electronic, pharmaceutical and medical technologies. British, Taiwanese, Korean, Indian, Filipino, and Cuban scientists, engineers, business managers, and laborers are the lifeblood of these dynamic firms and have become a visible sign of the modern American melting pot.

Business and Society Review (Spring 1991:36–40).

MORE BRAINPOWER

Increasingly, the business community has come to view immigrants as an essential source of new talent and brainpower. It isn't that Yankee ingenuity doesn't work anymore, industry leaders seem to be saying. Rather, the problem is that we need more of it.

Last October, the pleas of the business community for more highly skilled immigrants were at least partially answered. In the final hours of the final day of the 101st Congress, legislators passed a historic immigration reform bill that will swing open the golden gates to many more immigrants in the 1990s. This was the first such revision of America's legal immigration laws in some twenty-five years and only the fifth ever. Total immigration levels will be raised by roughly 30 percent—to 800,000 new entrants per year. Just as important, the number of new entrants selected on the basis of their high skills and education levels will be roughly tripled from 54,000 to 140,000 each year. At the same time, the major pillar of longstanding U.S. immigration policy—family unification—will remain fundamentally intact.

Yet in the aftermath of this new law, immigration remains one of the most contentious of national issues. Business interests, free-market think tanks, and ethnic groups continue their clamor for higher quotas; meanwhile, the general public remains skeptical about the wisdom of liberalized immigration rules. Some 70 percent of Americans, according to one recent public opinion poll, oppose higher quotas.

This is nothing new, of course. American attitudes toward the foreign-born have always been a curious paradox. Though a nation of immigrants, America has never warmly received the newest arrivals. As far back as the eighteenth century, a statesman as eminent as Benjamin Franklin derided the recent waves of German immigrants as "the stupidest of their race." Today, the standard stereotype of the contemporary immigrant is of the Third World exile secretly crossing the border and feeding off the U.S. welfare system.

RESTLESS NATIVES

Anti-immigrant sentiments are cultivated by an expanding network of vocal and well-funded nativist groups. The rallying cry for tighter border restrictions runs the gamut from A (the Audubon Society) to Z (Zero Population Growth) of politically influential Washington special interest groups. The movement often makes for strange bedfellows: It includes most major environmental and population control groups, which view immigrants as intensifying pressures on the environment; labor groups that decry immigrants as job competitors; and social conservative organizations that fear immigrants are diluting America's white, European heritage.

The umbrella organization for this network is the 50,000-member Federation for American Immigration Reform (FAIR). FAIR believes: "Many social and ecological problems stem from out-of-control immigration. They range from abuse of our natural resources to increasing taxes to support of an overburdened social services program."

Of course, these nativist groups are correct that immigrants are not an unmixed blessing. When they first arrive in America, the newcomers often impose costs on society through their use of schools, the medical care system, roads, and the physical infrastructure generally. In rapidly growing urban areas where problems of traffic gridlock and housing shortages are acute—Los Angeles, Miami, and Seattle, for example—public anxiety toward new foreign arrivals is understandable. Many Americans are particularly troubled by the perceived resistance of some immigrant groups to assimilate into the fabric of American society—manifested most noticeably through a reluctance to learn English. The recent boycott by blacks of Korean grocery stores in New York City is one dramatic example of the social and ethnic clashes that can arise between native-born Americans and new immigrant waves.

Hard-Headed Reasoning

As I have made evident over the years, I am committed to a liberal immigration policy. That [position is based], I think, on hard-headed economic grounds. As Germany, France, Switzerland, and other countries have come to rely on a large number of immigrant workers, or, as they are known in Germany, and elsewhere, guest workers, so we must rely for a wide variety of effort on willing and committed workers from our neighboring countries. And beyond that we need the inflow of educated and otherwise highly qualified talent that other countries can provide.

"We all look back with favor on our past immigration policies and what they have done for us. It is deeply inconsistent that we think the future to be different and, indeed, anomalous. Why is it that what contributed so much in the past should be so questioned in the present?

—John Kenneth Galbraith

These are all legitimate public concerns. Yet the important issue to most Americans is whether the United States can afford to take in substantially more immigrants. Will the benefits to the society of raising immigration to, say, one million visas per year, outweigh the costs? This question involves demographic, economic, and cultural considerations.

Of the first issue, demographics, the evidence strongly suggests that America can absorb additional immigrants. Immigration is not particularly high today in comparison with earlier periods of U.S. history. The new ceiling of 800,000 immigrants per year is still roughly 25 percent below the peak level of one million per year during the period of the great migration at the turn of the century. As a percentage of the U.S. population—a useful measure of the nation's ability to absorb new immigrants into the new economic and social infrastructure—America now accepts three immigrants for every 1,000 residents. This is five times below peak immigration rates and half the historical average. Our history as a nation, then, would suggest that we are nowhere near our capacity to take in new people. In fact, today, Australia, Canada, Sweden, and the United Kingdom have higher immigration rates than the United States.

Most immigrants who come to the United States as adults immediately enter the labor force. Can they be absorbed without risking job loss for many Americans? The latest information from the Census Bureau confirms that they can. America's labor force will grow slower in the 1990s than in four of the past five decades. Already, there are shortages of skilled workers in labor markets around the country, including Charlotte, North Carolina; Atlanta, Georgia; and Richmond, Virginia, according to the U.S. Department of Labor. The department's report shows that in the 1990s the labor force will grow at just one percent annually, but that the demand for technically skilled workers will be double this rate. This suggests that immigrants will be coming in greater numbers, just as they are most needed in the labor force.

A landmark study by the U.S. Department of labor on the impact of immigration on the labor market finds there is virtually no evidence that immigrants displace U.S. citizens from their jobs. "Neither U.S. workers in complementary jobs or most minority workers appear to be adversely affected by immigration," concludes the 1988 report. George Borjas of the University of California at Davis confirms this finding. Borjas, who has spent much of his professional career estimating the economic impact of immigrants, says: "The methodological arsenal of modern econometrics cannot detect a single shred of evidence that immigrants have a sizable adverse impact on the earnings and employment opportunities of natives in the United States."

"There is virtually no evidence that immigrants displace American workers."

My own research with Ohio University economists Richard Vedder and Lowell Galloway finds that, since the turn of the century, periods of very high immigration—such as the early 1900s—have been followed by periods of lower than usual unemployment and higher economic expansion. The flip side of the equation is also true: When immigration has been low due to restrictive laws, such as the late 1920s, the economy in subsequent years has been weak and joblessness high. In many ways immigrants have the effect of natural economic stabilizers; they tend to come when the economy is most eager to employ them and they tend to locate in areas where jobs are most plentiful.

Immigrants also fill vital niches in the labor market. A review of the occupational categories of the foreign-born shows that they are disproportionately employed in jobs with very high skill requirements—in science, medicine, and engineering—or in the lowest skilled service occupations, such as dish washing, providing child care, or picking fruits and vegetables. Some of these occupations, in fact, are so dominated by immigrants that without them whole American industries would have contracted or even disappeared by now. This is true, for instance, of much of the agricultural industry in California and Washington; the ranching industry in Idaho and New Mexico; the poultry industry in Maryland; and the garment district in New York. Mazaffar Christie, president of the International Ladies Garment Workers Union, insists that this domestic industry has been kept alive over the past decades only by the constant infusion of new immigrant workers. Similarly, if it were not for immigrant nurses and orderlies, *The New York Times* reports that some public hospitals in New York City would have had to close down. These hidden benefits of immigrant workers rarely surface in the debate over immigration policy.

IMMIGRANT EXPERIENCE

"Half of all U.S. engineering Ph.D.s are now awarded to immigrants."

It is not just semi-skilled industries whose survival and profitability depend on immigration. The high-technology industries of America are flourishing today largely because America has the stability to tap into the best and brightest talents from around the globe. A prime example is Intel Corporation, a Fortune 500 computer firm in California, where three members of the corporate management, including President and CEO Andrew S. Grove (from Hungary), are immigrants. Many of the most renowned computer chip innovations for the microprocessor in the 1970s and 1980s were invented by immigrants. "Our whole business is predicated on inventing the next generation of computer technologies," offers Dick Ward, an Intel vice president. "The engine that drives that quest is brainpower. And here at Intel, much of that brainpower comes from immigrants."

Dynamic Contribution

The major economic effect of immigration is to provide a steady stream of fresh human resources to the economy. Provided immigrants are attracted by the opportunities of the American economy rather than by the welfare provided by the American polity, they contribute greatly to the vitality of the economy. They are highly motivated, willing to work and venture, and bring in fresh insights. Immigrants have made a disproportionate contribution to dynamism of the economy because of these characteristics ever since our forefathers first landed in the New World.

—Milton Friedman

In 1988 the highly respected National Research Council examined the impact of foreign-born engineers on U.S. high-technology industries. It found that many U.S. industries benefit from the brainpower and talents of immigrants. The Council's overall conclusion is worth repeating: "Very significant, positive aspects arise from the presence of foreign-born engineers in our society. The diversity of intellectual backgrounds and experience that foreign-born engineers have brought in the past greatly contributed to U.S. engineering competence, and there are no reasons to believe that new immigrants will not contribute similarly."

EMINENT IMMIGRANTS

That assessment is not altogether surprising. The following statistics about the modern immigrants to America indicate that they play a vital, if underappreciated, role in keeping U.S. industry innovative and competitive:

- Half of all U.S. engineering Ph.D.s are now awarded to immigrants.
- Over 10,000 highly trained Asian immigrants are employed in the electronics and computer industry.
- Immigrant workers have a higher rate of starting new businesses than do American-born workers—9.2 percent versus 7.1 percent. Many of these businesses—Phoenix Laser Systems and Intel, to name two—create high-paying jobs for U.S. citizens.
- Thirteen of the seventeen high school valedictorians in Boston public high schools in 1989 were immigrants—from China, Vietnam, Portugal, Jamaica, France, Italy, and Czechoslovakia.

Foreign Capital

Few dispute the fact that immigrants enrich our society culturally. But many are concerned about the prospect that immigrants will displace present residents from their jobs. In fact, any such displacements are temporary. The major effect of a rising number of relatively low-skilled immigrants is to raise the real wages of skilled workers and managers and to raise the return on the existing capital stock.

—William Poole

Immigration is one of the few issues on which almost all economists agree on the positive economic effects. Last year I conducted a survey for the Hudson Institute and the American Immigration Institute of thirty-eight distinguished economists—past presidents of the American Economic Association and past members of the President's Council of Economic Advisers. Eight Nobel laureates were on the panel, including Milton Friedman, Theodore W. Schultz, George J. Stigler, James Tobin, and James M. Buchanan. The survey found that 80 percent of these world-class economists believe that immigrants have had, on balance, a "very favorable impact on the nation's economic growth in this century." Similarly, almost two-thirds endorsed higher immigration quotas as a way to "raise the standard of living in the U.S."

Assessing the cultural and social impact of immigration in contemporary America cannot so easily be measured in statistics and figures. Whether the new immigrants are integrating successfully into U.S. society is, to a large extent, in the eyes of the beholder. Many people who live near Little Saigon or one of the all-Hispanic neighborhoods in Los Angeles where English is often a second language complain that these new Americans are not Americanizing. One writer recently quipped that Los Angeles has become America's version of a Third World city.

Yet there is nothing new about immigrants settling in ethnic enclaves. Waves of German, Greek, Hungarian, Irish, Italian, Jewish, and Polish immigrants in Boston, Chicago, Milwaukee, and New York have left an endearing ethnic imprint on those metropolises. In the 1800s, German immigrants refused to learn English and steadfastly attempted to preserve their language until it finally died out. Then, as now, the complaint was the same; the "new" immigrants refused to assimilate. This raises the question: If Europeans settled among their own countrymen but eventually integrated into American society, why should we be so concerned that new Asian and Hispanic immigrants are following much this same pattern?

America is still the melting pot that it was fifty and 100 years ago, though the birthplaces of the new immigrants have changed. For instance, intermarriage rates among ethnic groups in America are higher than ever before. In 1980 census indicates that 30 percent of Mexican-Americans intermarry, as do 60 percent of "other Hispanics" and 40 percent of Chinese-Americans.

The concerns that English is becoming a second language and the United States is becoming a multilingual society are misplaced. In 1980, 98 percent of Americans spoke at least some English, according to the Census Bureau, a higher percentage than at any other time in American history. Almost all children of immigrants are proficient in English and their native language.

American immigration policy appears to have come to a critical crossroads as the United States prepares itself for the next century. There are those, such as conservative Pat Buchanan, who argue forcefully that America's strength lies in its "Euro-American" tradition. Millions of Americans share this view. But countless others, including many business leaders, insist that America's cultural diversity—its ability to attract the most hardworking, dedicated, and entrepreneurial talent from around the world—is the formula that constantly revitalizes the nation's energy and ambition. According to this view, immigration is America's greatest comparative advantage in the world.

The question of who will win this critical debate over the future of national immigration policy rages on and remains largely unresolved. If history is to be our guide then surely the latter view shall eventually prevail. It seems inconceivable that the value of the immigration process, which has benefitted America for more than two centuries, should now be doubted and distrusted.

Editor's Note: This article has been edited for publication.

Immigration Law Developments

Relief for Battered Spouses, Widows, and Abandoned Children

by the National Immigration Law Center

This article was written by the staff of the National Immigration Law Center, 1636 W. Eighth St., Suite 205, Los Angeles, CA 90017, (213) 487-2531.

SUMMARY

Between 1986 and 1991 there were sweeping reforms, legislative overhauls, or significant amendments to our immigration laws. By contrast, 1992 was relatively tranquil for immigration practitioners. Nevertheless, INS concentrated on implementing these statutory changes through final or interim regulations. This proved particularly significant for certain groups of persons who have been waiting for these regulations to remedy various past inequities. This article focuses on some of these groups who were most affected by INS's actions last year: battered women, widows, abandoned children, and the family members of legalized aliens.

VISA PETITIONS FOR SPOUSES

Overview of IMFA

The Immigration Marriage Fraud Amendments of 1986 (IMFA) imposed severe restrictions on aliens who obtain or attempt to obtain permanent residence based on marriage to a United States citizen. The most significant change was the creation of a new "conditional residence" status for these alien spouses. IMFA also imposed severe penalties on persons found to have entered into fraudulent marriages. Fortunately, some of the harshest aspects of IMFA were tempered by later provisions of the Immigration Act of 1990. Many of these provisions were implemented last year through INS regulations, policy memos, and modified application forms.

Clearinghouse Review (January 1993:1151–61).

Most alien spouses who immigrate through marriage to a United States citizen must obtain conditional resident status before they achieve the "unconditional" rights of other permanent resident aliens. This conditional status is imposed on aliens obtaining permanent resident status on or after November 10, 1986, if that status is based on a marriage that occurred within two years of either

(1) the alien's entry to the United States as a permanent resident or

(2) the alien's adjustment to permanent resident status within the United States.

Conditional resident aliens have the same rights, privileges, and responsibilities as other permanent residents. However, they must take steps to remove the conditional nature of their residence status or lose their lawful immigration status. Within 90 days before the second anniversary of the date on which these aliens obtained permanent residence, conditional residents must file a petition to remove the conditions on residence (INS form I-751).

Prior to December 1991, conditional residents could file either a "joint" petition to remove the conditions on residence with their spouse (I-751) or a petition to waive the joint petition requirement (I-752). After December 1992, conditional residents must file the same petition whether they are filing jointly with their spouse or seeking a "waiver." The earlier form I-752 has been eliminated.

If INS grants the I-751 petition and removes the conditional status, the conditional resident spouse is accorded full permanent resident status. INS can terminate the conditional status at any time during the two-year period, however, if it discovers that the marriage was dissolved, annulled, or was entered into fraudulently. If INS terminates the conditional status during the two-year period or denies the alien's petition to remove the condition, the conditional resident loses lawful immigration status and becomes subject to deportation.

Filing the "Joint" Petition

If the conditional resident is still lawfully married to the spouse through whom he or she obtained immigrant status, and if that spouse cooperates in completing the petition, then the couple can file a "joint" petition. On form I-751 both spouses must declare under penalty of perjury that

(1) the marriage was entered into in accordance with the laws in the jurisdiction in which it took place;

(2) the marriage was not entered into for the purpose of procuring an immigration benefit; and

(3) no fee was paid to anyone other than an attorney in return for the filing of the petition.

INS cannot deny or refuse to accept the I-751 joint petition based solely on the current viability of the marriage. In other words, if the marriage is failing at the end of the two-year period, even if the parties have separated or filed for a divorce, INS must still accept a timely filed joint petition. As long as the parties establish that the marriage was bona fide at the time of entry, INS cannot deny the joint petition on the grounds that the marriage is no longer viable. According to the INS general counsel, "present viability of a marriage is not one of the factors which the INA, as amended by the IMFA, lists as a consideration in adjudicating the I-751 petition."

Filing for a "Waiver" of the Joint Petition Requirement

In lieu of the joint petition, the conditional resident can request that the joint filing requirement be waived based on any of four grounds:

- the marriage was entered into in good faith, but the spouse has since died;
- the marriage was entered into in good faith but has been terminated through divorce or annulment;
- the marriage was entered into in good faith, but the conditional resident has been battered or subjected to extreme cruelty by the citizen spouse; or
- termination of permanent residency and deportation would result in extreme hardship.

For three of the above four waiver grounds, the applicant must prove that the marriage was entered into in good faith. The federal regulations state that INS will consider evidence relating to the amount of commitment shown by both parties to the marital relationship. To prove good faith, INS suggests submitting evidence regarding

(1) the extent to which parties shared financial assets and liabilities;

(2) the length of time the parties cohabited;

(3) the number of children born into the marriage; and

(4) any other pertinent evidence.

This is essentially the same type of proof needed to establish a bona fide marriage for purposes of obtaining conditional residency.

Death of the Spouse

If the conditional resident is submitting a waiver based on the death of his or her spouse, he or she should submit documentation establishing the death.

In addition, the conditional resident must still submit documentary evidence establishing that the marriage was bona fide. In almost all of these situations, INS will grant the request without requiring an interview. INS will be likely to investigate the matter further only if it suspected, in rare cases, that the conditional resident married someone in anticipation of his or her imminent death with the intention of thereby gaining immigration benefits.

Divorce or Annulment Waiver

To qualify for the second waiver, the conditional resident must demonstrate that the marriage has ended in either divorce or annulment. The Immigration Act of 1990 deleted IMFA's original double requirement that the marriage must have been terminated "by the alien spouse" and that the divorce or annulment must have been "for good cause." Now that these obligations have been eliminated, this waiver is available to all conditional residents whose marriages have failed, regardless of who was at fault for the breakup or who initiated the divorce or annulment proceedings.

INS has also allowed conditional residents to apply for this waiver if one of the parties has filed for dissolution but the divorce has not yet become final. In these cases INS would probably accept, but delay adjudicating, the waiver petition until it receives court documents indicating that the marriage has been officially dissolved.

Battered-Spouse Waiver

The Immigration Act of 1990 added an important option for spouses who are victims of battery or other forms of abuse. These spouses can now file for a waiver based solely on the ground that they or their children were subjected to such abuse. Under IMFA's original provisions these persons could seek a waiver based only on extreme hardship or termination of the marriage, and, in the latter case, only if the conditional resident was the first to file for divorce or annulment. As a results, many battered spouses elected to remain in abusive relationships, whole others felt compelled to file prematurely for dissolution of marriage. Now abused spouses have the option of either pursuing divorce, even if they did not initiate proceedings, or remaining married and removing their conditional status through the batter-spouse waiver.

The statute allows for the battered-spouse waiver if "during the marriage the alien spouse or child was battered by or was the subject of extreme cruelty perpetuated by his or her spouse or citizen or permanent resident parent." Interim regulations implementing the waiver further define the statutory terms and set forth the requirements for satisfying the waiver. The regulations clarify that the waiver is available to conditional residents, regardless of their current marital status. In other words, they may still be married and living with the abusing spouse, or separated, or divorced, or in the process of seeking divorce. As a practical matter, however, the battered-spouse waiver will probably be filed only by aliens who are not seeking divorce. Spouses who are divorced or have filed for divorce would normally file under the divorce/annulment waiver, due to its more relaxed proof requirements.

The new waiver is available to all spouses affected by the conditional residency requirements, whether their conditional residency was terminated prior to or after the creation of this waiver. Thus, both current and former conditional resident aliens can now take advantage of the 1990 statutory changes. To take advantage of the waiver, the spouse must not have departed from the country after the termination of the conditional resident status or be under an order of deportation.

Acts constituting battery or extreme cruelty include, but are not limited to, "any act or threatened act of violence, including any forceful detention, which results or threatens to result in physical or mental injury." Acts of violence shall include "psychological or sexual abuse or exploitation, including rape, molestation, incest [if the victim is a minor] or forced prostitution."

If the alien is alleging physical abuse, the alien can submit any credible evidence. This "may include, but is not limited to, expert testimony in the form of reports and affidavits from police, judges, medical personnel, school officials and social service agency personnel."

In the interim regulations, INS limits "extreme cruelty" to actions that qualify as "extreme mental cruelty." The agency also requires waiver applicants alleging extreme cruelty to furnish independent evidence from "a professional recognized by the [INS] as an expert in the field." Only licensed clinical social workers, psychologists, and psychiatrists fit that definition. The evaluation, as well as the waiver petition itself, must contain the professional's name, address, ID number, and the date his or her professional license expires.

Strict confidentiality is to be maintained regarding information contained in the waiver petition or supporting documents. The information is not to be released to any party without a court order or the written consent of the alien. Information may be released only to the applicant, his or her authorized representative, an INS officer, or any state or federal law enforcement agency.

Finally, the Immigration Act of 1990 requires the battered spouse not to have been "at fault in failing to meet the [joint filing] requirement." At first, the statute seemed to impose a "no fault" requirement: the battered spouse could take advantage of this waiver only if he or she were not at fault for causing the abusive action by the other spouse. But the interim regulations do not impose such a requirement, and to date INS has not interpreted this provision as requiring any further proof of eligibility. Therefore, it is unclear what, if any, meaning is to be placed on this statutory language.

Extreme Hardship Waiver

The conditional resident spouse may also claim a waiver based on "extreme hardship." Although the statute is silent on the issue, INS has stated that to claim the waiver, individuals who experience extreme hardship can be the conditional resident, children of the marriage, or the new spouse. The statute and regulations state that in assessing extreme hardship, INS shall take into account only factors that arose after the alien's entry as a conditional resident. For example, INS probably will not consider a preexisting medical problem that requires care and treatment in the United States. Medical problems that develop after entry into the United States, however, would be relevant. Political, social, or economic problems that have developed recently in the conditional resident's home country are other examples of relevant factors.

INS recognizes that a certain degree of hardship is likely to result from any deportation. INS will therefore grant the waiver only in cases in which the hardship is "extreme." Case law which has developed in the context of applications for suspension of deportation is relevant in defining extreme hardship. Those cases require more than the hardship ordinarily experienced by persons upon deportation, such as emotional strain incidents to relocation, separation from family and friends, and economic loss.

Suspension of deportation cases that have been particularly successful in proving extreme hardship have involved aliens with health problems for which adequate treatment was unavailable in the alien's home country. Economic detriment alone is usually insufficient unless the alien can show a complete inability to find work in the home country. But when economic hardship is combined with advanced age, illness, or family ties in the United States, INS is more likely to find extreme hardship. All possible equities in the case should be considered, especially those that demonstrate a special hardship. An unusually strong factor, together with more typical hardships such as psychological suffering, loss of ties in the community, and separation from family, will be very helpful.

Failure to Cooperate

If the marriage has not been terminated, but the citizen spouse will not cooperate in the filing of the joint petition, then the conditional resident must apply for one of the waivers. If the battered-spouse waiver is not appropriate, and if extreme hardship would be difficult to establish, then the only other option is for the conditional resident to file for divorce. If the facts of the case indicate that the waiver would be granted only under the divorce/annulment ground, filing for divorce may be the option to recommend, even if the conditional resident would otherwise want to stay married and continue efforts to reconcile with the citizen spouse. In such cases, the alien spouse's retention of lawful immigration status may be more important than the continuation of marriage. It is unfortunate and ironic that a law whose intent is to safeguard against fraudulent marriages could result in an increased number of dissolution of valid marriages.

Filing the Petition to Remove Conditions on Residence

The I-751 petition to remove conditions on residence must be filed, through the mail, with the INS Regional Service Center that has jurisdiction over the conditional resident alien's United States residence. The filing fee is currently $75.

If the conditional resident is in deportation proceedings at the end of the two-year period, the petition should still be filed with INS rather than with the immigration judge. In the deportation proceedings, however, the immigration judge has authority to review INS's decision on the joint petition or the waiver application.

ALIEN CHILDREN IN FOSTER CARE

Special Immigrant Status

The Immigration Reform and Control Act of 1986 created a means for some undocumented aliens to legalize their status, provided that they had resided in the United States since at least January 1, 1982. Some states and counties assisted alien children, who had been declared to be wards of the state, in their efforts to obtain lawful immigration status under this amnesty program. However, many of these children did not qualify for legalization because they could not establish that they had resided in the United States for the required time period. These children who remained in unlawful immigration status experienced difficulty qualifying for federal assistance programs. As a result, states and counties were forced to absorb a greater share of the costs of their support.

To remedy this problem, the Immigration Act of 1990 created a new "special immigrant" status for these children. Under section 153 of the act, a child may apply directly for permanent resident status if

(1) he is a dependent of a juvenile court and deemed eligible by that court for long-term foster care, and

(2) a court or an agency finds that returning the child to his or his parent's previous country of nationality or last habitual residence would not be in his best interest.

Few juveniles filed for special immigrant status because the 1990 statute failed to provide a complete remedy. Two major obstacles remained. First, almost none of the juveniles were eligible to "adjust" their status in the United States because they had entered the country illegally or had overstayed their initial visa. This meant that the children would have to return to their home country to receive their immigrant visas. The costs of such a trip, as well as the logistical problems of traveling alone, made the trip almost impossible for most of these children. Second, since the children were wards of the state and dependent upon foster care payments, they were all likely to be denied visas on the ground that they were public charges. The 1990 statute did not provide any waiver or exemption for this ground of exclusion.

On December 12, 1991, Congress made several important changes to the 1990 statute. A technical amendment allowed the alien children to adjust their status in the United States, regardless of their manner of entry into the country or their current immigration status. Juveniles therefore no longer need to leave the country to obtain their visas. The technical amendments also waived certain grounds of exclusion for these juveniles, most notably the public charge ground. Special immigrant juveniles can no longer be denied permanent resident status simply because they are indigent and receive foster care or other public assistance. In addition, grounds of exclusion relating to documentation requirements do not apply to the children. And finally, except for exclusion for criminal and national security reasons, the Attorney General is authorized to waive any other ground of exclusion for humanitarian purposes, for family unity, and for the public's best interest.

In an INS memorandum dated May 21, 1992, the associate commissioner for examinations instructed INS officers to begin processing these juveniles' applications for special immigrant status. Even though interim regulations regarding the processing of these applications had been issued on May 21, 1991, INS had stayed all adjudication until the technical amendments had been implemented. The INS memo also instructed INS offices to hold in abeyance applications from persons who are under age 21 but who are too old to qualify as "juveniles" under pertinent state law. The memo implied that when the agency issues final regulations, it intends to apply a uniform definition of "juvenile" to include all applicants under age 21.

The interim regulations and the May 21, 1992, memorandum define some key terms and set forth the procedure for filing for special immigrant status. The regulations define long-term foster care as "foster care that is of indefinite duration." The definition continues by stating that "[a] child who is eligible for long-term foster care will normally be expected to remain in foster care until [he or she] reach[es] the age of majority." This could present a problem for juveniles who are eligible for long-term foster care because the court has decided that family reunification is not possible, but who may not be in long-term foster care because the court has decided that adoption or guardianship is a better option. Unless this definition is modified in the final regulations, advocates and juvenile court judges may be forced to choose between securing permanent placement for abused and abandoned children (through adoption and guardianship) or securing lawful immigration status (by placing them in long-term foster care).

The interim regulations also require the applicant to remain a dependent of the juvenile court throughout the entire visa process. This could result in the denial of lawful immigrant status to some alien children who qualified as special immigrants when the law went into effect, but who have been or will be emancipated before INS adjudicates their application.

Juveniles who meet the requirements of the Immigration Act of 1990 and subsequent amendments complete form I-360 to establish eligibility as a special immigrant. The filing fee is $75. The application, filed with the INS district office where the child lives, is accompanied by

(1) an order establishing that the child is a dependent of a juvenile court and that the child has been deemed eligible for long-term foster care;

(2) evidence of a determination that returning the child to his or his parents' country of origin is not in the child's best interest (this evidence can be part of the same court order); and

(3) form G-28, notice of entry of appearance (if the applicant is represented by counsel).

An approved I-360 will not give the child the right to remain in the United States permanently. It should, however, provide future protection from deportation. The statute states that most grounds of deportation "shall not apply to a special immigrant described in section 101(a)(27)(J) based upon circumstances that exist before the date the alien was provided such special immigrant status."

Permanent Resident Status

To obtain lawful permanent resident status, the alien child should submit an application for adjustment of status (form I-485) along with the I-360 form for special immigrant status. To file the application for adjustment of status, an additional fee of $95 for children age 14 and under, and $120 for children over age 14, is required. The following documents relating to the child must be filed with the I-485 application: birth certificate, biographical information for children 14 or older (form G-325A), fingerprint card for children 14 or older (form FD 258), and three passport photos. To receive employment authorization prior to being granted permanent resident status, a special immigrant juvenile must submit a third application, form I-765, along with a $60 fee.

Since INS has now implemented the important 1991 technical amendments to the Immigration Act of 1990, juveniles who may qualify for the special immigrant status should be encouraged to apply. Because there is an annual limit of ten thousand visas for special immigrants, juveniles will have to compete for these visas with a variety of other immigrants who qualify for the special status under different statutory grounds. Priority for issuing the immigrant visas is based on the application date. Finally, the application for special immigrant status and for permanent residency should be filed and processed while the child is a dependent of the court because the juvenile court may terminate its jurisdiction over children approaching ages 18 or 21.

PERMANENT RESIDENT STATUS FOR WIDOWS AND WIDOWERS

In the past, problems often arose when a United States citizen died before the alien spouse had obtained immigrant status on the basis of the marriage. Marriage to a United States citizen alone does not confer any immigration rights or benefits to the alien spouse; the United States citizen must file a petition on the alien's behalf so that the spouse can become a permanent resident alien. If the citizen spouse died before filing the petition, immigration laws did not allow the alien spouse to initiate the procedure. And if the citizen spouse died after filing the petition but before the alien spouse had been granted the immigrant visa, INS could not grant the visa petition, and the alien could not obtain immigrant status.

INS recognized this problem but believed that it had little authority or discretion to grant immigrant visas to these widows and widowers. Congress finally addressed the problem in 1990. The Immigration Act of 1990 added provisions allowing widows and widowers to apply directly for an immigrant visa if, prior to the citizen spouse's death, the couple had been married for at least two years. The provisions required the widow or widower, however, to apply for permanent resident status within two years of the spouse's death. If the citizen spouse died before November 1, 1990 (the date the 1990 Act went into effect), the alien had until November 29, 1992 to apply for the visa. To be eligible for this latter benefit, the widow or widower must not have been legally separated from the citizen spouse at the time of his or her death, and must not have remarried in the meantime.

The widows and widowers must use a special form (form I-360) to apply for immigrant visas under the provision. The form must be accompanied by a fee of $75 and the following documentation:

(1) proof of the deceased spouse's United States citizenship;

(2) a marriage certificate issued by a civil authority;

(3) proof of termination of all prior marriages of both parties; and

(4) a death certificate issued by a civil authority proving the United States citizen's death.

If the petitioner cannot obtain these documents, he or she must show that they are "unavailable," either according to the State Department's Foreign Affairs Manual section on availability of documents, or through a letter from the local registrar of documents. If the above procedures are satisfied, the petitioner can submit secondary evidence, such as affidavits or church records, in lieu of the documents listed above.

Although the instructions on the I-360 form state that the deceased spouse must have been a United States citizen for at least two years prior to his or her death, the final INS regulations implementing the statutory provision have eliminated this requirement. As long as the marriage lasted at least two years, the length of the deceased spouse's status as a citizen does not matter.

Once the petition is approved, the immigration procedure is the same as those for immediate relatives of United States citizens who are alive. INS retains the petition if the person is eligible for adjustment of status; otherwise it forwards it to the State Department for visa processing abroad.

This change in the law for widows or widowers of United States citizens fails to provide any relief to the spouses of deceased lawful permanent residents (LPRs). LPRs, like citizens, must petition INS for legal immigration status for their spouses. However, LPR spouses cannot initiate the application process. If LPR dies before the immigrant visa is issued to the spouse, there is currently no statutory relief.

LEGALIZATION BENEFICIARY VISAS

Amnesty aliens who have obtained lawful permanent resident status can file a "second preference" visa petition for their alien spouse and unmarried children. But these visas are currently backlogged at least two and a half years; their availability in some cases depends upon the family member's nationality.

In anticipation of even larger backlogs forming in this visa category due to the 2.5 million amnesty aliens applying for their family members, in 1990, Congress created a new category of "transition visas" (also known as legalization beneficiary visas) for these spouses and children. It allocated an extra 55,000 visas a year for fiscal years 1992, 1993, and 1994 for these family members.

According to the State Department, the legalized alien follows the normal procedures when applying for a transitional visa. In other words, the legalized alien files a second preference petition for the spouse; this second preference petition will automatically be considered for a transition visa. As of October 1992, the State Department indicated that there is a two-year backlog in this transition visa category for "documentarily qualified" applicants. Document-arily qualified applicants are those who have an approved I-130 application and have complied with the first set of instructions from the State Department. These persons are waiting for the final instructions and a scheduling of their visa interview. These family members will therefore gain an advantage and time savings over other second preference applicants by qualifying for one of the transitional visas.

In INS's proposed regulations implementing the transitional visa pro-gram, INS imposed a requirement that the family relationship on which the visa petition is based must have existed at the time the petitioner obtained lawful permanent resident status. If the marriage occurred after the date petitioner obtained the status, the spouse would be ineligible for the transitional visa. The foregoing additional requirement, however, is not authorized by the statute, and INS dropped this requirement in the final regulations. Spouses and children of legalized aliens are eligible for transitional visas whether the family relationship was formed before or after the legalized alien obtained permanent residency.

Editor's Note: This article has been edited for publication.

A Rawlsian Analysis of the Immigration Act of 1990

Joan A. Pisarchik

INTRODUCTION

As a matter of both international and domestic law, a sovereign has the right to exclude immigrants from its territory. The procedures for exclusion vary from explicit requirements needed for admission, to delineating specific characteristics which, if possessed, will lead to automatic exclusion. In 1990, the United States employed a lottery system to award a portion of its visas. While this policy appears facially neutral, it is merely another procedure by which potential immigrants are excluded. The lottery is not open to all who seek admission. Instead, carefully tailored and highly specific statutory provisions detail those who are eligible to participate.

There are two ways to view the lottery. It can be seen as a less arbitrary way to allocate visas than previous policies, which were often formulated in response to crises, as opposed to a long range plan. Alternatively, the lottery can be viewed as a thinly disguised exclusionary policy similar to past United States policies, albeit packaged differently.

Immigration law has featured a consistency which is absent in many other areas of law. The lottery system is not an exception and its consistency with former United States policies of exclusion will be highlight in this Note. As a thinly disguised nativist policy, the lottery can be viewed as coming full circle, returning to the racist and nativist policies seen in immigration law from 1920 to 1950.

COMPONENTS OF IMMIGRATION LAW

Elements traditionally considered by government in creating an immigration policy include economics, race, nationalism, and foreign policy. The current immigration policy reflects the balance among these four factors. As a fifth factor, this Note will discuss the moral concerns involved in immigration. The theories of John Rawls will provide the framework for the analysis which will

Georgetown Immigration Law Journal, Volume 6 (1992:721–44).

constitute an examination of what the relevant moral concerns are, and whether these moral considerations have any force in shaping immigration policy. The four factors, as manifested in immigration law, have been upheld by United States courts as valid exercises of legislative will. Courts have traditionally refused to involve themselves in close examination of immigration laws, basing their deference on principles of international law and freedom of the Executive to conduct foreign policy.

THE RAWLSIAN FRAMEWORK

The dominance of plenary power leaves little room at the policy-making level for discussion of moral concerns and how, if at all, they should be regarded in the formulation of immigration policy. Natural rights of people to migrate have been sacrificed to rights of the nation incident to sovereignty. This motion is in direct contrast to the ideas of thinkers, such as John Rawls, who distinguish between the claims of

> liberty and right on the one hand and the desirability of increasing aggregate social welfare on the other; and that we give a certain priority, if not absolute weight to the former. Each member of society is thought to have an inviolability founded on justice . . . which even the welfare of everyone else cannot override. . . . Therefore in a just society the basic liberties are taken for granted and the rights secured by justice are not subject to political bargaining.

Rawls believes that the "first virtue of social institution" is justice. If laws or institutions are unjust, they should be changed or abolished. Rawls does not presuppose that all people will have equal rights. However, those who disagree about which conception of justice is correct may still agree that an aspect of justice is the lack of "arbitrary distinctions . . . between persons in the assigning of basic rights and duties."

His "conception of social justice . . . provid[es] . . . a standard whereby the distributive aspects of the basic structure of society are to be assessed." What rational people would choose, behind a veil of ignorance, as equal liberty will become the principles of justice. If rational people viewed themselves as equals, presumably they

> would not agree to a principle which may require lesser life prospects for some simply for the sake of a greater sum of advantages enjoyed by others. . . . No one has a reason to acquiesce in an enduring loss for himself in order to bring about a greater net balance of satisfaction.

If immigration policies were made from behind the veil of ignorance, presumably free migration would be the rule. Those determining policy would be aware of the unequal distribution of resources, but would not know how they would be affected by it. Therefore, they would choose open immigration because they themselves might be the ones wishing to utilize it in the future.

Under liberal theory, the rights of an individual are independent of his or her identity as a member of a particular community or nation. Our policies, however, differentiate among would-be immigrants largely on the basis of group identity or nationality. Identity thus becomes the greatest barrier to immigration, one that can be overcome only by a showing of special skill or some other desirable trait which makes the immigrant acceptable despite his or her nationality. If, as Rawls contends, "social justice is the principle of rational prudence applied to an aggregative conception of the welfare of the group," and can be applied globally, then United States immigration policies traditionally have been illiberal, drawing distinctions among potential immigrants based solely on nationality or special skills possessed. United States policy admits those people deemed to be best for United States interests. The total global good may be increased by the addition of talented and skilled immigrants to the United States. However, this policy disproportionately benefits the United States and maintains the status quo for those who are worst off. This may be the correct result under utilitarian theory, but it fails to take into account any distinction between persons.

In a Rawlsian framework, two different principles are initially available for ordering society. Basic rights can be assigned unequally, or social and economic inequalities can be accepted, but only "if they result in compensating benefits for everyone, and in particular for the least advantaged members of society." Similarly, on a global scale, nations may attempt to alleviate inequality with respect to unequal distribution of resources and unequal levels of economic development by migration. This allows for three possible justifications for freedom of movement: basic liberty; fair equal opportunity; and the difference principle.

A basic liberty, garnering the greatest protection, is that of internal movement. Under a Rawlsian system, it can be restricted only when it impinges on another basic liberty. Economic considerations and the preservation of the income level of citizens do not qualify as basic liberties. However, exclusion is often justified by economic considerations, such as concern that immigrants will take jobs away from citizens and drive down wages, thereby lowering the standard of living. It would be difficult to imagine a scenario in which a basic liberty or civil right was trampled on by movement of persons into and out of a country. Global migration, however, is not viewed by policymakers as similar to internal movement. Instead, national boundaries, which some argue are morally arbitrary, have become significant in the denial of global freedom of movement because they serve to maintain privileges for an elite group.

If movement is not a basic liberty, perhaps it may be justified as fair equal opportunity. This means that everyone has the equal right of access to a desirable social position, based on one's qualifications. It assumes that the "distribution of natural assets [to] those . . . [of] the same level of talent and ability . . . should have the same prospects of success regardless of their initial place in the social system." The main reason that people desire to move is to improve their condition or career prospects, thus linking social and geographical mobility. This equal right of access, like a basic liberty, cannot be overcome by economic considerations.

United States policies, however, have jealously guarded domestic economic well-being against a potential influx of these who could have the effect of lowering our standard of living. Currently, preference visas are awarded to those who are highly educated or skilled, such as scientists and professionals. There is no corresponding visa allocation for persons with less education or a low level of skill. This reflects our desire to recruit only those with superior intellects or skills, while excluding those whom we view as a threat to the economic well-being of our working-class. As a result, equal access for all is impossible, due to these requirements.

Rawls' difference principle views the unequal distribution of primary goods, "things that every rational man is presumed to want," such as rights or wealth, as acceptable only if those who are in the worst position are made better off than under any other feasible plan. Some of these primary goods need not be scarce, although the use of artificial constructs, such as political boundaries and visas, have served to make them scarce.

If visas may be viewed as primary goods, tied to the job market, among other things, then under the difference principle visas would be issued to alleviate the suffering of the greatest number of the most disadvantaged. In theory, some liberties are given up for economic and social gains. However, through the use of boundaries, restrictions, and requirements developed by governments as tools of exclusion, not only have liberties been relinquished, but there has been no corresponding economic or social gain on a global scale.

Additionally, immigration policies affect the distribution of income, presumably with the income of new aliens increasing while the income of citizens decreases. However, would-be immigrants are generally those who are worst off because they have the fewest social and economic rights. They are the recipients of unequal treatment and such inequality is allowable in a Rawlsian framework only if everyone in society benefits, and particularly if the least advantaged members of society benefit. Current immigration policy keeps those who are most disadvantaged in the same position, while guarding the rights of the privileged. The drawing of political boundaries prevents both global free movement as a basic liberty and the chance to gain fair equal opportunity.

Immigration Reform and Control Act of 1986

The main focus of the Immigration Reform and Control Act of 1986 (IRCA) was to address illegal immigration and to attempt to stop or severely impede it. Nonetheless, it may be informative to place IRCA in the larger context of United States policies, and the other goals it seeks to achieve, and to see how IRCA relates to the 1990 Act, as the two are temporally close.

IRCA granted amnesty to millions of illegal aliens, many of whom were from Mexico and Latin America. To the extent that the 1990 Act is reminiscent of earlier acts, it may be viewed as a response to IRCA, an act that legalized many illegal aliens and tipped the numerical balance far away from the preeminence formerly enjoyed by European nations. The lottery could be viewed as trying to rectify this perceived problem and to bring people into the United States who have been viewed traditionally as similar to ourselves. Thus, the 1990 Act could be viewed as a racist policy because it is seeking more "good aliens" in order to preserve the status quo or at least to slow the proportional growth of Third World immigration, both legal and illegal.

Immigration Act of 1990

At first glance, the lottery system appears to be a less discriminatory and less arbitrary way to determine who will be admitted to the country, compared to past policies, which focused closely on individual and group criteria. Upon closer inspection, however, the lottery is analogous in outcome to past laws although it uses a different process to achieve the result. Instead of specifically excluding certain groups, group identity is specified for those who are desired for admission. The wording of the statute is irrelevant because the result, admission of those deemed acceptable, is the same in both cases.

The 1990 Act and the lottery provision can be analyzed in the same ways in which the earlier acts have been analyzed, as a continuance of classical immigration law and restrictive nationalism. Under this analysis, the 1990 Act first will be looked at in terms of the four factors which are dominant in policy formation: economics, racial moods, nationalism, and foreign policy. Second, as a fifth category, the lottery and the tension between the lottery and the moral and ethical concerns about human migration will be explored. This focuses on the tension between public policy and liberal principles, due to the lottery's emphasis on group identity over that of the individual. Finally, the lottery will be analyzed in Rawlsian terms, using his three principles, with greater emphasis on the difference principle.

Section 1153 of the 1990 Act addresses diversity immigrants. It calls on the Attorney General to identify high and low admission regions and states and to calculate the numbers of immigrants admissible from various areas. There are no visas available for people from the high-admission states. Section 1153 also requires immigrants to have a high school education or its equivalent, or to have two years of work experience in a field that requires at least two years of training or experience.

Section 1153 also contains the lottery provision. It states that "notwithstanding the numerical limitations in . . . the Immigration and Nationality Act, there shall be made available to qualified immigrants . . . 40,000 immigrant visas in each of fiscal years 1992, 1993, and 1994." Qualified aliens are those who: (1) are not from states contiguous to the United States; (2) have employment secured in this country; and (3) are otherwise admissible. The visas are available to those who apply in chronological order. The 40,000 person lottery, however, is subject to the restriction that forty percent of the visas be allocated to "natives of the foreign state . . . which received the greatest number of visas issued under section 314 of the Immigration Reform and Control Act." The Irish are the beneficiaries of this provision.

The 1990 Act highlights the right of the sovereign to exclude immigrants for any reason. This is the hallmark of classical immigration policy. Economics appear to be the primary motivation behind many of the provisions, especially the lottery, followed by concerns about race and nationalism. Foreign policy considerations appear insignificant, but there is little doubt that the Supreme Court would exercise deference to the legislature if any cases arise under the 1990 Act. Plenary power would seem to remain intact.

Persons wishing to immigrate under any part of the 1990 Act must meet educational requirements, possess skill and experience in some field, or have family members in the United States. Additionally, lottery applicants must have secured employment in the United States prior to admission. This excludes many people from the poorest nations who are unable to meet the requirements and are unlikely to become eligible at any time if they are forced to remain in their native countries. The reality of these requirements is that the immigrants who are eligible for admission will disproportionately reflect the total immigrant population. Only the most qualified persons, according to Western standards, will be admitted, perpetuating the notion of who is desirable and worthy of admission to the United States.

The stringent requirements which must be met show that the lottery lacks the randomness that is usually associated with lotteries because the pool has been artificially limited, notably and expressly excluding Mexicans. The exclusion of great numbers of Mexicans, due both to numerical limits and skill or educational requirements, means that there are proportionally more visas for persons wishing to immigrate from other areas. In addition, Europeans are likely to be better educated than many groups of potential immigrants and more likely to be already employed when they arrive in the United States. This means that those chosen through the lottery will reflect the bias in favor of educated European persons. Instead of desiring a variety of people, the lottery works to maintain uniformity of immigrants, albeit through a disguised process. The criteria and numbers of immigrants allowed per region ensure that the new immigrants will be a fairly homogeneous group resembling their predecessors.

The McCarran-Walter Act prohibited the use of race as an absolute bar to immigration, but the 1990 Act seems to reflect racial considerations and tensions in border states and large cities, arising from the influx of legal and illegal immigrants from Central and South America. Moreover, the 1990 Act ignores population growth and widespread poverty in Central America, and especially in Mexico. This has been accomplished by narrowly tailoring regional definitions and groupings in the 1990 Act and then allowing the Attorney General to establish numerical limits. The non-lottery provisions of the 1990 Act provide for six regions and define them as: (1) Africa; (2) Asia; (3) Europe; (4) North America (other than Mexico); (5) Oceania; and (6) South America, Mexico, Central America, and the Caribbean. The exclusion of Mexico from the North American region and inclusion with Central and South America is highly suspect. Presumably, the preponderance of North American immigration to the United States would be from Mexico. The effect of grouping Mexico with Central and South America is to reduce proportionately the number of Mexicans who will be able to enter the United States legally. The 1990 Act appears to have grouped the most desperate countries into the same region, thereby severely limiting immigration from them while granting more spaces to areas which are less likely to have as many people desiring to come to the U.S., such as Canada, Europe, and Oceania.

This policy is illiberal because it defines people and their rights in geographic terms. Within each region, people are subdivided by education and work experience or training; the acceptability and amounts are defined according to Western standards. This is contrary to liberal thought which considers political boundaries to be morally arbitrary and illegitimate when they are used to protect certain privileged groups while denying others access to a better life. Geography is the final hurdle for those who are otherwise qualified. It enables policymakers in the United States to tailor carefully the racial and ethnic mix of immigrants, while ensuring that they are ready to contribute to the economy of the United States upon admission.

Under a Rawlsian analysis, the 1990 Act keeps immigration subservient to the whims of sovereigns. Freedom of movement between countries remains something less than a basic liberty or even an issue of fair equal opportunity. The 1990 Act strives to exclude those who may be most in need of escape from their native lands. The definition of regions and the skill requirements keep those in greatest desperation out of the United States. The 1990 Act is another instance of guarding the economy and standard of living from the perceived threat and fear of an influx of immigrants.

In order to comport with the difference principle, those who are the most disadvantaged would have to be made better off than under any other feasible plan. In this respect, the regional construct of the 1990 Act may be one of the harshest provisions. It does nothing to further the interests of those who are the worst off. It is not difficult to conceive of numerous other ways in which regional boundaries could have been drawn to promote the interests of the poorest people, who are unable to qualify for visas under current law. The lottery has the same effect through its careful enunciation of those who are permitted to participate. The denial of participation to the worst off reinforces their position and maintains the status quo.

CONCLUSION

United States immigration policy has been a steady progression and refinement of former laws, plus responses to current real or perceived threats to factional domestic interests. The 1990 Act and the lottery are not divergent branches of policy. Rather, the 1990 Act could be viewed as closing the circle which began in 1921, for very little has changed. There are no doubts under international law or United States law about the right of a nation to exclude whomever it chooses, or to set up elaborate conditions for gaining entry. Indeed, people are excluded for a myriad of reasons, many of them economic but few, if any, moral. The consistency of immigration policy in the United States is remarkable, especially in its resistance to updating the law to reflect current global reality. There has been a population explosion and concomitant proliferation of poverty, yet immigration law remains parochial, failing to respond to those who are most desperate in the global community.

Editor's Note: This article has been edited for publication.

The Move to Employment-Based Immigration in the Immigration Act of 1990

Towards a New Definition of 'Immigrant'

William V. Roebuck, Jr.

INTRODUCTION

The recent Immigration Act of 1990 ("The Act"), passed in Congress on October 27 and signed into law by President Bush on November 29, 1990, is the most extensive reform of the legal immigration laws of the United States passed in the last quarter century. The Act is long and complex, with provisions affecting a wide range of immigration issues. The Act continues the established policy of favoring family reunification by increasing the number of visas available for this purpose, and underlines the importance of a newer policy, the strengthening of the economy and American competitiveness, by nearly tripling the number of visas available for employment-based immigrants. The Act also reopens the door to immigrants from Ireland, Italy, Poland, and other countries "that traditionally were sources of immigration in the past," but whose citizens had been "foreclosed from immigrating due to the vagaries of the 1965 law." The Act makes further critical changes in the immigration law provisions relating to exclusions (barring from entry) and deportations based on health and national security grounds, and eliminates much of the archaic language and many of the specific provisions originally enacted as part of the McCarren-Walter Act of 1954 (which banned entry into the United States "on the basis of homosexuality and ideology").

Of all the changes made to the Act, the most significant is the move to employment-based immigration. The move represents a fundamental change in United States immigration policy; one brought about by a variety of factors including changed social and economic circumstances, the experience gained from nearly twenty-five years with the old policy, and the changing views of immigration experts and constituencies. This Article will focus on this aspect of the new immigration law by explaining its legal aspects, describing the legislative background, and exploring some of the rationales and criticisms of this new approach to United States immigration law.

North Carolina Journal of International Law and Commercial Regulation, Volume 16 (1991:523–39).

THE ACT

The Immigration Act of 1990 nearly triples the number of visas available based on employment criteria, from 54,000 to 140,000. This number is subdivided into several different employment-related categories. Forty thousand visas are set aside for "priority workers," a category which includes "aliens with extraordinary ability in the sciences, arts, education, business, or athletics;" outstanding professors and researchers; and "certain multinational executives and managers." Aliens admitted under this category of "priority workers" must be seeking entry to "continue work in the area of extraordinary ability" and their entry must be shown to be of "substantia[l] benefit prospectively" to the United States.

The second allotment of employment-based visas, also numbering 40,000, is for "aliens who are professionals with advanced (masters' or higher) degrees or who have exceptional ability in the sciences, arts, or business." In addition, to obtain a visa in this category, the alien must show that his "services . . . are sought by an employer in the United States." In determining whether an immigrant has exceptional ability, the possession of a degree or professional license will not "by itself be considered sufficient evidence of such exceptional ability."

The third major category for employment-based immigration, also with an annual allotment of 40,000 visas (plus any visas not used in the above-mentioned categories), is for "skilled workers, professionals, and other workers." Skilled workers are defined as "those capable of performing skilled labor (requiring at least two years training or experience), not of a temporary or seasonal nature, for which qualified workers are not available in the United States." "Professionals" in this category should have a baccalaureate degree to accompany their professional status. "Other workers" are immigrants who are capable of performing "unskilled labor, not of a temporary or seasonal nature, for which qualified workers are not available in the United States." Immigrants in this third major category must have labor certification from the Secretary of Labor showing that there are insufficient qualified workers in the United States to perform such work.

The most detailed provisions of the employment-based immigration component deal with visas set aside for "employment creation." These visas are for immigrants seeking to enter the United States "for the purpose of engaging in a new commercial enterprise." The number of annual visas designated for this category is limited to 10,000. The alien must invest one million dollars in a new commercial enterprise which will "benefit the United States economy and create full-time employment for not fewer than ten United States citizens" or lawfully admitted aliens who are authorized to work. There are no requirements concerning what type of business investment must be made. Such "industrial policy tests" were rejected as stifling to entrepreneurial creativity.

Of these 10,000 annual visas, 3,000 will be set aside for "targeted employment areas." Such an area is defined as either a rural area or an area "which has experienced high unemployment (of at least 150 percent of the national average rate)."

To ensure that visas granted for employment creation actually serve that purpose, the Act establishes strict oversight procedures. Visas in this category are granted on a conditional basis for two years. If during that period, the Attorney General determines that the alien entrepreneur has not properly fulfilled the requirements for investment and establishment of the commercial enterprise, the Attorney General shall terminate the permanent resident status of the alien and his family. Such termination proceedings may be brought on several grounds: first, if the Attorney General determines that the commercial enterprise was established solely as a means of evading the immigration laws of the United States; second, if the commercial enterprise was not established; third, if the alien did not invest the requisite capital; fourth, if the alien was not sustaining the investment and the establishment of the enterprise throughout the two year period; or fifth, if in some other way the alien did not conform to the specified requirements.

To have the conditional status lifted, the alien entrepreneur must petition the Attorney General, supplying the necessary facts and information, and submit to an interview, during which such information would be corroborated. Failure to file the petition or have the interview would be grounds for termination of permanent resident status. If the alien entrepreneur receives a favorable determination from the Attorney General, the conditional status is removed. Otherwise, the alien entrepreneur's permanent status is terminated. An alien who knowingly establishes a commercial enterprise in order to evade any provision of the immigration laws could be subject to up to five years imprisonment.

To complement the employment-based immigrant visa program, the Act establishes a three-year pilot program to assist the Secretary of Labor in determining labor shortages or surpluses in up to ten occupational classifications. Where there is a labor shortage with respect to an occupational classification, certification by the Secretary of Labor for petitions in that classification is automatic.

ANALYSIS

Sponsors and supporters of the Immigration Act of 1990 (and its preliminary formulations in the House and Senate) have offered different justifications supporting the emphasis on employment-based immigration. First, they point out that family reunification is still the "cornerstone" of legal United States immigration and that the reforms aimed at increasing employment-based immigration do not require a cut in the number of visas for family-sponsored immigration. Supporters also point out that employment-based immigration is not a new policy. Under prior law, there were categories for skills-based admissions. The reason the reform has struck many as a very radical change is because the old system had functioned in such a way that family-sponsored immigration almost totally dominated the supply of visas.

Employment-based immigration has also received support because it encourages diversity and innovation, two of the traditional justifications for United States legal immigration policy. Data indicate that a policy favoring skills-based immigrant admissions tends to open up "immigration channels for applicants from ethnic groups and countries of origin which, for one reason or another, [were not] present in previous immigration streams." Such a policy would not, as some critics of the reform have charged, favor European immigration and shut the door on immigrants from developing countries.

Employment-based immigration is also justified on several economic grounds. Some experts believe that employment-based immigration will help the United States confront a skilled-worker shortage and will increase American competitiveness. According to this view, the same declining transportation and communications costs "which have facilitated the increase in international trade [have] also heightened the international competition for skilled immigrants. There is now not merely a national labor market for skilled immigrants, for skilled workers; there is now an international labor market for skilled workers." If the United States does not look to its economic self-interest and compete for these immigrants, other countries will reap the benefits. There already exists in the United States a demand for highly-skilled workers which employment-based immigration will help to meet.

A focus on immigrants with skills not only helps American competitiveness, it also benefits the American economy in two ways. First, it expands the productive capacity of the economy: "[T]he potential for job creation by immigrant scientists, engineers, and entrepreneurs can be substantial." Second, such a focus would improve "the relative earnings of lower skilled U.S. workers." Such an effect is more easily understood by looking at the consequence of *not* focusing on skills in implementing an immigration policy. Statistics show that the lowest-skilled immigrant workers who have family already in the United States will predominate. This increases competition among low-skilled workers for jobs and drives down wages. Immigration of more highly skilled workers tends to reduce "relative differentials in wages . . . thereby promoting the policy objective of narrowing the inequality of income, reducing poverty and welfare dependency."

The investor visa program, authorizing visas for immigrants who can invest one million dollars in a business and create ten jobs for American workers, is a more focused application of this general view that highly skilled immigrants in certain fields can create job opportunities for Americans and increase both the productive capacity of the economy and American competitiveness. This program, according to its proponents, would "generate over eight billion dollars annually in new investment in small and independent U.S. businesses and provide up to 100,000 new jobs for Americans. . . ." Such programs have been tried with great success in Canada and Australia, and have served as examples to which supporters of the new policy have pointed. Failure to enact such a program, it was argued, would have discouraged productive investment, undercutting the "vigorous efforts by various states and regions to attract foreign investment that will create jobs. . . ." Supporters countered the charge that visas were "up for sale" by pointing out that:

> [o]ur entire immigration preference system makes choices based on individuals' attributes and circumstances. Individuals who have acquired the ability to invest and actively manage new enterprises to the direct benefit of U.S. workers and our economy, are not so less honorable or desirable than individuals who have acquired doctoral degrees or exceptional abilities in the arts and sciences, which also benefit our nation.

Certain social and economic developments that have taken place since the family-sponsored immigration system was last examined in the 1960's justify a shift to a more employment-based immigration policy. First, because of tremendous reductions in transportation and communications costs, immigration is no longer the "gut-wrenching experience" it used to be. Previously, it "meant the virtual severance of all ties with family members who remained behind. This has not been the case for several decades. . . ." Second, the mid-1960's was a very different period, in economic terms, from the 1990's. What was justifiable in terms of the assimilation of immigrants then is less justifiable now. The mid-1960's was a "period of low and declining real costs for energy, unprecedented growth in productivity, shrinking unemployment and rapidly expanding real GNP per capita. Most important, it was a period during which Americans believed all these trends would continue indefinitely." The times and corresponding expectations have changed. Slower economic growth, lower increases in productivity, increased international competition, and America's "declining position as a world leader in technology" required a reevaluation of United States immigration policy.

Many who supported the general idea of increased employment-based immigration qualified that support in one critical way. They argued that any increase should be tied to employer sponsorship and that labor certification requirements, indicating real labor shortages, should be strictly enforced. The employer sponsorship and labor certification requirements that remain in the new law, in the second and third categories respectively, are vestiges of prior law and could be interpreted to indicate congressional reservation about moving fully to an independent immigration system that is not based on any specifically demonstrable labor need for each immigrant. Supporters of employment-based immigration split on this issue. Labor groups, like the AFL-CIO, supported the employer sponsorship and strict labor certification provisions: "worked [sic] based admissions to this country must be limited to admissions based on real need that cannot otherwise be met in the short term. Such a need must be *demonstrated,* not simply asserted."

Others questioned the efficacy of having either the government or employers attempting to determine labor shortages. Such a system, critics asserted, could not work. An immigrant could not be made to stay in a particular place with a particular job once given a visa. Second, the Department of Labor was incapable of determining where labor shortages existed. The market system and worker/employer negotiation, these critics argued, did a better job of identifying and rectifying such shortages than a government bureaucracy. Finally, such policies would lead to strong political pressures on the Department of Labor to certify (or not certify) a shortage in a particular category, with employers and employees exerting pressure in opposite directions. Despite such questioning, labor certification of some kind, to indicate that immigrants would not (in theory at least) be taking away jobs from Americans, proved a political necessity and remained in the final bill as enacted into law. It served supporters well in their efforts to justify the new law.

The employment-based immigration portion of the new law represents less than a quarter of the total number of immigration visas that were to be available. Nevertheless, the law was seen as a fundamental shift away from a nearly total focus on family-based immigration. It was inevitable that such a shift, although relatively small, would attract criticism; some of it cogent and probing.

First, critics felt that the employment-based immigration program came at the expense of family-sponsored immigration. Although supporters of the new law pointed out that no cuts were made in family-sponsored immigration (and in fact such allotments were increased), the political shift away from family-sponsored immigration would greatly reduce any *increases* in allotments for family visas. Further, some adjustments in policies for family-based immigration were viewed as new restrictions. Because the shift in emphasis represented a fundamental change in priorities, some critics recommended that the employment-based component be enacted on a trial basis. Accompanying this type of criticism was a reminder of the economic benefits of family-based immigration: the family provides a safety net for immigrants, helping them to assimilate and to find jobs; and families also provide child care and other services which "assist the immigrant's adjustment and social well-being" and thereby relieve drains on government-provided social services.

Critics also questioned the key justification for the partial shift to employment-based immigration. There was no labor shortage, in their view, to justify an influx of skilled and semi-skilled immigrants. Instead, the real economic problems were high unemployment and a lack of job training and technical education. Employment-based immigration was the wrong solution to such problems. A variation on this argument was that even if a labor shortage existed, there was "no data to support the conclusion that the shortage of skilled workers in the United States [was] due to the quality of persons immigrating under the [old] preference system." Focusing on immigration to solve this problem, instead of focusing on the education system and on better government planning, would drastically alter the immigration system to the detriment of family-based immigration with little or no guarantee that the changes would have any effect on the problems.

The investor visa program was harshly criticized as amounting to a "visa for sale" program. Given the damage this would do to the traditional view of the United States as a haven for immigrants from around the world, any economic benefits would be unjustified. Critics failed to recognize that the program was limited in scope and had been developed from provisions of the prior immigration laws.

The move to create completely separate tracks for family-sponsored and employment-based immigration also drew criticism. The argument against this move was based on functional grounds: the program would not work as planned. The separation of "family connection immigrants and independent immigrants may not be realized or only imperfectly so, because of strenuous competition likely to occur between the two groups over time." Immigrants admitted on the basis of employment would use family-sponsorship categories to bring over their spouses and children, thus increasing demand for these visas and creating longer waiting periods. Instead of separating the two tracks the new law would merge them by increasing demand on both tracks:

> These dynamics could imply an increased 'gaming' of the system through multiple applications, and an expanded effort by immigrants to seek the quickest route of entry—whatever it may be—depending on such variables as country of origin, family size, and nature of family relationships with persons in the United States.

One final criticism leveled at the employment-based system was that it amounted to too little, too early. That is, until *illegal* immigration was better controlled, nothing should be done to increase levels of legal immigration, even if employment-based immigration made up part of that increase. Second, the change to employment-based immigration was far too modest. A more radical overhaul of the immigration system was needed, which would severely restrain if not eliminate family-sponsored immigration and put an employment-based system in its place.

CONCLUSION

The decision to include an employment-based component in the new immigration law represents a fundamental shift in immigration policy. The reform is not unprecedented, however, since some of its elements were taken from policies and procedures present (but largely neglected) in the Immigration Act of 1965. Nor is the reform disproportionate, since the employment-based component represents a relatively small portion of the total allotment of annual visas. In addition, this component, though not a trial program *per se, is* subject to review (as is the entire immigration legal system) by an independent commission established by the Immigration Act of 1990. Despite these somewhat tentative measures and the built-in safeguard of review, the new component of employment-based immigration did manage to embrace many of the critical reforms in immigration law that have been proposed with growing intensity by various experts and groups over the last decade. That mix of old and new, after some initial criticism and suggestions, eventually attracted widespread support, even from groups which had opposed earlier formulations of the law.

Obviously, Senators and Representatives, experts and lobbyists all had their private agendas to pursue. What is unique about U.S. immigration, however, is that it encompasses certain shared values and traditions present on anyone's agenda as an American, for the United States is a nation of immigrants. As Senator Kennedy put it, "what we are really talking about is how all of us basically arrived here. Whether it was 300 years ago or 100 years ago, it was immigration and immigration policy that really defined how America became America." With the passage of the Immigration Act of 1990, a slight addition to the definition of immigrant has been made. With time, we will know whether that new definition of immigrant is workable and enduring.

Editor's Note: This article has been edited for publication.

Gender and Persecution

Protecting Women Under International Refugee Law

Linda Cipriani

INTRODUCTION

The human displacement resulting from World Wars I and II led to the adoption, first by the League of Nations and later by the United Nations, of international agreements to protect refugees. Today, the international law on refugees consists of the Statute of the Office of the United Nations High Commissioner for Refugees (Statute), The Convention Relating to the Status of Refugees (Convention), and the Protocol Relating to the Status of Refugees (Protocol). These treaties define "refugee" as a person with a well-founded fear of persecution due to his or her race, religion, nationality, political opinion or membership in a social group. At the time these treaties were ratified, international concern was focused on educated Europeans left homeless after the Second World War as well as those fleeing communism. Today, most refugees are "victims of violence or natural disasters, not ideological perse-cution." Some have argued that this calls for a new definition of refugee. One proposed change has been to include as refugees women who face persecution because of their gender.

Because asylum is not granted specifically for gender-based persecution, there are no statistics indicating how many women flee their countries due to such persecution. Women fleeing gender-based persecution may, instead, claim persecution on other grounds which are recognized by the treaties, such as political opinion. In recognition of the persecution some women may face, the United Nations High Commissioner for Refugees (UNHCR) and the European Parliament have taken limited measures to extend protection to these women under the "social group" category of the refugee treaties. Some have argued that further measures should be taken to consider women facing severe vio-lence or discrimination as a social group because asylum could be given under existing laws. Yet, successfully claiming membership in a social group has proven to be very difficult because the UNHCR has given little guidance as to whom this category was meant to apply. Additionally, the UNHCR has

Georgetown Immigration Law Journal, Volume 7 (1993:511–48).

stated that "[m]ere membership of [sic] a particular social group will not normally be enough to substantiate a claim to refugee status."

The definition of refugee should be expanded to include those with a well-founded fear of persecution because of their gender. This would protect women from institutionalized misogyny in which the government carries out, sanctions, or ignores oppression of or violence against women because they are women. The most notorious example of such persecution is probably Islam with its strict rules regarding the status and behavior of women. However, similar conditions exist in India under the Hindu religion, in Africa under tribal laws, and in Latin America under the tradition of *machismo*. Clearly, these practices reflect cultural or religious traditions that outsiders often cannot understand. Nevertheless, if a government forces these traditions upon a woman who rejects them, this may amount to persecution.

EXAMPLES OF PERSECUTION OF WOMEN

Religion, Culture, and Gender

Clearly, the treatment of women described in this Article can be justified on religious grounds. The right to freely practice one's religion is protected by many international agreements. However, international agreements guaranteeing the freedom of religion permit the state to restrict such practice in order to protect the rights of others. One such agreement is the International Covenant on Civil and Political Rights which states that the "[f]reedom to manifest one's religion or beliefs may be subject only to such limitations as are prescribed by . . . the fundamental rights and freedoms of others." Religious practices which impinge on the fundamental rights of women could be subject to limitation without being considered a violation of religious freedom. The state must show that the restriction was necessary (*i.e.,* that it was taken to achieve a permissible aim and is proportionate to that aim). This Covenant also provides that any one of its provisions may not be interpreted so as to allow for the destruction of any one of the other freedoms recognized by it. A state would, thus, not be able to rely on the principle of freedom of religion to deny women rights guaranteed by other provisions of the covenant such as the right to consent to marry, or to live free of discrimination because of one's sex.

This conflict between religious freedom and women's rights raises the problem of which rights prevail in such a situation. Rights that have achieved the status of peremptory norms, such as the prohibition of slavery, torture, genocide, or systematic racial discrimination, must clearly prevail over the right to manifest religion. Some of the practices mentioned herein should clearly be absolutely prohibited because they violate peremptory norms. For example, the practice of *sati* and bride-burnings in India is a violation of the right to life as is the murder of "dishonored" women in Iran or Pakistan; and the selling of child brides to Muslims is arguably a form of slavery as are the Africa practices of *levirate* or *sororate*.

Some of the practices mentioned in this Article do not fall into this category of peremptory norms, so the problem of which right should prevail, freedom of religious practice or gender equality, becomes more difficult. One possible solution that has been offered is to balance the competing interests by considering: the relationship between the specific equality right and goal of gender equality; the significance of the religious law to the religion; the effects on other human rights; the degree of conflict between the religious and gender rights; the cumulative effects of multiple restrictions on either rights; and the proportionality of the restriction. Clearly this approach is extremely complex and leaves a great deal of discretion up to those persons performing the balancing act. Yet, until there is universal consensus to give women's rights priority over religious traditions, this may be the only way to resolve a conflict between the two competing rights.

The restrictions on women's rights described herein can also be justified on cultural grounds. Similar to freedom of religion, the freedom to practice one's culture is protected by treaties such as the International Covenant on Economic, Social, and Cultural Rights. This right, however, is limited so that cultural practices cannot violate fundamental human rights. Therefore, a similar argument that was made above regarding conflicts between freedom of religion and gender equality can be made for conflicts between cultural practices and women's rights. Cultural practices that violate fundamental rights of women should be absolutely prohibited. For example, genital mutilation of young girls in Africa and the Middle East is arguably a violation of the peremptory norm against cruel or inhuman treatment and should therefore be prohibited. Again, the balancing approach would be used with cultural practices that restrict those rights that are not peremptory norms. In this way, a resolution of the conflict between cultural practices and gender equality can be achieved. The remainder of this Article will examine the refugee laws and how they can protect women from the persecution that can result from these religious and cultural practices.

THE DEFINITION OF REFUGEE IN INTERNATIONAL LAW

As noted above, the only current, binding international agreements regarding refugees are the Statute of the UNHCR, the UN Convention and the Protocol. Many international and regional agreements address the plight of refugees. The United Nations Declaration on Human Rights (1948) and the Declaration on Territorial Asylum guarantee the right to asylum, but they are not binding treaties. In addition, there are several regional agreements dealing with the rights of refugees such as the Organization of African Unity's Convention Governing Specific Aspects of Refugee Problems in Africa (1969), and the Organization of American States' Caracas Convention on Diplomatic Asylum (1954), and the Caracas Convention on Territorial Asylum (1954).

The Statute of the UNHCR has adopted a three-pronged definition of refugee. First, it includes those people who were considered refugees under either: The Constitution of the International Refugee Organization, or the Arrangements of 12 May 1926 and 30 June 1928, the Conventions of 28 October 1933 and 10 February 1938, and the Protocol of 14 September 1939. Second, it includes those who, due to the events occurring before January 1, 1951, are outside their country of nationality (or, for stateless persons, their habitual residence), have a well-founded fear of being persecuted for their race, religion, nationality, or political opinion, and are unable to seek protection from their own government. The refugees' inability to receive protection from their own government differentiates refugees from ordinary aliens. Third, the statute extends to those who meet the requirements of the second definition but removes the temporal limitation of January 1, 1951.

The Convention has adopted only the first two parts of the UNHCR definition of refugee. It recognizes as refugees those with a well-founded fear of persecution because of their race, religion, nationality, or political opinion due to events occurring before 1951. According to the Statute, the High Commissioner has authority to protect refugees irrespective of any dateline. Therefore, a person who meets the criteria of the Statute qualifies for protection by the UNHCR regardless of whether or not he is recognized as a refugee under the Convention.

The Protocol serves to broaden further the Convention's definition of refugee by removing the limitation that allowed refugee status for persons fleeing events that occurred before January 1, 1951. As a result of the Protocol, refugee status can potentially be extended to anyone having a well-founded fear of persecution because of his or her race, religion, nationality, or political opinion regardless of whether or not those fears are based on events occurring before 1951. In addition, the Protocol expanded the definition of refugee even further by including persecution based on membership in a particular social group. The Protocol adopts all of the articles of the UN Convention so that those states that are contracting parties to the Protocol but never ratified the UN Convention are essentially parties to the Convention as well.

TOWARD A BROADER DEFINITION OF REFUGEE

The international community is now beginning to recognize the need for broadening the definition of refugee to include those fleeing gender-based persecution. In April of 1984, the European Parliament adopted a resolution which called on states to recognize the right "of women in certain countries who face harsh or inhuman treatment because they are considered to have transgressed the social mores of the country" to be considered a "social group" within the meaning of the definition of refugee in the Convention. In May of 1985, the Dutch Refugee Association organized a seminar in which thirty-seven representatives and women refugees from various countries met in the Netherlands to discuss women refugee issues. The participants formulated ten recommendations, the first of which was that "Governments should recognize as forms of persecution, leading to the granting of refugee status, social and institutional forms of oppression of women which contravene international judicial standards and constitute violation of human rights, and should take measures to bring this to public attention."

One method of granting refugee status to persecuted women is to consider them a "social group" within the meaning of the Convention. In October of 1985, the UNHCR's Subcommittee of the Whole on International Protection considered a Note on the International Protection of Refugee Women. It acknowledged that there were a number of cases in which women sought asylum pursuant to the Convention due to the treatment of women in their country. States were asked to consider the resolution of the European Parliament in 1984 and adopt its conclusions.

Unfortunately, the UNHCR chose not to follow the model of the European Parliament. Instead, the UNHCR Executive Committee Report left the option open to individual states:

> The Executive Committee . . . recognized that States, in the exercise of their sovereignty, are free to adopt the interpretation that women asylum-seekers who face harsh or inhuman treatment due to their having transgressed the social mores of the society in which they live may be considered as a 'particular social group' within the meaning of Article 1 A(2) of the 1951 United Nations Refugee Convention.

By leaving it up to the states, this provision may be enforced or ignored inconsistently in the international community. The following cases illustrate this problem.

In November of 1986, five Iranian nationals, one of whom was a woman, sought political asylum in the Federal Republic of Germany. The woman claimed that she was subject to special reprisals because of her sex. The Federal Office granted the applicants asylum because of their well-founded fear of persecution due to their political activities. In addition, the woman was found to have belonged to a specific social group, Iranian women, that was subject to persecution specific to that group. The Office held that "the ideologically based power of men over women, results in a general political repression of women in defiance of their individual liberties and human rights."

In a similar case coming out of the United Kingdom, the court denied asylum based on the social group category even through it recognized that women could be protected under this category. The way the court applied the law, however, clearly indicates the problem of protecting persecuted women as a social group rather than recognizing gender as a basis of persecution. In this case, an Iranian woman sought asylum in the United Kingdom based on the position of women in Iran. Her application was denied. One of the conclusions of the Appeal Tribunal was that the "social group" provision means membership in a group that can be identified and has common practices or beliefs, but that there was no evidence that Iranian women considered themselves a social group. Another conclusion was that

> [o]pposition to Islamic rules remains individually based. Therefore even if the penalties that flow from a westernized approach amount to persecution, this would not be persecution within the Convention on the Status of Refugees, 1951.

The United States agrees with such a narrow reading of the term and would likewise make it difficult for women to rely on this category to flee gender based persecution. The Ninth Circuit has been the only circuit to develop a test for what constitutes a social group. In a 1986 decision, *Sanchez-Turijillo v. INS,* the court stated:

> The phrase "particular social group" implies a collection of people closely affiliated with each other, who are actuated by some common impulse or interest. Of central concern is the existence of a voluntary associational relationship among the purported members, which imparts some common characteristic that is fundamental to their identity as a member of that discrete social group.

The second Circuit recently relied on this definition to deny a woman refugee status. In *Gomez v. INS,* a Salvadorian woman sought asylum because she had been repeatedly battered and raped throughout her youth by Salvadorian guerrillas. She claimed that because of these attacks she became a member of a social group singled out for persecution in El Salvador. The court relied on *Sanchez-Trujillo* to deny her refugee status. It held that she "failed to produce evidence that women who have previously been abused by the guerrillas possess common characteristics—other than gender and youth—such that would-be persecutors could identify them as members of the purported group." In addition, there was no indication that the plaintiff would be singled out for persecution again.

The inconsistent use of the social group category, as indicated by the above cases is clearly the result of the UNHCR's failure to define it in precise terms. Scholars and practitioners who attempt to define it consider such factors as ethnic, cultural, and linguistic origin, education, family background, economic activity, shared values, outlook, and aspirations. They also consider relevant the attitude toward and treatment of the purported social group by others, in particular, state authorities. In the countries described herein, however, women do not seem to be perceived of by their government or the rest of society as a cohesive group.

As an alternative to obtaining refugee status as a social group, persecuted women could seek protection under the political opinion or religion category. Yet a woman's refusal to abide by the traditions of her country is not based on any political opinion or religious belief she may hold. Rather, it is based on her personal distaste for that particular tradition.

A third method of enabling women to achieve refugee status is to expand the definition of a refugee to include anyone having a well-founded fear of persecution because of gender. If the Convention recognized persecution because of gender, individual women who opposed the rules and traditions of their society and were persecuted because of it would be protected. Women would then just have to prove that they were persecuted because they were women and would not have to show they were members of a social group of persecuted women with common beliefs and practices.

GENDER AND PERSECUTION

The definition of refugee in the Convention should be expanded to include gender-based persecution for several reasons. The persecution suffered by women as illustrated in Part II is consistent with the definition of persecution in the UNHCR's *Handbook on Procedures and Criteria for Determining Refugee Status* (*Handbook*): the drafters of the original definition contemplated further expansion to include future concerns; and the international community already condemns persecution of women.

To argue for an expansion of the definition of refugee to include gender-based persecution, first, "persecution" must be defined. Unfortunately, the treaties do not define this term. In addition, case law on this topic is limited because concern with what constitutes a "well-founded fear" has dominated asylum determination and preempted inquiry into "persecution." However, the *Handbook* does give some indication of what this term means.

The *Handbook* states that there is no universally accepted definition of persecution and that attempts to formulate such a definition have not been successful. However, it does give some indication as to what persecution includes. A "threat to life or freedom" or "other serious violations of human rights" always constitutes persecution. Discriminatory treatment constitutes persecution in certain circumstances such as when one faces "serious restrictions in his right to earn his livelihood . . . or his access to normally available educational facilities." Discriminatory measures that are not in themselves serious may give rise to a reasonable fear of persecution if they produce, in the person concerned, a feeling of insecurity and apprehension regarding future existence. Persecution also includes a combination of factors that cumulatively portray an "atmosphere of insecurity." Although persecution is normally a result of government action, "where serious discriminatory or offensive acts are committed by the local populace, they can be considered as persecution if they are knowingly tolerated by the authorities or if the authorities refuse, or prove unable, to offer effective protection."

This provision is especially significant because this convention, if amended to include gender-based persecution, could offer protection to women in circumstances which are normally considered within the "private" sphere of international law. International law has allowed the particular concerns of women to be ignored because of its structural distinction between public and private spheres. The public sphere of international law governs relations between states, while the private sphere consists of problems within the state where international law has no recognized legal interest. This distinction could exempt states from responsibility for religious or cultural practices that persecute women unless their agents were directly responsible and that responsibility could be imputed to the state. However, this provision does not allow this public/private distinction to be used and will extend refugee status even to those whom their own government will not protect.

The treatment of women outlined herein could be considered "persecution" under the *Handbook*. The examples given in Part II indicate that women are deprived of the right to work, to attain education or training, and to enter into marriages freely, are deprived of control over their own persons, and are considered in the eyes of the law as inferior to men. These laws and practices clearly fall into the categories of persecution given in the *Handbook*. In some countries, there may be no single event that could be seen as persecution that would qualify a woman as eligible for refugee status, but all the factors together would create an atmosphere of well-founded apprehension regarding a woman's security.

One could also look to the drafting history of the refugee treaties for a better sense as to what the drafters meant to include as refugees. Clearly, the issue of protecting women from persecution was not on their minds in the late 1940s and early 1950s. At the time, the U.N. was attempting to restore order back into a world torn apart by two world wars and the expansion of communism in a relatively short period of time. However, the drafting history indicates the goals of the Contracting Parties which may be used to justify the addition of sex-based persecution in the treaties.

During the August 6, 1949 meeting of the Economic and Social Council, France and Belgium presented a draft resolution for the formation of a High Commissioner's Office to protect refugees. Both countries stated that their policy in extending refugee protection was to go beyond national interests and to consider "humanitarian motives" rather than political ones. This motive was considered essential to a majority of the Contracting Parties as the present Statute of the UNHCR states that its work is humanitarian in nature and non-political in character.

In January and February of the following year, the Ad Hoc Committee on Statelessness and Related Problems met to draft a statute for the U.N. High Commissioner on Refugees. The Committee debated whether the definition of "refugee" should include all refugees irrespective of their origin and date of departure from their country. The Committee concluded that it was too difficult for governments to sign a blank check and undertake obligations to future refugees whose origin and number were unknown. It also thought that because refugees may become the charge of a U.N. agency, the categories of individuals protected should be specified, in line with previous U.N. documents. As a result, the Committee drafted a definition of "refugee" that excluded events occurring after January 1, 1951, and required a well-founded fear of persecution due to race, religion, nationality or political opinion. The definition was limited in this way in order to address contemporary problems and to avoid the uncertainty of attempting to meet future needs.

On August 16, 1950, the Economic and Social Council discussed the definition of refugee for the purposes of a General Assembly resolution which was later to become the Statute for the U.N. High Commissioner on Refugees. All the delegates agreed on the universal nature of the principle of protecting refugees; however, there was disagreement as to who was a refugee. Canada argued that the term should have the broadest definition possible under the statute. It found the resolution definition too narrow, but it voted for the draft resolution, reserving the right to expand the definition at a later date. The United Kingdom and China felt the same way, but refused to vote for the resolution. Belgium, Denmark, and Pakistan also argued for a broader definition and abstained. The draft resolution was adopted by a vote of nine to zero with six abstentions. It is significant that all the abstentions were because of the fear that the definition was too narrow and would not protect those who should be considered refugees.

A few days before the Statute of the UNHCR was adopted by the General Assembly, there were more debates regarding the definition of the term refugee. Belgium, Canada, France, Israel, Turkey, the United Kingdom, the United States, and Venezuela presented an amendment to the proposed definition that would add a provision that "the contracting states may agree to add to the definition of the term 'refugee' contained in this article persons in other categories, including such as may be recommended by the General Assembly." When the Statute was adopted two days later, however, it did not contain this provision.

The debates over the definition of "refugee" indicate clearly that there was disagreement as to whether it should be defined broadly or narrowly. A narrow definition was finally adopted because countries did not want to commit themselves blindly to accepting future refugees, and because it was in line with past U.N. decisions. The opinions of the countries that abstained in the August vote indicated a recognition by them that the definition might be broadened in the future. The amendments presented by the group led by Belgium in December of 1950 also indicate a recognition that the definition of refugee may need amendment in the future. Clearly, many countries in the working group foresaw a time when the definition of refugee would have to be expanded to meet new problems that might arise.

Expanding the definition of refugee to include gender-based persecution would also be consistent with the international community's commitment to promoting human rights and the rights of women, as well as providing concrete protections, where now there are often little more than indefinite commitments toward eliminating gender-based discrimination. The international community has already condemned through various treaties such as the Charter of the United Nations (U.N. Charter), the Universal Declaration of Human Rights, and the Convention of the Elimination of All Forms of Discrimination Against Women (CEDAW). One of the purposes of the U.N. Charter is to achieve international cooperation in promoting human rights and fundamental freedoms without regard to gender differences. All members of the U.N. are obligated to abide by this provision. Women all over the world are being denied what the international community has recognized as fundamental freedoms, such as the right to life, education, employment, and entering marriage freely, because they are women. By not protecting those women who seek refuge, U.N. members are avoiding one of their obligations under the U.N. Charter.

The Universal Declaration of Human Rights, which codifies customary international law, states that everyone is entitled to its rights and freedoms without discrimination of any kind including gender discrimination. In addition, Article 7 states that "[a]ll are entitled to equal protection against any discrimination in violation of this Declaration. . . ." The Declaration ensures that men and women have equal rights in marriage, and that everyone has the right to own property, the right to work and free choice of employment, and the right to education. Current refugee laws do nothing to protect women from persecution which denies these human rights. Ignoring the plight of these women directly conflicts with the preamble of the Declaration, which states that every organ of society shall teach and promote respect for these rights and freedoms and secure their universal recognition and observance.

The CEDAW also calls for equality between the sexes and imposes an obligation on states to modify or abolish discriminatory laws. Among other things, the CEDAW holds that all State Parties shall ensure political equality, educational equality, equality in the work place, legal equality, and equality in marriage. Its ability to protect women, however, is hampered by the fact that it is among the most heavily reserved human rights conventions. Twenty-three of the 100 member states made eighty-eight substantive reservations and an additional twenty-nine reservations to dispute resolution procedures. Because the drafting commission wished to encourage widespread acceptance of the CEDAW, reservations compatible with its object and purpose were permitted. However, many of the reservations failed to meet this compatibility test and pose a threat to achieving the goals of the CEDAW.

For example, one of the most significant articles of the treaty is Article 2, which requires states to pursue a policy of eliminating discrimination against women, yet, many states made reservations to it. Bangladesh made a general reservation to this article stating that it does not consider itself bound by it as it conflicts with *Sharia* law based on the *Qur'an*. Iraq's reservation to this article went without explanation. Libya, Tunisia, and Egypt's reservations stated they would comply with Article 2 but only to the extent it did not conflict with domestic policies based on Islam.

Article 15 obliges states to accord women legal equality. However, several reservations were made to this article as well. Thailand made a reservation to the provision declaring null and void all contracts which restrict women's legal capacity. Brazil made a reservation to the provision guaranteeing women's equal rights to freedom of movement and choice of residence or domicile.

The most heavily reserved of the substantive articles is Article 16, which requires states to eliminate discrimination in marriage and family relations. This article is a key provision of the treaty as the CEDAW addresses both public and private discrimination which occurs de facto and de jure. A reservation to this article would allow women to suffer discrimination in the most pervasive aspect of their lives: the home. Yet Brazil and Korea reserved to this article without explanation. Bangladesh reserved to parts of Article 16 (equal rights during marriage and its dissolution and over children) stating that they conflicted with *Sharia*. Egypt's reservation explains its adherence to Article 16 must be without prejudice to Islamic laws which ensure a just balance between spouses.

Reservations by a state to so many articles of the CEDAW may indicate a systematic purpose not to be bound by the major goals of the treaty. For many countries, ratification of the CEDAW seems to be a formality which may win political points abroad but which has little substantive effect at home. Thus, women who face sex discrimination even in countries which have ratified the CEDAW have little real recourse to improve their condition. Expanding the definition of "refugee" to include persecution because of gender would give women all over the world more protection when their country's commitment to eliminating discrimination proves to be little more than words on paper.

ABSORBING A FUTURE WAVE OF WOMEN REFUGEES

One problem that potentially arises from any expansion of the definition of refugee is how to absorb the influx of claimants caused by the new provision. In a world that is already overburdened with those fleeing not only persecution but war and natural disaster, this is clearly an important concern. A definition that includes persecution based on one's sex would probably not result in a flood of refugees. First, many women in the countries described herein may not feel that their cultures, religions, or legal systems persecute them. Second, others who feel that they do face some persecution may not be willing to leave their country, family, or friends because of it. Third, women who do feel that they are victims of persecution may already be seeking refugee status by attempting to base their claim on one of the provisions already in the treaties, such as persecution because of their political opinion or religion. Adding gender as one more ground for refugee protection, therefore, would ensure protection for those women who truly believe their society was persecuting them and would not encourage those women who would not normally seek refugee status in this manner. In addition, the international community would be fulfilling its commitment to protect women from human rights abuses.

Expanding the definition of refugee in this way raises the additional problem of protecting women fleeing gender-based persecution when they reach their country of refuge. Women refugees face unique security, economic, and educational problems. The UNHCR, currently headed by a woman, Sadako Ogata of Japan, has become increasingly concerned with the special problems that women refugees face, particularly in the area of personal security. In addition to the security problems that all refugees face, women need special protection against manipulation, sexual and physical abuse, and protection from sexual discrimination in the delivery of goods and services.

The plight of women in war-torn Bosnia-Herzegovina exemplifies the special security problems faced by women. Croatian and Muslim women fleeing "ethnically-cleansed areas" have been subjected to rape and sexual torture in detention camps at the hands of Serbian soldiers and some have been forced into prostitution. The sexual abuse of some of these women has been especially severe as they have been repeatedly raped until they become pregnant. These women are only released during the last stages of pregnancy after it is too late to have an abortion. Their captors tell them to take good care of the child and to raise a Serbian soldier-hero. The rape and subsequent pregnancy have an especially harsh impact on Muslim women because of the importance Islam puts on the virginity of women. Officials of Bosnia-Herzegovina fear tens of thousands of rapes have been carried out on Muslim and Croatian women. The reports of rape are so extensive that some analysts think it is systematic.

Although the conditions endured by these women are extreme and some forms of the abuse may be particular to the ethnic conflict that now divides the region, they do highlight some of the security problems all women refugees face. Women who flee gender-based persecution are especially susceptible to these problems. These women will probably continue to face other abuse from those men who still wish to impose cultural, religious, or social customs on them. They will be especially vulnerable because, unlike many women refugees who come with husbands or other family members, they will probably come to the country of refuge alone or with only their children.

The UNHCR has outlined several proposals in order to deal more effectively with these sorts of physical security problems. Among its suggestions are: designing refugee camps to promote greater security (including special accommodations for women, improved lighting, reduced use of closed facilities or detention centers where women are more likely to be victims of violence); placing trained international staff (including more women) in border areas, reception centers, and refugee camps; employing social workers to work with refugee women to identify and remedy any problems they are having; providing emergency relocation; ensuring reunification with family; establishing law enforcement mechanisms to identify and prosecute abusers; reviewing legal codes in refugee camps to protect women; and educating women regarding their legal rights.

The UNHCR has also recognized that becoming a refugee can drastically alter women's social and economic roles. They may find themselves either alone, or as sole supporter of their families. This would be especially true for women fleeing gender-based persecution as the persecutors are often their husbands or parents. When they attain refugee status, they have to be able to support themselves and possibly their children. This may be a new experience for some of these women. The UNHCR has committed itself to integrating women into protection and assistance programs. These programs focus not only on women's new social and economic roles but also on how to ensure their increased participation in the community.

One way to improve women's economic role is to focus on education and skills training. The UNHCR has recognized that its record on providing educational opportunities is poor, especially for females. The skills that women bring with them are not usually directly relevant to their experiences in a refugee camp. Additionally, cultural constraints prevent women from undergoing training or taking jobs. The UNHCR has proposed several measures to overcome these and other related problems. Women refugees must be given equal access to eduction and training programs, they must be integrated into any refugee aid and development programs, cultural biases in these programs regarding women's roles must be recognized and projects must be monitored to ensure adequate household income.

The women who flee gender-based persecution would need special protection from the UNHCR even after leaving their home countries. Much of the needed assistance would be available in the policies and programs, described above, which are already in place.

CONCLUSION

The refugee laws formulated fifty years ago are no longer able to deal with all the refugee problems that arise today. The persecution women face in various parts of the world should not be ignored; protection should be extended to those who seek it and who can prove a well-founded fear of persecution. The European Parliament has already taken steps to protect those women who face persecution because they have transgressed the social mores of their countries. The UNHCR has encouraged the international community to extend protection to these women under the social group category. However, it is clear that calling these women members of a social group does not go far enough to ensure that they are not forced to go back to their homes where they may face violence and oppression. In addition, it relegates gender-based persecution to a position less important than, for example, persecution based on politics or race. The international community must go further to protect the fundamental rights of women, the majority of the world's population and the world's refugees.

Editor's Note: This article has been edited for publication.

The Exclusion from the United States of Aliens Infected with the AIDS Virus

Recent Developments and Prospects for the Future

Juan P. Osuna

INTRODUCTION

Few issues in immigration law have caused as much controversy in recent years as the exclusion from the United States of aliens infected with the human immunodeficiency virus (HIV), the precursor of AIDS. While seemingly a straightforward question, the issue is actually quite complex and has a long and volatile history. Moreover, it involves a series of sub-issues, such as whether all aliens, or only those seeking to immigrate permanently, should be excluded; what weight should be given to various factors, such as public health considerations and cost concerns; and what message the exclusion sends to the public at large.

The exclusion of HIV-infected aliens has undergone changes since 1987, when the ban on entry was formally put in place. Yet, the fact remains that what was established in 1987 is still in place today: the United States has the ability to exclude immigrants infected with HIV. Whether President Bill Clinton will someday attempt to rescind the ban, as he promised, or whether the ban is here to stay remains unclear. Recent legislative and administrative maneuverings, however, have ensured that, at least for the foreseeable future, the ban will remain in place.

This article discusses the exclusion of HIV-infected aliens, beginning with 1987. The article then reviews administrative and congressional events since President Clinton took office in January 1993. Finally, it attempts to foresee what the future holds for the exclusion policy.

Houston Journal of International Law, Volume 16 (1993:1–41).

BACKGROUND

Exclusion on Health Grounds

Every alien seeking admission to the United States, whether as an immigrant or a nonimmigrant, must establish that he or she is "admissible." To determine admissibility, the Immigration and Nationality Act (INA), the basic immigration law of the United States, lists several "grounds of exclusion." For years, the INA included thirty-three grounds. The Immigration Act of 1990, however, consolidated these into nine grounds, and made additional significant changes. Both before and after the 1990 Act, the INA included specific health-related grounds of exclusion, and in 1987 those grounds became the subject of controversy as the debate over the exclusion of aliens infected with the AIDS virus heated up.

AFTER THE IMMIGRATION ACT OF 1990

On October 27, 1990, Congress approved the Immigration Act of 1990 (IMMACT 90), the most far-reaching reform of U.S. immigration laws since 1952. Then-President George Bush signed the legislation into law on November 29, 1990. The 1990 Act affected almost every major provision of the immigration statutes, including the grounds of exclusion.

The 1990 Act changed the health-related exclusion grounds to provide for the exclusion of any alien who is determined, according to PHS regulations, to have a "communicable disease of public health significance"[1] or a physical or mental disorder that might pose a threat to the alien or others. A separate provision of the 1990 Act provides for a waiver of excludability under certain circumstances for aliens falling under this section.

Soon after the 1990 Act became law, the PHS announced that it would remove HIV infection from the list of diseases, and in January of 1991, the agency formally published proposed regulations to remove HIV from the list. The PHS, in fact, proposed removing all the diseases from the list, except for infectious (active) tuberculosis. The PHS justified the proposal by explaining

---

1. Id. § 601, 104 Stat. at 5067 (codified as amended at 8 U.S.C. § 1182). The legislative change in the language of the INA did not change the authority of the PHS to list the excludable diseases, but Senator Helms interpreted the change as nullifying his 1987 amendment. 139 Cong. Rec. S1721 (daily ed. Feb. 17, 1993) (statement of Sen. Helms). During the 1993 debates on the HIV exclusion, Senator Helms said that during the congressional debates over the 1990 Act, "[w]ithout any consultation nor any warning, a little provision was slipped in that rendered nugatory the 1987 Helms amendment." *Id.*

that HIV is not transmitted casually, but instead through either sexual intercourse or the sharing of contaminated injection equipment. The PHS noted that "[t]he risk of (or protection from) HIV infection comes not from the nationality of the infected person, but from the specific behaviors that are practiced." Utilizing current medical knowledge and epidemiological principles, the PHS determined that admission of HIV-infected aliens into the United States would not significantly increase the risk of HIV infection to the U.S. population, particularly since HIV infection was already prevalent within the United States.

The outcry in response to the proposal was immediate and fierce. Legislation was introduced in Congress that would continue to exclude HIV-infected aliens, and fifty-seven Republican members of the House of Representatives sent a letter to HHS Secretary Dr. Louis W. Sullivan urging him to keep HIV on the list of diseases. By May 1991, the PHS had received over 40,000 overwhelmingly negative letters in response to its January proposal. As a result, the PHS on May 31, 1991, published new interim regulations that kept HIV and the other seven diseases on the list of contagious diseases. The PHS explained that "[i]n view of the extent of the public comment" it needed more time to review the issue. By the summer of 1991, however, indications were that the Bush administration had decided not to remove HIV from the list at all.

Predictably, the reversal sparked criticism from supporters of lifting the HIV ban. For example, the Eighth Annual International Conference on AIDS was initially scheduled to be held in Boston in the summer of 1992. The organizers of the conference moved it to Amsterdam, however, to protest the U.S. HIV policy. Among the many critics of the policy were members of Congress, with one saying that "[o]ur immigration policy toward HIV infected people reflects the Bush administration's continuing capitulation to hysteria, bigotry, and irrational fear. Once again, George Bush has embarrassed and isolated the United States in the international community."[2]

Central to the arguments that the exclusion of HIV-infected persons represents bad public policy were concerns that the exclusion serves to diminish and undermine educational efforts about AIDS. One of the keys to combating the disease, many argued, is education, and specifically efforts to inform the public about how HIV is transmitted and what people can do to protect themselves. Excluding persons infected with the AIDS virus, therefore, sends the message that HIV is casually transmitted, thereby misinforming the public, stigmatizing HIV-infected persons, and decreasing awareness about the disease.

---

2. 138 Cong. Rec. H6253 (daily ed. July 21, 1992) (statement of Rep. Jim McDermott (D-Wash.))

Typical of this argument is the following statement by the American Public Health Association: "We cannot afford to send mixed messages about such a serious disease as HIV infection. The public is not at risk of HIV from casual contact with individuals with HIV infection or AIDS. As physicians and scientists concerned with the health of Americans we must say so. Failure to change the immigration policy would do serious harm to the credibility and confidence we have all struggled to maintain during the HIV epidemic."[3]

Another example was a July 1991 letter by 85 physicians and health care workers from medical centers around the United States to the Centers for Disease Control. In that letter, the physicians said that "[t]he notion that the threat of HIV comes from outside of the United States and can be avoided through exclusion of HIV-infected immigrants and travelers is medically and epidemiologically incorrect and is a potential threat to the public health. The American public must understand that it can only protect itself from HIV infection by refraining from high risk behaviors."[4]

THE CLINTON ADMINISTRATION

The HIV controversy entered a new phase with the victory of Bill Clinton in the 1992 presidential election. During the presidential campaign, Clinton released a ten-point plan for immigration that vowed to end "the cynical politicization of federal immigration policies" and follow public health recommendations that HIV be removed from the list of diseases.

Shortly after he took office on January 20, 1993, there were indications that President Clinton was preparing to make good on his campaign promise to lift the HIV ban. In February 1993, the PHS approved a draft of final regulations that would once and for all remove HIV from the list of contagious diseases. As an indication of how explosive the HIV exclusion issue had become by that time, the PHS stated that the Centers for Disease Control had received almost 175,000 comments in response to the proposed regulations and the interim regulations. Thirty-five percent of those comments supported keeping HIV on the list, while sixty-five percent supported deleting it.

The PHS draft proposal was prompted in part by concerns for Haitians infected with HIV and detained at the United States' naval base at Guantanamo Bay, Cuba. The Haitians were part of the exodus from Haiti that began in September 1991, when the Haitian military overthrew the democratically-elected President of Haiti. The Haitians were interdicted by the U.S. Coast

---

3. Letter from William H. McBeath, Executive Director, American Public Health Association to Senator Edward M. Kennedy (Feb. 11, 1993), *reprinted in* 139 CONG. REC. S1714, S1715 (daily ed. Feb. 17, 1993).
4. Letter from 85 physicians, *supra* note 104, at S1717.

Guard on the high seas and taken to Guantanamo, where they were screened for "bona fide" claims to asylum in the United States based on possible persecution in Haiti. Except for the HIV-infected Haitians, all of the interdicted Haitians determined to have such claims were taken to the United States to pursue asylum. The HIV-positive Haitians, however, were detained on Guantanamo. An internal memorandum accompanying the 1993 PHS draft rule referred to the plight of the Guantanamo Haitians.

While reiterating many of the previous arguments in favor of lifting the HIV ban, the PHS draft regulations also attempted to address increasing concerns that the admission of HIV-infected aliens would burden an already overburdened health-care system in the United States. The PHS noted in the draft that in the 1990 Act Congress retained the "public charge" exclusion ground, which bars the entry of aliens who might become a "public charge" at any time. The PHS thus argued that while Congress was clearly concerned about the economic burdens that might result from admitting aliens with certain health conditions, including HIV infection, Congress chose to address these concerns through the public charge exclusion ground.

Predictably, President Clinton's proposal to lift the HIV ban created a storm of controversy. As in 1987, Congress entered the fray in a major way, this time largely to prevent the President from proceeding with the removal of HIV from the list of diseases. Senator Helms introduced a general bill to control the spread of AIDS, and one section of that bill reiterated that the President should include HIV infection on the list of contagious diseases. In the House of Representatives two bills were introduced that would deem HIV a communicable disease for purposes of exclusion. Representative Bill McCollum (R-Fla.) introduced one of these, H.R. 985 on February 18, 1993, and it became significant later in 1993 during final congressional action on the HIV exclusion.

The HIV controversy in Congress, however, focused on Congress' consideration of legislation reauthorizing many of the programs of the National Institutes of Health (NIH), which is part of HHS. Among the first bills that the 103rd Congress considered after it convened on January 20, 1993, were S. 1 in the Senate and H.R. 4 in the House of Representatives, companion bills to reauthorize the NIH programs.

Speaking in support of his amendment, Senator Nickles called President Clinton's proposed change in policy "a serious mistake," because "if [one] change[s] this policy and allow[s] more people to come into the country that are HIV positive, if they do not change their social behavior, the disease will spread faster throughout the United States." Senator Dole also expressed support for Senator Nickles' amendment, arguing that while some of the fears about the spread of AIDS are unfounded, the United States is facing an epidemic, "one that will call on all our resources to address." Senator Dole was unable "to see how permitting more people infected with the AIDS virus into America will in any way contribute to the health and well-being of the American public, or help us resolve the very serious issues facing us here at home."

Senator Alan K. Simpson (R-Wyo.) disputed the Clinton administration's view that HIV is not "a disease of public health significance." He asked:

> [I]s a disease which has reached epidemic proportions, killing more than 175,000 fellow Americans and infecting as many as a million-and-a-half more, a disease of public health significance? . . . [I]s a disease which renders its victim terminally ill in every single instance, with medical care expenses reaching as much as $100,000 or more, a disease of public health significance?

The answer to both questions is yes, he argued.

Some even thought the Nickles amendment did not go far enough. Senator Trent Lott (R-Miss.), for example, argued that the amendment should be extended to the other sexually-transmitted diseases on the contagious diseases list. Still, Senator Lott supported the Nickles amendment because it "protects public health" and "helps contain the spread of a tragic disease."

Senator Kennedy, however, argued that while public health concerns are indeed paramount, it should be the health professionals of the PHS that make such decisions. "Do you know what we did in 1990 in the Immigration Act?" he asked his colleagues. "We said, let us make science and science policy the guiding factor in terms of excluding those individuals who have diseases that are going to pose a public health threat to American citizens. So we do so with tuberculosis."[5] Senator Kennedy's comments were echoed by Senator Dianne Feinstein (D-Cal.) who told her colleagues that because "politics have dominated the discussion around the AIDS epidemic" for too long, public health decisions should be carried out by the federal government's health officials.

Cost Concerns

The debate over the exclusion of HIV-infected aliens currently largely turns on concerns about potential costs to the health-care system, and such concerns were evident in the Senate debate. The concerns first surfaced in 1991, when many conservative members of Congress and others objected to lifting the HIV ban on the grounds that aliens infected with the AIDS virus would impose an additional burden on an already overwhelmed U.S. health-care system.

The cost argument was probably the argument that persuaded the greatest number of senators to support the Nickles' amendment. Senator Nancy Landon Kassebaum (R-Kan.) made this clear when she noted that "[two] years ago

---

5. 139 Cong. Rec. S1712 (daily ed. Feb. 17, 1993).

when this issue was considered in the context of the upcoming World Conference on AIDS in Boston, the debate focused at that time largely on the issue of whether foreigners with AIDS would pose a public health risk to American citizens. Today, however, the chief issue has become cost, and I believe that it does need to be addressed."[6]

Senator Kassebaum argued that it was important that "we not simply support an AIDS ban out of fear, that entrance to the United States will pose an immediate contagious risk to Americans." She noted that public health experts stress that no such threat exists, and that the ban is therefore not justifiable on public health grounds. However, given that a single AIDS case is estimated to cost about $102,000 over the patient's lifetime, Senator Kassebaum said, "I think we deserve to know a lot more about how many AIDS-infected immigrants we are going to see in coming years if this ban is lifted."[7]

Another member who noted the cost concerns was Senator Phil Gramm (R-Tex.): "We have 37 million people who are not covered by health insurance. We have Americans now who cannot afford to get health care in their own country. What kind of logic is it that we should be bringing people who are sick from other countries into our country to pay their medical bills when we cannot pay the medical bills of our own people?"[8] "Compassion," Senator Gramm said, "ought to begin at home."[9]

Senator Helms, the original sponsor of the 1987 legislation, also added his voice to those expressing concerns about the expense of AIDS treatment. He focused in part on the HIV-infected Haitians at Guantanamo, noting that were it not for his amendment in 1987, they would have been allowed to enter the United States. Permitting the Guantanamo Haitians to enter would mean a potential cost to taxpayers of $20 million in medical bills alone, he argued. Moreover, in citing a WHO estimate that fifteen percent of the population of Haiti has AIDS, Senator Helms suggested that additional costs would be incurred as thousands entered the United States with the disease. Senator

---

6. 139 CONG. REC. S1709 (daily ed. Feb. 17, 1993).

7. *Id.* Senator Kassebaum acknowledged the procedural issue of whether the exclusion of HIV-infected aliens should be dealt with through regulations or whether Congress has a say in the matter. Under normal circumstances that issue is worth debating, she said, but "these are not normal circumstances, and tragically, AIDS is not just another disease." *Id.* at S1709–10. Senator Kassebaum also pointed out that the AIDS exclusion exists "in large part" because of congressional action. *Id.* The Senate originally approved the AIDS immigration exclusion in 1987. *Id.* at S1710.

8. *Id.* at S1720.

9. *Id.*

Connie Mack (R-Fla.) echoed these concerns, noting that his home state of Florida would be disproportionately burdened by allowing the Guantanamo Haitians into the United States, where they could seek medical treatment.

Senator Kennedy, however, did not believe that the Nickles amendment dealt with the cost concerns as other medical conditions, such as renal failure or cancer, were not addressed. Immigrants can have all kinds of other diseases, he noted, yet they are not excluded because of cost concerns. Moreover, Senator Kennedy disputed suggestions that lifting the exclusion would result in thousands of HIV-infected aliens entering the United States and posing a cost burden. Two years ago, he noted, only 450 out of 700,000 immigrants tested positive for the AIDS virus and were thus excluded. Last year only 600 tested positive. He emphasized that the INS already has the authority under the public charge exclusion ground to exclude from the United States any alien who is likely to become a public charge and thus become a burden on the local community. Senator George J. Mitchell (D-Me.), the Senate Majority Leader, also spoke against Senator Nickles' amendment and in favor of Senator Kennedy's amendment, reiterating that the Kennedy amendment would mandate that the Attorney General make recommendations to ensure the exclusion of aliens likely to become public charges, thereby addressing the cost issue.

Allegations of Bias

During his statements on the Senate floor, Senator Kennedy suggested other more nefarious motivations behind the HIV ban. Referring to the plight of the HIV-infected Haitians at Guantanamo, Senator Kennedy suggested a racial motivation behind the exclusion in general and Senator Nickles' amendment in particular:

> [W]hat the supporters of the Nickles amendment are saying—and we all know what they are saying here today—is you have 268 black Haitians in Guantanamo Bay, 40 children and 2 have HIV, and 20 pregnant women. Many of them have been found to be in incredible fear of persecution if they go back to Haiti. The proponents of this amendment say, 'Send them back. Send them back. We do not care.'[10]

Senator Nickles strenuously objected to Senator Kennedy's statements and disclaimed any racist motivation. Senator Kennedy also argued that the HIV exclusion was motivated in part by anti-homosexual bias. He noted that the debate was similar to the congressional reaction to President Clinton's proposal to lift the ban on homosexuals in the U.S. military. Senator Barbara Boxer (D-Cal.), who supported Senator Kennedy's amendment, agreed, saying

---

10. 139 Cong. Rec. S1712 (daily ed. Feb. 17, 1993).

that "[w]e do not want to rely on politicians when we deal with health issues because they just might try to make political points based on fear and division in the politics of hate."[11] Once again, however, Senator Nickles disputed that assertion. He argued, "This amendment is not born out of hate. This amendment is not born out of fear. This amendment is not born out of homophobia."[12]

While it is unclear how many Senators were motivated by anti-gay bias, it was clear that such was at least one of Senator Helms' motivations. He said, "I had reached the conclusion that every possible concession had already been made to the AIDS lobby and to the homosexual rights movement which feeds it. But the Clinton administration's kowtowing to this arrogant and repugnant political group is beyond belief," Senator Helms said.[13] Senator Helms argued that Americans rightly feel outraged at President Clinton who, "after breaking promise after promise, has made clear that about the only citizens who need show up to pick up their campaign IOU's are the radicals in the organized homosexual movement."[14]

CONCLUSION

What is the status of the AIDS ban now, and what does the future hold? After years of controversy, we now have a statutory ban. More than anything else, the intent of the House-Senate conferees on S. 1 clearly appeared to codify current administrative practice. This intent was evident not only from the language of the conference report, but also from statements made on the House and Senate floors during final passage of the conference report. Thus, it appears that little has changed. Certainly, the final version of the ban gives greater flexibility to the executive branch than the numerous provisions of the Nickles amendment.

The codification is significant, however, for two main reasons. First, there is now clearly no discretion left for the HHS Secretary to decide whether or not HIV infection is a "communicable disease of public health significance" for immigration purposes. Congress' direct amendment of the statute leaves no room to maneuver: HIV *is* a "communicable disease of public health significance," and HHS cannot conclude otherwise. This represents a clarification of sorts. Before, it was unclear whether HHS could amend the list of

---

11. *Id.* at S1722.
12. *Id.* at S1723.
13. As a measure of the intensity of the debate, Senator Helms, before his statement on the Senate floor, noted that he was "adjust[ing] . . . [his] hearing aid" to "accommodate the decibels of the Senator from Massachusetts." *Id.* at S1720 & at S1721.
14. *Id.*

diseases to remove HIV without prior congressional approval. Now, there is no question that removing HIV from the list clearly requires congressional action, since S. 1 explicitly placed HIV on the list.

Second, there are concerns as to whether S. 1 definitely means a codification of prior practice across the board, including prior practice on testing of aliens and granting of waivers. Certainly, some members of Congress, such as Senator Kassebaum, argue that there is no change, and that prior practice on waivers and testing continues unchanged. However, the language in the S. 1 conference report is remarkably vague and brief for such an important and controversial issue. The conference report only states that "the Conferees intend these provisions to be a codification of current administrative practice."[15]

In the end, therefore, the long-term impact of the HIV exclusion will largely depend on how the Clinton and subsequent administrations implement the exclusion. The conference committee on S. 1 clearly opted to continue allowing the executive branch substantial discretion on the issue. The only issue where the executive now has no discretion, in fact, is whether to keep HIV on the list at all. On all other related matters, such as testing and waivers, the INS, State Department, and HHS still retain widespread discretion.

It is likely that the Clinton administration will continue the prior practice of testing immigrants, but not nonimmigrants. President Clinton clearly did not fulfill his campaign pledge to remove HIV from the list of diseases altogether, but that failure was primarily the result of overwhelming congressional opposition to lifting the ban, as evidenced by the substantial margins by which the ban passed both chambers of Congress. Thus, the administration will probably change little in its implementation of the ban. Moreover, given the President's prior stated opposition to the ban, it is highly unlikely that his administration will implement the exclusion in a way that expands its effect, such as testing nonimmigrants or restricting the types of waivers allowed.

One hint of how the Clinton administration might handle the HIV exclusion issue came in June 1993, when the administration paroled into the United States 139 HIV-infected Haitians who had been held at the U.S. naval base at Guantanamo Bay, Cuba since early 1992. The administration transported the Haitians to the United States after a federal judge in New York ordered the government to release the Haitians, who had all been deemed to have plausible claims for asylum in the United States but who had been prevented from entering because of their HIV status.

In addition, the Clinton administration decided not to appeal the judge's order. This brought sharp reaction from members of Congress, who argued that the President was ignoring S. 1 and allowing the entry of aliens who would

---

15. H.R. Conf. Rep. 100, 103d Cong., 1st Sess. 118 (1993).

pose significant costs for the health-care system. Many members, especially those who represent congressional districts in Florida, urged the administration to seek a stay of the court order or to appeal to a higher court. The administration declined to do so.

The Haitian episode was important for two reasons. First, it offered a glimpse of the general inclination of the Clinton administration towards the HIV issue. While clearly obligated to treat HIV-infected persons as excludable from the United States, the manner of implementation of the exclusion is critical. The decision to not appeal the court order on the Guantanamo Haitians suggests that the administration will administer the exclusion in a compassionate and flexible way.

Second, the reaction to the administration's decision not to appeal suggests that the HIV issue is not one that will go away soon. Opposing advocates will continue to hammer away on the issue and "test cases" such as the Haitians will continue to feed the controversy accompanied by the charges and counter-charges of racism and discrimination and by the concerns about public health and medical costs.

In more ways than one, therefore, the more things changed with the HIV issue over the past year, the more things remained the same. While Congress clearly intended to codify prior administrative practice into the law in S. 1, it also codified the controversy that has been brewing since 1987. Perhaps that is not surprising, since the HIV exclusion remains one of the most emotional and important issues in immigration law.

Editor's Note: This article has been edited for publication.

Haitian Refugee Center, Inc. v. James Baker, III

The Dred Scott Case of Immigration Law

Thomas David Jones

INTRODUCTION

"It is unconscionable that the United States should accede to the Protocol and later claim that it is not bound by it. This court is astonished that the United States would return Haitian refugees to the jaws of political persecution, terror, death and uncertainty when it has contracted not to do so. The Government's conduct is particularly hypocritical given its condemnation of other countries who have refused to abide by the principle of non-refoulement. As it stands now, Article 33 is a cruel hoax and not worth the paper it is printed on. . . ."

On December 16, 1990, Jean-Bertrand Aristide, a Roman Catholic priest and populist politician, was elected president of the Haitian republic. Aristide was the first democratically elected president in Haiti's politically turbulent history. Subsequently, on September 29, 1991, less than a year later, a military junta composed of Brigadier General Raoul Cedras, Colonel Aliz Silva, and Colonel Henri Marc Charles seized political power by *coup d'etat.* The overthrow of the Aristide regime precipitated an internal armed conflict that culminated in the weakening of the rule of law and the suppression of fundamental human rights.

Both the United Nations (hereinafter "UN") and the Organization of American States (hereinafter "OAS") responded to the violent political upheaval by passing resolutions in support of the restoration of democracy and condemning the *coup d'etat.* The UN and OAS demanded the return of Aristide to power and declared the Cedras regime illegal under international law. Many of the member states of these international organizations applied economic sanctions against the Haitian military junta in an effort to force the restoration of democracy under Aristide's leadership. An embargo was instituted by the OAS and the United States against the Cedras regime. Recently, officials of the United States captured the oil tanker, *Fayou K,* which allegedly delivered 250,000 gallons of diesel fuel to Haiti in defiance of OAS and United States economic embargoes. In May 1992, OAS foreign ministers agreed that

Dickinson Journal of International Law, Volume 11 (1992:1–48).

it had become necessary to strictly impose sanctions against the military regime in Haiti. To date, the junta has refused to reinstate President Aristide. The foreign ministers now hope that intensification of sanctions will force the military-backed leadership to restore Aristide to power. There was almost unanimous support of a proposal by OAS Secretary-General Joao Baena Soares to "ban ships that do business with Haiti from OAS members' ports, restrict air traffic to Haiti and deny travel visas to Haitians who support the [present] government." The foreign ministers acknowledged that such action might aggravate the already serious refugee problem.

As a by-product of the political conflict in Haiti, thousands of Haitians have fled and continue to flee the country in search of refuge in the United States. Approximately 30,000 Haitian refugees have been intercepted by the United States Coast Guard. Since May 15, 1992, the United States Coast Guard has intercepted 2,106 Haitians on the high seas. As is demonstrated in this article, the efforts of these Haitian refugees to gain admission to the United States by claiming political refugee status have been fraught with difficulty. The preceding assertion is buttressed by the Eleventh Circuit's decisions in the appeals litigated by the Haitian Refugee Center, Inc. (hereinafter "HRC") discussed herein.

ANALYSIS OF HRC I, HRC II, AND HRC III

The case of *Haitian Refugee Center, Inc. v. James Baker III,* might best be characterized as the *Dred Scott* case of immigration law. In *Dred Scott v. Sandford,* the United States Supreme Court (hereinafter "Supreme Court"), through Chief Justice Taney, decided that the temporary residence of a slave, Dred Scott, in free territory did not free him under the common law doctrine articulated in *Somerset v. Stewart.* Lord Mansfield in *Somerset* held that a slave was *sui juris,* a free man, once he entered a jurisdiction that did not acknowledge slavery, even though the slave escaped and was recaptured by the master. The Supreme Court decided that the federal courts which heard Dred Scott's claim did not have jurisdiction to determine his claim. Slaves were not citizens within the meaning of the Constitution and therefore did not enjoy the rights, privileges and immunities guaranteed those who were citizens of the United States. Slaves were property owned by their masters. The most famous passage from the decision states:

> They had for more than a century before been regarded as beings of an inferior order, and altogether unfit to associate with the white race either in social or political relations; and so far inferior that they had no rights which the white man was bound to respect; and that the negro might justly and lawfully be reduced to slavery for his benefit. . . . This opinion was at that time fixed and universal in the civilized portion of the white race. It was regarded as an axiom in morals as well as in politics, which no one thought of disputing, or supposed to be open to dispute; and men in every grade and position in

society daily and habitually acted upon it in their private pursuits, as well as in matters of public concern, without doubting for a moment the correctness of the opinion.

The Court of Appeals for the Eleventh Circuit essentially held that Haitian refugees, though seized by the United States on the high seas, have no substantive legal rights under the Constitution which a domestic court is bound to accept. Like fugitive slaves, these refugees have been returned to their symbolically political masters with a clear and probable consequence of punishment, persecution, or death. There is probative evidence that such persecution and death has occurred.

Unlike the Supreme Court's opinion in *Dred Scott v. Sandford,* the court of appeals opinions in *HRC I* and *HRC II* provide legal conclusions supported by scant analysis. In *HRC I,* the court of appeals devotes two paragraphs to its discussion of Article 33 of the 1967 Protocol. The court summarily concluded, without analysis, that the provision was not self-executing. The plaintiffs had no cognizable legal rights pursuant to Article 33. It is impossible for one to know why the court of appeals decided that Article 33 was not self-executing because the majority of the Court fails to supply a principled or reasoned basis for its decision-making. Judge Hatchett in his dissenting opinion argued that Article 33 of the 1967 Protocol is self-executing and applies extraterritorially. His position is the better viewpoint. Judge Hatchett's position relies on the law as set forth in *United States v. Postal.* The Court of Appeals for the Fifth Circuit there held:

> The question whether a treaty is self-executing is a matter of interpretation for the courts when the issue presents itself in litigation . . . and, as in the case of all matters of treaty interpretation, the courts attempt to discern the intent of the parties to the agreement so as to carry out their manifest purpose. . . . The self-executing question is perhaps one of the most confounding in treaty law.

It is the general consensus that it is necessary to consider to several factors in determining whether a treaty is self-executing or directly applicable in domestic law. In determining self-execution, courts consider the intent of the parties, the treaty's legislative history, negotiations, and the subsequent judicial construction of the parties.

In the instant case, the weight of the evidence is clearly in favor of self-execution or direct applicability as suggested by Judge Hatchett. The strongest evidence in favor of the self-executing nature of the 1967 Protocol is its legislative history and its subsequent domestic construction. During the Senate deliberations on the 1967 Protocol, the State Department stated that no domestic legislation was required to implement the 1967 Protocol. Congress adhered to the belief that no amendment to the Immigration and Nationality Act was necessary to comply with the Protocol's provisions. In addition, the Senate committee report which recommended accession to the 1967 Protocol suggested that the United States would be automatically bound to apply articles

2 through 34 of the convention. The subsequent judicial constructions of the 1967 Protocol also militate in favor of a conclusion that the 1967 Protocol is self-executing. The Board of Immigration Appeals in *Matter of Dunbar* described the 1967 Protocol as self-executing. Also, it is worth noting that the INS Guidelines specifically refer to Article 33 of the 1967 Protocol and the 1951 Refugee Convention. The INS Guidelines state, in relevant part:

> C. INS officers shall be constantly watchful for any indication (including bare claims) that a person or persons on board the interdicted vessel may qualify as refugees under the United Nations Convention and Protocol.

Under the heading "AUTHORITY," the INS Guidelines provide:

> 4. Article 33, United Nations Convention and Protocol Relating to the Status of Refugees.

Moreover, Executive Order 12324 states that in actions taken beyond the territorial waters of the United States "no person who is a refugee will be returned without his consent." Executive Order 12324 admonishes the Attorney General to strictly observe "our international obligations concerning those who genuinely flee persecution. . . ." Both the INS Guidelines and Executive Order 12324 support the position that compliance with Article 33 is mandatory. Thus, it is reasonable to conclude that Article 33 is self-executing.

There is a view which holds that those treaties which create individuals rights and duties are self-executing. Apparently, the United States Court for the Eleventh Circuit shares this view. In *United States v. Bent-Santana,* the court of appeals stated:

> It is settled principle of both public international and American constitutional law that unless a treaty or intergovernmental agreement is self-executing—that is, unless it expressly creates privately enforceable rights—an individual citizen does not have standing to protest where one nation does not follow the terms of such agreement.

Article 33 of the 1967 Protocol creates the individual right of nonrefoulement. The court of appeals overlooked its own decision. However, it must be reiterated that the court of appeals, in its brevity, failed to disclose the underlying basis for its decision that Article 33 was not self-executing. It is, therefore, difficult to criticize its conclusion. Nonetheless, whether one considers the 1967 Protocol self-executing or denies that it is self-executing, one should not allow the "tyranny of terminology" to annul international treaty obligations. The United States is no less bound by those norms articulated in the 1967 Protocol. As a party to the 1967 Protocol, the United States has agreed to comply with the provisions stated therein. As a matter of fundamental fairness, justice, and good faith, the government should not now be heard to argue that it is not bound to comply with a provision of a treaty because there is no implementing legislation. If implementing legislation was necessary to give domestic, legal effect to the 1967 Protocol, the Unites States should have passed such legislation within a reasonable time of its adherence to the treaty in 1968. The Reporter's Notes to § 111 of Restatement 3rd of Foreign Relations Law of the United States suggests that the United States is obliged to comply with the provisions of a treaty at the moment it comes into force. A failure or delay on the part of the United States to take the appropriate action to implement a treaty may constitute a breach of the government's international obligation. The Restatement Third specifically provides that,

> if the Executive Branch has not requested implementing legislation and Congress has not enacted such legislation, there is a strong presumption that the treaty has been considered self-executing by the political branch, and should be considered self-executing by the courts. (This is especially so if some time has elapsed since the treaty has come into force. In that event, a finding that a treaty is not self-executing is a finding that the United States has been and continues to be in default [of its international obligation] and should be avoided.

The 1967 Protocol has been an international obligation of the United States for the past 24 years. The government's dilatory behavior has resulted in a failure to promulgate implementing legislation. To condone such state conduct vitiates the sanctity of the treaty negotiation process and the value of international law.

Article 26 of the Vienna Convention on the Law of Treaties provides that "[e]very treaty in force is binding upon the parties to it and must be performed by them in good faith." The preceding legal norm codifies the fundamental principle of international law governing the observance and sanctity of treaties, *pacta sunt servanda*. Judge Lauterpacht of the International Court of Justice stated in the *Norwegian Loans* case: "Unquestionably, the obligation to act in accordance with good faith, being a general principle of law, is also part of international law." Article 27 of the Vienna Convention states that "[a] party may not invoke the provisions of its internal law as justification of its failure to perform a treaty." Also, the Vienna Convention provides that a state is obligated to refrain from behavior which would defeat the object and purpose of a treaty, if the state has either signed the treaty or has exchanged instruments of ratification, acceptance, or approval. The Permanent Court of International Justice held that "a state cannot adduce as against another state its own Constitution with a view to evading obligations incumbent upon it under international law or treaties in force." Thus, the United States cannot invoke the internal or domestic rule of non-self-execution to justify the failure to enforce Article 33 of the 1967 Protocol, a treaty it has ratified. The government's argument that it is not bound to enforce the treaty obligation because the 1967 Protocol is not self-executing constitutes a failure of the United States government to act in good faith and violates the international norm of *pacta sunt servanda*. Article VI, clause 2, of the United States Constitution provides that treaties are a part of the supreme law of the land. The judiciary is legally required to enforce these international obligations. It is not textually demonstrable that the self-execution rule is an exception to the preceding constitutionally mandated, legal principle.

The court of appeals, in its effort to "expedite disposition of the appeal," disregarded the well-reasoned *amicus curiae* brief filed by the Office of the United Nations High Commissioner for Refugees (hereinafter "the High Commissioner"). The High Commissioner argued that Article 33 of the 1967 Protocol memorializes an independent fundamental right, exclusive of any question of admission to the United States territory or the grant of asylum. The High Commissioner further argued that Article 33 guarantees that no refugees will be returned to the frontiers of a country where they may be persecuted or murdered and its prohibition applies extraterritorially on the high seas. Where the refugees are intercepted is an irrelevant consideration.

> Article 33 identifies the place to which no refugee may be sent, no exception is provided that conditions the obligation on the place from which a refugee is returned. The obligation arises wherever the government acts.

The High Commissioner began its discussion by demonstrating that international law is a part of the law of the United States. The domestic courts of the United States are bound by international common law or customary international law. The principle of nonrefoulement is embodied in the 1951 Refugee Convention, and the 1967 Protocol and is a customary rule of international law. Consequently, the United States is legally obligated to observe these international legal norms. The High Commissioner noted that none of the parties to the 1967 Protocol have made reservations thereto. The High Commissioner observed that reservations to Article 33 are prohibited by Article 42 of the 1951 Refugee Convention and Article 7 of the 1967 Protocol. The High Commissioner revealed that the United States has supported the universal application of the principle of nonrefoulement by stating:

> [O]n November 25, 1974, U.S. Representative Clarence Clyde Ferguson, Jr. made a statement to the Third Committee of the U.N. General Assembly concerning the subject of refoulement. Ambassador Ferguson stated:
> "Once again my government wishes to stress, in this forum, the overriding importance among the High Commissioner's manifold activities of his function of providing international protection for refugees. It is difficult to overemphasize the significance to refugees of ensuring liberal asylum policies and practices, and above all in making certain that no refugee is required to return to any country where he would face persecution. It is the High Commissioner's task to work unceasingly toward affording such guarantee. His chief tools in so doing are the 1951 Convention and the 1967 Protocol Relating to the Status of Refugees. As the Committee knows, Article 33 of the Convention contains an unequivocal prohibition upon contracting states against the refoulement of refugees *in any manner whatsoever* to territories where their life or freedom would be threatened on grounds of race, religion, nationality, membership of [in] a particular social group or political opinion.

My government joins with the High Commissioner in condemning the inhumane practice of refoulement. The principle that refugees must not be repatriated against their will, and the right of a refugee to seek and secure asylum, have become even more firmly embedded international law."

Additionally, the High Commissioner concluded that the principle of nonrefoulement is an absolute obligation with no territorial limitations. No limitation appears in the text of Article 33. Again, the High Commissioner stated:

It is significant that the principle of *non-refoulement*—perhaps the foremost principle of international law protecting refugees—is stated in mandatory terms as an absolute obligation, and that no territorial limitations appears in the language of Article 33. When the drafters of the 1951 Convention as a whole wished to condition the rights of refugees on their physical location or residence, they did so expressly in the language of the treaty. Thus, in the article on the separate matter of 'expulsion' immediately preceding Article 33, the 1951 Convention expressly limits the scope of the right to 'a refugee' 'lawfully in the territory. . . .' Article 4 on freedom of religion and 27 on the issuance of travel documents state, also expressly, that States' obligations under these articles are limited to refugees who are present in the territory of the State. Article 18 on rights to self-employment and 26 on freedom of movement clearly state that their scope is limited to refugees lawfully on the territory of the Contracting State. Similarly, Articles 15, 17(1), 19, 21, 23, 24, and 28 (regarding, respectively, rights related to association, employment, exercise of the liberal professions, housing, public relief, labor conditions, and travel documents) all are expressly conditioned on the refugee's legal status on [sic] the territory of the State. In stark contrast to all of these provisions, Article 33 contains no such restriction. To the contrary, Article 33 prohibits the return of refugees 'in any manner whatsoever.'

In supporting its interpretation that the 1967 Protocol applies extraterritorially, the High Commissioner relied on the statement of United States delegate, Louis Henkin, who stated:

The Committee had, it was true, decided to delete the chapter on admittance, considering that the convention should not deal with the right of asylum and that it should merely provide for a certain number of improvements in the position of refugees. It did not, however, follow that the convention would not apply to persons fleeing from persecution who asked to enter the territory of the contracting parties. Whether it was a question of closing the frontier to a refugee who asked admittance, or of turning him back after he had crossed the frontier, or even of expelling him after he had been admitted to residence in the territory, the problem was more or less the same. Whatever the case might be, whether or not the refugee was in a regular position, he must not be turned back to a country where his life or freedom could be threatened. No consideration of public order should be allowed to overrule that guarantee, for if the State concerned wished to get rid of the refugee at all costs, it could send him to another country or place him in an internment camp.

Finally, the High Commissioner stated that the United States responded to the Indochina "boat people" by granting political asylum and resettling them, with few exceptions. In its report to Congress for Fiscal Year 1984, the Office of the U.S. Coordinator of Refugees' Affairs of the State Department advised that

> "[d]espite the heavy burden often imposed by enormous numbers of refugees, asylum countries generally have not forcibly repatriated refugees against their will to countries [from] which they have fled."

Accordingly, as suggested by Judge Hatchett, only Haitian refugees are intercepted at sea and forced to return to their country of origin where they may suffer persecution or death. The United States government might attempt to justify its interdiction procedure pursuant to the bilateral treaty which permits interdiction. This treaty was concluded between the United States and the notorious Duvalier regime. In light of the presence of an illegal military junta which has overthrown the democratic Aristide government, the United States government should not use this bilateral agreement as justification for returning refugees to a regime that the United States has condemned and is now subjecting to economic sanctions. Such a bilateral treaty conflicts with the customary international norm of nonrefoulement. The norm of nonrefoulement is a human rights norm and is *jus cogens*. There can be no derogation from such a norm unless it is supplanted by a peremptory norm of equal importance on the international normative hierarchy. Thus, the court of appeals inadequately justified its ruling that Article 33 of the 1967 Protocol is not self-executing or directly applicable.

In *HRC I,* the court of appeals further decided that the plaintiffs' First Amendment claim of access to the interdictees could not support injunctive relief granted by the district court, since the district court did not predicate its decision on this claim or require the defendants to allow HRC access to the detained Haitians. The court of appeals did not reach the First Amendment issue. Perhaps, the failure of the district court to order the defendants to allow the HRC access to the interdicted Haitians was a simple matter of oversight. The district court did hold that there was a substantial likelihood that the plaintiffs would succeed on the First Amendment claim at trial. The court of appeals analysis is sound on this issue. The error was that of the district court.

Furthermore, the district court failed to grant the plaintiffs relief on its claim that the APA provided judicially enforceable rights. The court of appeals held that because the plaintiffs did not cross-appeal on the denial of the APA claim, it could not properly uphold injunctive relief based on the claim. Judge Hatchett argued that the court of appeals had jurisdiction to resolve all issues raised and decided by the district court. The decision of the court of appeals to not rule on the APA claim due to plaintiffs' failure to cross-appeal is a valid procedural practice. Counsel for plaintiffs had the opportunity to cross-appeal on this issue and did not do so. It is impossible to know whether counsel for plaintiffs failed to cross-appeal because of a view that its position on the APA claim was not strong or whether the failure to cross-appeal was due to neglect.

Nevertheless, it was plaintiffs' counsel's duty to cross-appeal. Having not cross-appealed, the plaintiffs cannot be heard to complain of the court of appeals' refusal to consider the issue, *sua sponte.*

In *HRC II,* the court of appeals was again faced with the APA claim when the district court issued a temporary restraining order based on the APA claim, enjoining repatriation of Haitian interdictees. The court of appeals invoked the district courts' prior denial of the APA claim and adopted the district courts' reasoning for denying injunctive relief based on the claim. The court of appeals characterized the district court's order as a preliminary injunction and decided to review the order. The district court's order was stayed pending appeal. Here, the court of appeals was in error because the district court considered an APA claim that was different from the APA claim decided in *HRC I.* The district court in its Order Memorializing Oral Rulings explains:

> The court recognizes its previous determination that plaintiffs had not shown a likelihood of prevailing under the APA [Dec. 3, 1991]. That determination was based on Congress' broad grant of discretion to the President in establishing the interdiction program. However, the court now has the benefit of the thorough briefing of the APA issue before the Eleventh Circuit Court of Appeals, as well as the Court of Appeals' December 17, 1991 per curiam opinion. In this new light, the court now finds a substantial likelihood of success, based in part on the distinction between the President's discretion in establishing the program and subordinates' discretion or lack thereof in following program procedures and guidelines.

Clearly, the opinion of the court of appeals indicates that it believed the APA claim ruled upon in *HRC II* already had been ruled upon in *HRC I.* Hence, the court of appeals was in error.

After issuing two brief, analytically deficient opinions, the court of appeals in *HRC III* produced a substantial judicial decision with sustained legal analysis. First, the court of appeals concluded that 5 U.S.C. § 701(a)(1) of the APA did not authorize judicial review of an agency decision where relevant statutes precluded review. The court of appeals gave a restrictive reading of the relevant provisions of INA. Applying a plain meaning approach to the construction of 8 U.S.C. §§ 1253(h), 1252(b), 1105(a) and 1158(a) would lead to the conclusion that these provisions apply only to aliens within the borders of the United States. Unfortunately, the drafters of these provisions could not have foreseen the circumstances of the case, *sub judice.* Though, technically outside of the borders of the United States, the Haitian interdictees were seized or "captured" and detained on property leased by the United States at Guantanamo Bay. Other Haitian interdictees were held on United States Coast Guard cutters. These interdictees were physically prevented from reaching the shores of the United States. Since the interdictees were on United States property, leased or owned, they should have been viewed as constructively within or at the borders of the United States. It is the opinion of this writer that although the court of appeals strictly construed the relevant provisions of the INA, as amended by the Refugee Act of 1980, its construction has some analytical merit. Judge Hatchett's dissent does not refute the Court's construction of 8 U.S.C. §§ 1253(h), 1252(b), 1105(a), and 1158(a).

The court of appeals' opinion that judicial review was not permissible pursuant to § 701(a)(2) because the action was committed to agency discretion is weakly reasoned. The plaintiffs argued that the President's subordinates failed to properly carry out the procedures mandated by the INS Guidelines. Consequently, the conduct of these low-level subordinates would be subject to review. As argued by Judge Hatchett, the case of *Jean v. Nelson* supports the plaintiffs' position. In *Jean v. Nelson,* plaintiffs were Haitian refugees who were detained in various facilities in southern Florida until the INS could determine their asylum claims. The majority of the court remanded the case to the district court with instructions to reconsider the issue of whether low-level officials had abused their discretion in implementing the Executive branches parole policy for Haitians. The majority of the court ruled:

> The question that the district court must therefore consider with regard to the remaining Haitian detainees is thus not whether high-level executive branch officials such as the Attorney General have the discretionary authority under the Immigration and Nationality Act (INA) to discriminate between classes of aliens, but whether lower-level INS officials have abused their discretion by discriminating on the basis of national origin in violation of facially neutral instructions from superiors.

Further, the court of appeals continued:

> Nevertheless, since the discretion of lower-level immigration officials is circumscribed not only by legislative enactments but also by the instructions of their superiors in the executive branch, our conclusion that the Executive's policy is consistent with the power delegated by Congress does not end the process of judicial inquiry here. The district court must still determine whether the actions of lower-level officials in the field conform to the policy statements of their superiors in Washington.

Oddly, there is absolutely no discussion of *Jean v. Nelson* by the majority of the court in *HRC III.*

The court of appeals also decided that the exception to 701(a)(2), which permits a court to review agency action where the agency violated its own rules, was not applicable. The court of appeals characterized the INA Guidelines as mere internal operating instructions. There was evidence that government officials were not complying with the INS Guidelines promulgated pursuant to Executive Order 12324. These Guidelines were adequate binding regulations to which the agency was required to adhere. They are extraordinarily detailed and specific in nature. They refer to both the 1951 Refugee Convention and the 1967 Protocol as authority. The majority's opinion that there was no law or binding regulations limiting agency discretion and against which agency discretion could be reviewed is a clearly erroneous legal conclusion.

The court of appeals further held that HRC had no First Amendment right of access to the Haitians. Again, the court of appeals ignored the teachings of *Jean v. Nelson* in which the majority of the court ruled:

> The Supreme Court has repeatedly emphasized that counsel have [sic] a first amendment right to inform individuals of their rights, at least when they do so as an exercise of political speech without expectation of remuneration.

As asserted by Judge Hatchett, *Jean v. Nelson* does not base counsel's First Amendment right of access on the underlying rights possessed by clients. Additionally, it is uncontestable that the government allowed others access to the Haitian interdictees while denying the same right to HRC. The conduct of the government was inherently unfair, unjust, and discriminatory. The majority's speculation that the government would have to assist HRC in its exercise of its right of access finds no support in the record. There was no evidence that the government would have to go to great expense in actualizing HRC's right of access. The suggestions of the court that the contrary would be true is a view sown out of the gossamer seeds of speculation and conjecture.

Perhaps, the most extraordinary ruling of *HRC III* was the majority's pronouncement that

> [t]he plaintiffs also claim that customary international law, or international common law, creates enforceable rights. This claim is meritless and does not warrant discussion.

Again, the majority of the court reached a legal conclusion without any supportive analysis. It is impossible, therefore, for one to adequately criticize such a ruling, since the majority has failed to apprise the parties or readers of a rational basis for its legal decision. The majority ignored the Supreme Court's holding in the *Parquete Habana,* declaring international law or the law of nations an integral part of the law of the United States. The United States is bound by customary norms of international law. It is beyond dispute that the principle of nonrefoulement is considered a customary norm of international law by most of the countries of the world. The principle is so important that both the 1951 Refugee Convention and the 1967 Protocol prohibit reservations to Article 33. The court of appeals' dismissal of the importance of international law in the HRC litigation case reveals a lack of respect for the law of nations.

Finally, it is surprising that plaintiffs' counsel did not raise the issue of discrimination based on race or national origin in its arguments before the court of appeals. The issue was raised in *Jean v. Nelson* where the court of appeals remanded the case for consideration of whether low-ranking, subordinate, executive officials were properly executing the immigration policy of the

President without discrimination based on national origin. Judge Hatchett, without alleging discrimination based on race or nationality, suggests the possibility of disparate treatment in his dissenting opinions. In *HRC I* Judge Hatchett wrote:

> . . . Under existing law, any refugee may reach the shores of the United States and thereby acquire the right to enforce the United States immigration laws in the United States courts, except Haitian refugees. Only Haitian refugees are interrupted in international waters and repatriated to their country of origin. . . .
> The government seeks to convince this court that its interdiction program was instituted as an effort to save the lives of Haitian refugees travelling in unseaworthy vessels. But the government's own brief shows that the program was instituted in 1981, long before the current immigration wave. . . . The primary purpose of the program was, and has continued to be, to keep Haitians out of the United States.

In *HRC III,* Judge Hatchett stated:

> . . . [T]he capture of Haitian refugees in international waters is authorized under a 1981 agreement between the Reagan administration and the totalitarian government of Jean-Claude "Baby Doc" Duvalier. The record does not disclose such a agreement with any other country.
> . . . Haitians, unlike other aliens from anywhere in the world, are prevented from freely reaching the continental United States. . . .

There is extant other evidence of discrimination against Haitian refugees by the United States government. The interdiction process began in 1981. From 1981 to August 1986, only two Haitian refugees were permitted entrance to the United States. More than 9,000 were repatriated during the same period. The following Tables, prepared by Amnesty International USA, reflect the disparity of treatment accorded Haitian refugees who have applied for political asylum in this country between June 1982 and September 1989.

Amnesty International USA has concluded that the INS is biased against asylum seekers of certain nationalities. In *Reasonable Fear: Human Rights and United States Refugee Policy,* Amnesty International USA charges that "the most compelling evidence of bias . . . appears in cases of Salvadoreans, Guatemalans, and Haitians." The norm of nondiscrimination is irrefutably an accepted norm of customary international law which binds all states in the international community. It would be morally repugnant and hypocritical if discrimination on the basis of race, color or nationality were permitted by the United States on the international level when it is has been outlawed on the domestic level.

CONCLUSION

Recent studies and reports, including a report published by the State Department, ineluctably demonstrate that political persecution and human rights violations continue to be a severe problem in Haiti. The State Department found that "[t]he military's human rights record improved under the Aristide government, but that trend was reversed following the September coup. . . ." Another report reveals that the infamous Tonton Macoutes of the Duvalier regime have become operative and have mobilized "against all supporters of ousted president Aristide." Thus, the claim that the Haitian refugees are merely economic refugees and not political refugees is not supported by the evidence.

The HRC plaintiffs exhausted all judicial remedies. They were unsuccessful in a petition to the United States Supreme Court that requested a ban on repatriation. However, as a direct result of the HRC litigation, several bills have been introduced by various members of Congress to give Haitians who are in the United States or "in the custody or control of the United States (including on Coast Guard vessels on the high seas)" protected status and to halt the repatriation process.

Though President Bill Clinton promised to reverse former President Bush's policy of returning Haitian immigrants to Haiti after intercepting them at sea, President Clinton has now retreated from his campaign pledge. President Clinton has stated: "For the time being this [policy of forced repatriation] is the right policy. . . . Those who leave Haiti by boat for the United States will be intercepted and returned to Haiti by the U.S. Coast Guard." President Clinton has suggested that more consular officials may be dispatched to Haiti to facilitate the processing of asylum applications. President Clinton may also ask Caribbean countries to give Haitians temporary refuge.

Recently, Haitian detainees have protested the dissimilarity of treatment accorded them as compared to Cuban refugees. Cuban refugees who arrive in the U.S. are released to relatives without applying for asylum. These Cubans qualify for permanent residency after one year of residency. This process is sanctioned and established under the Cuban Adjustment Act of 1966.

An appeal to the legislative branch of government is the forum of last resort. This author submits that such an appeal should include legislation that redefines and broadens the definition of political refugee. The poignant and perspicacious observations of the editor of the *Washington Post* are noteworthy:

> The test for admission to this country is whether the refugees have reason to fear political persecution if they return home. For people from communist countries that used to be taken for granted.
>
> For increasing numbers of refugees worldwide, as for the Haitians, the fear of political persecution is no longer a useful test. Haiti isn't a communist despotism. It's in a state of anarchy in which armed men roam the streets knowing that there is neither an independent police force nor a judiciary capable of calling them to account. . . . They fear robbery and murder. They fear starvation in a country that was desperately poor to begin with and is now under international sanctions that have cut off the meager trade on which it lived— except perhaps for the drug trade.

The United States ought not try to repatriate any Haitians by force until the Organization of American States has gone farther in its efforts to reestablish a legitimate government there and reduce the level of violence. It's understandable that the Bush administration does not want to incite a further migration of Haitians to this country. But it is ludicrous to tell Haitians that they aren't real refugees because they aren't fleeing the right kind of tyranny.

Editor's Note: This article has been edited for publication.

The International Refugee Regime

Stretched to the Limit?

Gil Loescher

International institutions traditionally have had difficulty addressing refugee problems, particularly during times of great disorder and structural change within world politics—for example, during the First World War when multinational states and empires disintegrated and after the Second World War when the global structure shifted from a multipolar to a bipolar system. Over 70 years ago, the world community established an international refugee regime to regularize the status and control of stateless people in Europe. Since then, international laws specifying refugees as a unique category of human rights victims to whom special protection and benefits should be accorded have been signed and ratified by over a hundred states and enforced for several decades.

Like international institutions, however, states also have been traditionally ambivalent about international cooperation over refugee issues. On the one hand, states have a fundamental, self-serving interest in quickly resolving refugee crises: Refugee movements create domestic instability, generate interstate tension and threaten international security. Thus, states created the international refugee regime prompted not by purely altruistic motives, but by a desire to promote regional and international stability and to support functions which serve the interests of governments—namely, burden sharing and coordinating policies regarding the treatment of refugees.

On the other hand, state independence is also an issue: States often are unwilling to yield authority to international refugee agencies and institutions and consequently, impose considerable financial and political limitations on their activities. For example, the first intergovernmental activities on behalf of refugees during the interwar period (1921–1943) were limited to specific groups of European refugees. The series of international organizations created to deal with these situations possessed limited mandates of short duration. Although governments met in the early Cold War period (1949–1951) to create the contemporary international refugee regime and formulate rules and decision making procedures, they sought to limit once again the regime's responsibilities in the context of the emerging global refugee problem. The great

Journal of International Affairs, Volume 47 (Winter 1994:351–77).

powers were unwilling to commit themselves to indefinite financial costs and large resettlement programs.

Nonetheless, despite state reservations, significant intergovernmental collaboration on the refugee issue did in fact occur, and the responsibilities accorded to the international refugee regime steadily expanded, with assistance and protection granted to a progressively larger number of refugees. In the post-Cold War era, however, the number of displaced people in situations of internal conflict, state disintegration and environmental degradation is growing rapidly. The refugee regime—ill-equipped to address the causes of a crisis, the numbers caught up in it or its consequences—is once more in danger of being overwhelmed.

Having presented an overview, the article examines the dynamics of regime change through the five periods during which the international refugee regime confronted significant challenges to its authority and adapted to those specific needs: the interwar period; the immediate post-Second World War era; the period of expansion into the Third World during the late 1950s through most of the 1970s; the decade of the 1980s, when the regime faced long-standing refugee problems resulting from superpower involvement in regional conflicts; and finally, the post-Cold War era, during which internal displacements and repatriations in situations of civil conflict assume primary importance for international organizations and governments. Next, this article analyzes the characteristics of many of today's displacements, the challenges they pose to the international refugee regime and the kinds of policy responses required—not only to alleviate human suffering, but also to contribute to greater stability and security in the future. Finally, the article concludes with suggestions for new alliances and new actors for forging a way through the present crisis.

DYNAMICS OF REGIME CHANGE

The 1980s: Dealing with Refugee Outflows from Superpower Rivalry and Regional Conflicts

Until the late 1970s, the relatively liberal attitude of most states and their willingness to accept additional responsibilities to assist refugees and strengthen measures to protect them characterized the post-Second World War regime. During the 1980s, however, states within the regime began to develop not only restrictive but also conflicting policies regarding the refugee issue. In addition, despite its phenomenal organizational growth during the 1970s, the international refugee regime still fell short in addressing the new and seemingly intractable refugee problems of the decade.

The intensification of the Cold War during the 1980s shifted the structure of the bipolar conflict: Both established third world governments and their opposing political forces collected external Western patrons and enjoyed relatively easy access to weapons. As a result, internal wars in Indochina, Afghanistan, Central America, the Horn of Africa and Southern Africa became protracted and debilitating affairs. Such conflicts perpetuated endemic violence which, in turn, generated large waves of refugees.

In light of such developments, during the 1980s, long-term care and maintenance in enclosed camps for the majority of refugees fleeing regional conflicts in Africa, Asia and Central America characterized the global refugee relief situation. The international community failed to devise comprehensive or long-term political solutions or to provoke any alternatives to prolonged camp existence. At the same time, a growing number of Third World refugees appeared on the doorsteps of Western countries to seek asylum. Unlike in earlier periods, these refugees were no longer confined to their regions of origin, and now travelled directly to Western countries by air transport.

Refugees' Problems in the Post-Cold War Era

The 1990s represent a new era for refugees. The end of the Cold War brought about major changes in the general pattern of refugee emergencies and challenges posed to the international refugee regime in providing relief and protection. Most major refugee crises of the 1990s have been triggered by internal conflicts in which ethnic identity is a prominent element in both the goals and methods of adversaries. The number of wars involving secession and state formation are increasing. In such conflicts, civilians are often used as weapons and targets in warfare, and large-scale displacements comprise a political strategy in claiming control over territory. Refugee movements are more likely the result of ethnic, communal and religious conflicts—fueled by the increasing availability of arms, due to the breakup of the Cold War—as well as of sharp socio-economic divisions and human rights abuses. UNHCR must confront refugee emergencies in rapid, sometimes overlapping, succession. Refugee crises in Iraq, Bosnia, Croatia, Kenya, Somalia, Bangladesh, Nepal, the Caucasus, Tajikistan, Benin, Ghana, Rwanda and Burundi strain the capacities of the organization almost to the breaking point. At the same time, UNHCR is trying to resolve the long-standing refugee problems of the previous decade primarily through repatriation in the context of continuing instability and insecurity.

It is time for a major debate about how the United Nations, regional bodies and states can effectively intervene in internal conflicts and humanitarian emergencies. The most difficult political and humanitarian questions confronting the international community in the 1990s are how governments and international organizations can intervene to prevent refugee flights within countries or across international borders; how they can provide assistance and protection to internally displaced people when their own governments object to such intervention as an infringement of sovereignty; or, when, as in Somalia,

Liberia, Haiti or Bosnia, it is impossible to determine the legitimate government or authority in the country. The most immediate short-term problem for international agencies is to determine when and how repatriation and reintegration are most appropriate, particularly as some past regional conflicts in Central America, Indochina and Africa subside.

THE CHALLENGES FACING UNHCR: INSTITUTIONAL CONSTRAINTS AND POTENTIAL PROBLEMS

For the past 40 years, UNHCR has worked with people fleeing to countries of asylum where they require protection and assistance. UNHCR staff focused their activities on assisting refugees in camps and on negotiating with host governments for support. UNHCR assisted refugees on the assumption that once the conflict has ended, the refugees would return home and the old socio-political and territorial order would be re-established. Internally displaced persons were aided only in so far as home governments allowed it.

Since the end of the Cold War, UNHCR has adopted new criteria in serving refugee populations: Now, UNHCR focuses on meeting the immediate needs of refugees, returnees and internally displaced people who live in conditions of inter-communal violence, shifting borders and on-going conflict. In countries of asylum across the world, UNHCR has extensive experience in aiding refugees on the basis of its mandate and well-defined international refugee instruments. But in countries undergoing civil wars, UNHCR staff find themselves not only working with governments, but also with opposition groups, guerrilla forces and political factions. UNHCR staff are now engaged alongside U.N. peacekeeping forces in anarchic and unstable countries which lack viable national and local structures. Their duties include protecting civilians against reprisals and forced displacement; relocating and evacuating civilians from conflict areas; and assisting besieged populations, such as those in Sarajevo, who are either unable or unwilling to move from their homes. Frequently, however, UNHCR lacks any firm institutional and legal basis for this work.

The Challenges of Working in Internal Conflicts

In the post-Cold War era, the international community is emphasizing the underlying causes of the refugee problem. Such a policy includes early warning, preventive diplomacy and ensuring respect for human rights. UNHCR itself has started to develop strategies and approaches intended to address the root causes of refugee flows before they start and to reduce or contain population movements which have already begun.

This shift to a preventive strategy, however, cannot be accomplished easily or quickly. Working in countries of origin differs substantially from working in countries of asylum. Unlike in countries of asylum, UNHCR must work with governments as well as opposition movements and guerrilla factions. UNHCR is ill-equipped to respond to the needs of internally displaced people and returnees who live amid conditions of inter-communal violence and on-going conflict. For example, UNHCR staff experience serious difficulties in reaching displaced people, especially in areas contested by both governments and armed opposition groups, and many UNHCR officials lack prior experience in working with internally displaced populations. Furthermore, most staff are not recruited or trained to work in situations where local populations view both the displaced and returnees as the enemy and U.N. assistance as favoring one side to the disadvantage of the other. In situations such as in Bosnia, the Caucasus or Tajikistan, UNHCR uses humanitarian and legal interventions similar to those used by the International Committee of the Red Cross (ICRC), but its staff lacks the special training, skills and experience of ICRC staff members.

A major obstacle to taking a more active role in refugee protection in countries of origin derives from the international refugee regime itself. The regime was designed to be non-political and strictly humanitarian, a strategy employed to receive permission to work in host countries and to secure funding from donor governments. UNHCR, as it is presently structured, is not mandated to intervene politically against governments or opposition groups, despite documentation of human rights violations. In addition, UNHCR staff are often unfamiliar with human rights and humanitarian law and are uncertain of how governments and opposition groups will react to their interventions using these protection norms.

Warring parties in internal conflicts perceive humanitarian assistance and one of several weapons of warfare which is another weakness of current relief operations. For example, food assistance is very often used as a political weapon. Adversaries divert assistance from the proper recipients for military or political goals while denying assistance to certain populations and geographical areas by blocking access to international agencies. If UNHCR is to respond effectively to enlarged population flows resulting from the consequences of the increasing number of internal wars, it must both reorganize the staffing, training and operations of the organization to reflect new roles and endow it with the necessary resources, tools and mandate to do its job effectively.

The Inadequacy of the Existing Resource Base

The 1990s presented UNHCR with several new emergencies that greatly increased its overall expenditures. In 1991, as a result of emergency relief operations in northern Iraq and the Horn of Africa, total voluntary fund expenditures amounted to $862.5 million, an increase of almost 60 percent over 1990. In 1992, new refugee and humanitarian crises in the former Yugoslavia, Bangladesh, the Horn of Africa and Southern Africa, as well as continued responsibilities in northern Iraq and new repatriation programs in Cambodia, Ethiopia and Mozambique, pushed UNHCR expenditures over $1 billion. The sums required for UNHCR operations in 1993 are estimated to be in the range of $1.3 billion.

In addition to the high costs of responding to refugee crises, internal displacements and repatriations, humanitarian missions today are likely to be protracted affairs with no clear outcome. In the former Yugoslavia, for example, UNHCR committed approximately one-quarter of its staff and one-third of its total resources worldwide to providing assistance and protection to nearly four million people. UNHCR is now in danger not only of overextending itself because of its involvement in vicious and intractable conflicts, but also of exhausting the political interest of donor governments in continuing to fund such protracted operations, even in high-profile situations like Bosnia-Herzegovina.

One of UNHCR's most significant weaknesses is its dependence on *voluntary* contributions to carry out existing and new programs. The flow of assistance from donor governments is neither reliable nor always in the most appropriate form. In addition, funding is frequently provided late and is often earmarked for particular uses with political overtones.

In the past, donor governments have made funding contingent upon external political factors. Today, however, these governments are less influenced politically by refugee situations, which they view as local or regional problems of little or no foreign policy or security value. Funding is now more likely to be cut back in favor of the domestic priorities of these industrialized states. Major powers are reluctant to provide funds for humanitarian programs when internal conflicts in aid recipient countries continue unabated. Thus, despite the clear link in situations involving displacement and regional security, such as in the Caucasus and Central Asia, there is weak donor interest in funding a comprehensive strategy for dealing with refugees and internally displaced people. It is a tragic irony that major Western donors appear to have lost political incentive for providing generous support to new programs at a point when many political barriers to effective humanitarian actions have disintegrated.

Inadequacy of Existing Mandates in International Humanitarian Law

While there is a clear mandate for the protection and the provision of humanitarian assistance to refugees, existing political, diplomatic, economic and legal mechanisms are insufficiently developed to cope with the increasingly complex and volatile population movements of the post-Cold War period. In particular, there are no specific international organizations mandated to protect and assist the internally displaced. At the same time, the political issues involved, particularly state sovereignty and non-intervention in domestic affairs, make the issue of the internally displaced one of the most challenging problems confronting the international community in the 1990s.

Further, existing human rights and humanitarian laws offer internally displaced persons little protection. These also do not adequately cover forcible displacements and relocations, humanitarian assistance and access, the right to food and the protection of relief workers. In particular, public emergencies and internal violence fall outside the scope of the Geneva Convention of 1949 and Additional Protocol II of 1977. As a result, many human rights provisions are suspended when the security of a state is suspended. It is precisely in these conditions that internal displacement often occurs.

THE WAY AHEAD: THE NEED FOR NEW ALLIANCES AND NEW ACTORS

Hindered both by its dependence on voluntary contributions to carry out its programs and its need to obtain the approval of host governments before intervening, UNHCR cannot resolve the problems of refugees, returnees and internally displaced people single-handedly. More attention must be focused on a range of players including development agencies, human rights networks, peacekeeping and conflict resolution mechanisms and the traditional relief organizations—all of which must be involved in finding innovative approaches and collaborations to resolve conflicts and their accompanying displacements.

Interagency cooperation is the key to a more effective response to the problems of displacement. If UNHCR hopes to ensure cooperation in achieving a solution to displacement and phasing out the political source of such operations in the future, it must continue to work at improving coordination with other international, regional and non-governmental agencies, particularly in strategic planning and in making legal and institutional arrangements with other agencies charged with responding to refugees.

Department of Humanitarian Affairs

Making the system work better requires a more effective division of the labor among the actors involved in responding to the humanitarian, political and security dimensions of internal conflicts. The U.N. General Assembly took an important first step in December 1991 in creating the Office of the Emergency Relief Coordinator, charged with providing a focal point, within governments and between governmental and non-governmental organizations for communication during U.N. emergency relief operations. In early 1992, Jan Eliasson, the Emergency Relief Coordinator, become the first Under Secretary-General in the newly formed U.N. Department of Humanitarian Affairs (DHA). The creation of the DHA was an essential step in clarifying and assigning responsibilities to U.N. agencies in complex emergencies. This is particularly apparent in situations where mandates overlap or where no entity has a clear mandate to act; in making quick decisions on the best coordinating mechanisms to respond to humanitarian emergencies at the field level; and in negotiating access for these agencies without waiting for a formal government request. Donor states influential in the creation of the DHA envision the office gathering data and managing information, mobilizing resources and orchestrating field activities, negotiating a framework of action with political authorities and providing overall leadership to humanitarian aid efforts.

Unfortunately, in the past two years, the vision has not been realized. Lack of adequate staff in the field, a rapid succession of humanitarian crises in the post-Cold War period, and incompletely established and largely untested mechanisms for interagency coordination have caught the DHA unprepared, to assume its intended leadership role in most recent emergencies. Perhaps the greatest difficulty confronting the DHA is that the specialized agencies such as UNHCR and others possess a high degree of constitutional autonomy and consistently resist any attempt by the DHA to impose strong authority over their actions in humanitarian emergencies. If the DHA's presence is to lead to improvements in the response capacity of the United Nations, the significance of its coordinating role must be recognized by UNHCR and other agencies. The DHA must also be fully equipped both politically and financially to undertake effectively its assigned tasks.

Coordinating Relief and Development

Closer coordination between United Nations Development Programme (UNDP) and UNHCR represents a key solution to situations involving refugees, returnees and the internally displaced. Cooperation between these agencies already takes place in quick impact projects (QIPs) aimed at assisting a variety of displaced groups in Central America, Mozambique and Cambodia. In addition, in recent years in the Horn of Africa, UNHCR and UNDP established joint management structures to create preventive zones and cross mandate programs to stabilize and prevent displacement in border areas.

Although there have been greater efforts at UNDP-UNHCR coordination in field operations, far more effective interagency planning, consultation and implementation are required. The roles and responsibilities of the UNDP and UNHCR in such efforts continue to be determined on an *ad hoc,* situation-by-situation basis. In most countries, humanitarian or emergency relief aid is administratively and programmatically divorced from developmental concerns. Thus, a "development gap" exists between short-term humanitarian relief assistance and long-term development. Through QIPs, UNHCR attempted to fill this gap in Central America, the Horn of Africa and Indochina where there are large returnee and displaced populations. But QIPs, because of their small size and limited nature, have only partially filled the gap between immediate assistance and longer-term development, highlighting the fact that UNHCR is not a development agency. The task of the overall rehabilitation of these communities must be carried out by UNDP, or by other U.N. agencies, which can more appropriately deal with reconstruction and development. This requires a full transfer of responsibility from UNHCR to UNDP after the immediate emergency relief phase is over—again, an idea that UNDP consistently resists because it views itself as having a development, and not even a partially emergency, focus. Interagency coordination is especially important in the large-scale repatriations which UNHCR is planning for the 1990s.

In countries such as Afghanistan, Ethiopia, Cambodia and Mozambique, a precondition for successful returns is development aid and reintegration assistance aimed at alleviating extreme poverty in countries of origin. Without improved and established economic prospects in these countries, political instability and new displacements are likely to occur. A focus on safety of return and reintegration involves rethinking the roles and mandates of international organizations and NGOs; shifting their operational priorities from receiving countries to countries of return; training agency staff to work in development as well as relief assistance; and closer cooperation and coordination between development and refugee agencies on the one hand, and human rights and refugee agencies on the other.

Greater Human Rights Monitoring and Enforcement

Greater development assistance alone is not enough to create safe conditions for those returning home: international cooperation must also ensure democratization and respect for human rights. However, neither good governance nor respect for human rights falls within UNHCR's domain. The existing U.N. human rights machinery needs to be strengthened and applied more effectively to deal with refugees, returnees and the internally displaced, for it is integral to the success of U.N. peacemaking.

In recent years, the U.N. human rights system has demonstrated its potential capabilities to respond quickly to a select number of human rights emergencies involving the internally displaced. In 1992, it called an unprecedented meeting of the U.N. Commission on Human Rights and appointed a special *rapporteur* to investigate human rights abuses of minority populations in Bosnia and to make recommendations to the Security Council. Similarly, an incriminating U.N. report on human rights violations in Iraq, including the alleged forced deportation and murder of the Shi'ite population by the Iraqi army, provided humanitarian justification for the establishment of an air exclusion zone over southern Iraq.

At the same time, the United Nations Centre for Human Rights, through its Advisory Services, has worked on a number of U.N. peacekeeping or peace-enforcement missions, providing significant technical assistance and cooperation to the U.N. human rights presence in the field, for example, in El Salvador, Somalia and, now, in Cambodia. These actions underscore both the potentially key role of the U.N. human rights machinery and the growing involvement of the Security Council in humanitarian matters, and the recognition that the promotion and protection of the human rights of refugees, returnees and the internally displaced are an integral part of U.N. peacemaking.

At present, the U.N. human rights program is grossly understaffed and underfunded. The advisory services section of the Centre for Human Rights, for example, has an annual budget of approximately $700,000. This is a minuscule sum in view of both the massive amounts currently being spent on relief and peacekeeping operations and the potential of the advisory services section to strengthen civil society, promote democratic and pluralistic institutions and procedures and, thereby, to prevent human rights abuses and mass displacements.

If the United Nations hopes to respond more effectively to the refugee crises, it must strengthen its capacity to monitor developments in human rights issues. A greater protection role in the field should be granted to U.N. human rights personnel. At present, the U.N. Centre for Human Rights has country expertise but no field presence. In the short-term, the Centre can strengthen its coverage in the field by the continued expansion of its advisory services and technical cooperation. In addition, by offering services such as training judges, strengthening electoral commissions, establishing ombudsmen, training prison staff and advising governments on constitutions and legislation regarding national minorities and human rights, the Centre is likely to be more successful in its activities and less threatening to governments than in more straightforward, fieldwork-oriented human rights monitoring.

In recent years, there has been much discussion about the creation of special human rights machinery for the internally displaced. At its 1993 session, the U.N. Human Rights Commission reappointed the Special Representative on the Internally Displaced to monitor mass displacements of people, collect information on violations of their human rights, and help to sustain a positive dialogue toward achieving solutions with governments of the country of origin. But the Special Representative must be given proper political support and funding to carry out his or her tasks effectively. A General Assembly Resolution confirming the role and mandate of the Special Representative is now required to institutionalize this office further. A significant first step toward trying to deal with the problem would be to designate a permanent representative for the internally displaced. This representative could undertake fact-finding missions, intercede with governments, embark on activities which strengthen institutions that sustain democracy and civil society, publish reports and bring violations to the attention of human rights bodies and the Security Council.

Recently, there have been attempts to create closer linkages between UNHCR and the human rights organs and activities of the U.N. system. In 1992, for example, the Centre for Human Rights and UNHCR drafted a memorandum of understanding so that human rights information collected by UNHCR could be forwarded to the Centre for Human Rights. At the end of 1992, UNHCR and the Centre established a joint working group to study mechanisms and approaches for enhanced and continuous collaboration. Such consultation should be strengthened to ensure that displacements emanating from human rights violations are brought to the attention of the Commission on Human Rights, and that the work of the Centre's advisory services section adequately addresses human rights issues associated with refugee movements and internal displacements.

Military Involvement in Future Refugee Emergencies

The emergencies in the post-Cold War era have highlighted the need for more effective interface between humanitarian relief and political and security considerations. Relief programs frequently now run alongside peacekeeping efforts or other types of military intervention. Indeed, humanitarian aid is likely to become increasingly militarized, especially because of the heavy casualties among relief workers and fighting, for example, in Mozambique and Bosnia. Recent experience has demonstrated that the military has instant access to a range of material and logistical resources which simply are not available to UNHCR and other humanitarian organizations. With the greater use of military convoys and the need for security training among UNHCR staff, UNHCR field operations in conditions of continuing conflict are, in fact, becoming increasingly militarized.

While the potential for cooperation between humanitarian organizations and military forces should not be discounted, it is evident that the objectives and working methods of the two groups of actors are different, and, in some cases, contradictory. As relief operations in countries such as Iraq and Somalia have indicated, military forces rarely, if ever, have a purely humanitarian agenda. Moreover, they are generally unwilling to work under external direction, even in operations conducted under U.N. auspices.

Recent experiences in Bosnia also demonstrate that the provision of military security for relief operations can compromise the neutrality of UNHCR and its staff, and can even threaten the delivery of humanitarian assistance. Military intervention may also have an adverse impact on the resolution of conflicts. In the struggle to provide aid to the displaced and other war victims, the resolution of the root causes of the conflict can easily become increasingly peripheral.

In future operations, there should be greater efforts to ensure the complementarity of humanitarian and political objectives. If military intervention for humanitarian purposes is undertaken, it should fit into an integrated humanitarian/conflict resolution framework, and humanitarian assistance and the protection of refugees and displaced persons should not be subservient to or compromised by the political and military decision-making process and priorities. Any humanitarian action needs political support, but humanitarian agencies and military forces should work as partners in situations where humanitarian and political objectives carry equal weight.

The U.N. Secretary-General should ensure that the peacekeeping, peace-making and humanitarian components operating in complex emergencies are better coordinated. Further, the Secretary-General should ensure that each of these components embraces an explicit humanitarian mandate that recognizes the primacy of human rights and refugee protection in the conduct of peace-keeping activities. This would prevent the recurrence of situations, as have occurred in Bosnia and Somalia, where U.N. military or civilian staff have failed to prevent or ameliorate human rights abuses, claiming that such action is beyond their mandates. In the long-term, the DHA should be given the necessary capacity and ability to coordinate all the dimensions and actors involved in refugee emergencies.

CONCLUSION: FUTURE INTERNATIONAL COOPERATION AND THE GLOBAL REFUGEE PROBLEM

The refugee emergencies of the post-Cold War era highlight the fact that combatting the causes of forced migration cannot proceed solely within the mandate of international humanitarian organizations. The global refugee problem is not a humanitarian problem requiring charity but is a political problem requiring political solutions, and as such it cannot be separated from other areas of international concern such as migration, human rights, international security and development assistance. Such an approach raises complex questions of harmonization of efforts, coordination, determination of institutional responsibilities and allocation of resources. Thus, the challenge of the 1990s for the international community will be to respond not only to the immediate humanitarian problems of displaced people, but, in the long-run, also to confront the conditions which lead to these dislocations. These are political tasks requiring a more active role from national policymakers and a greater willingness to utilize fully the U.N. and regional mechanisms on security, peacekeeping and peacemaking and human rights in anticipating as well as reacting effectively to refugee incidents around the world. A more comprehensive and effective international response to refugee problems will require adequate and readily available resources. UNHCR, the Office of the Emergency Relief Coordinator, and other U.N. agencies cannot accomplish their missions unless the major donor states, including the United States, are prepared to bear a greater financial burden. Greater interagency cooperation, financial support and reinforcement of existing institutional mechanisms are the only effective ways for the international community, both to manage interdependent issues like refugee movements, and to ensure long-term global strategic stability.

Editor's Note: This article has been edited for publication.

An Ephemeral Victory for Refugees

Temporary Protected Status Under the Immigration Act of 1990

Dolly Z. Hassan

No Congressional acts are more complex in scope or more controversial in execution than those dealing with the problems of refugees and their claims for asylum. Since the early 1980's, a consensus has developed that there is "a 'crisis' in asylum in America." With the arrival in the U.S. of tens of thousands of refugees, mostly from the war-ravaged countries of Guatemala, Nicaragua and El Salvador, the situation has reached a critical point. The Urban Institute in Washington, D.C. has estimated that there are between 500,000 and 850,000 Salvadorans living in the U.S., and approximately 400,000 to 600,000 of them are living here illegally, a number representing 10% of the entire population of El Salvador. These refugees, most fleeing violence at home, chose to seek safe haven in the United States in spite of having little hope of receiving documentation or other permission to remain in the U.S. from the Immigration and Naturalization Service (INS). This explosive growth in the number of undocumented refugees eventually forced Congress to accept the necessity for a policy that would accommodate these individuals despite a growing resistance by many constituencies to any new waves of immigration.

The Immigration Act of 1990 [hereinafter 1990 Act], the fruit of years of rancorous debate, contains the U.S. government's measured response to this problem. In a portion of the 1990 Act, U.S. legislators, led by Congressman Joseph Moakley (D. Mass.) and Senator Dennis DeConcini (D. Ariz.), have adopted the twin provisions of Temporary Protected Status for nationals of certain designated countries and Special Temporary Protected Status for Salvadorans. While these measures and the legislative history regarding their enactment suggest that Congress has recognized the inadequacies of current law, the measures themselves are riddled with problems that might well prevent them from having any long-term positive effect on the problems they were enacted to solve.

ILSA Journal of International Law, Volume 15 (1992:33–60).

THE SEARCH FOR REFUGE

For over a century the inscription on the base of the Statue of Liberty, "Give us your tired, your poor, Your huddled masses yearning to breathe free," has been accepted as an open invitation by millions of immigrants. Driven from their native lands, often by political instability, social upheaval, natural disaster, and persecution, these immigrants arrived seeking refuge in the United States. Until about twenty years ago, their main concerns upon arrival in this country had to do with establishing themselves in spite of the xenophobia that has always infected the darker side of the American character. Today, in addition to dealing with a freshly virulent wave of nativism, their greatest problems involve first, entering into the U.S. undetected, and later, avoiding deportation from this country, a place of "first asylum" for most refugees. Unfortunately for these latest refugees, they have been manipulated by forces beyond their control to flee to the United States at precisely the same time that the United States has decided that it is unable—or unwilling—to grant legal immigration status to the thousands of individuals arriving daily at its ports and borders seeking safe haven.

Reception of Asylum Seekers in the United States

Despite massive and escalating human rights violations in many Latin American countries, U.S. administration officials and immigration restrictionists persist in arguing that aliens arriving in America today come seeking economic fortune, not fleeing persecution at home. Thus, strenuous and calculated efforts have been made to deter asylum seekers from coming to the United States. Asylum seekers are often subject therefore to long-term detention under abominable conditions and are then either encouraged to or forced to leave the United States.

This response comes as the result of a new wave of anti-refugee sentiment that emerged with the arrival of thousands of Indochinese refugees in the late 1970's and "took root with a vengeance in the summer of 1980" when 125,000 Cubans arrived in the Mariel Harbor boatlift. During this same period, Haitians fleeing the brutal Duvalier dictatorship also began to arrive by boat, and the United States implemented a unique policy of discriminatory treatment towards them. In 1981, the United States government established the Interdiction Program allowing the U.S. Coast Guard to board and turn back all U.S.-bound vessels sailing from Haiti—even if they were in international waters—as long as they carried Haitians intending to enter the U.S. Haitians who were able to evade the Coast Guard but were captured after landing were detained and automatically deported regardless of any asylum claim they might be entitled to make. Some observers attribute this treatment to the U.S. government's friendship with the Haitian regime, while others attribute it to racism and the fear of a "black tide."

The U.S. response to Salvadoran refugees has become victim to these same impulses. In spite of ample documentation detailing human rights violations by the militarily-controlled Salvadoran government, the U.S. government has adamantly refused to recognize Salvadorans as having a legitimate claim to safe haven in this country. Ignoring all evidence to the contrary, the U.S., in order to further its foreign policy objectives, continues to depict human rights conditions in battle-torn El Salvador as "improving." This diplomatic conclusion, as one scholar observes, "would be jeopardized by granting asylum to Salvadorans." Thus, the State Department has followed a policy of excluding from the U.S. "Salvadoran communist troublemakers." This policy is reflected in INS practices which exhibit a pattern of systematically pressuring Salvadorans to relinquish any asylum claim they might have and to accept, however unwillingly, repatriation.

After years of this unethical treatment, the judiciary was moved to intervene. The court in *Orantes-Hernandez v. Meese,* for example, resisted the government's claims that human rights conditions in El Salvador were improving:

> People from a wide cross-section of Salvadoran society suffer human rights abuses. . . .
> The form of the persecution includes the following: arbitrary arrest, short term detention, torture including the use of electric shock, *capucha,* beatings, rape, "disappearance," extra-judicial executions, abductions, threats against family members, intimidation, forced ingestion of food, false imprisonment, mock-executions, sleep deprivation, mass killings, and forced relocations. . . .
> The persecutors are primarily Salvadoran military and security forces. . . .
> The widespread acceptance of voluntary departure is due in large part to the coercive effects of the practices and procedures employed by the INS . . . INS agents directed, intimidated, or otherwise coerced Salvadorans within their custody, who had not expressed a desire to return [by using] a variety of techniques to procure voluntary departure, ranging from subtle persuasion to outright threats and misrepresentation.

The court ordered the INS, first, to cease coercing detainees into signing "voluntary departure" forms; second, to inform them of their right to apply for political asylum; and third, to facilitate, rather than to interfere with, their right to seek counsel in deportation proceedings. Subsequently, the court was forced to issue a contempt order on the grounds that the INS had violated certain provisions of the injunction.

American popular reaction to immigrants (including Salvadorans) since the 1970's has been notably mixed. While clerics and their lay supporters established sanctuary movements to attempt to assist and lead to safety Central Americans who were the victims of persecution and war, others called out for the U.S. to regain control of its "porous borders." In order to garner support, immigration restrictionists often warned of the "Silent Invasion" of immigrants crossing U.S. borders, taking jobs from American citizens and weakening the economy through excess reliance on social benefit programs. These calls persisted in the face of several studies which showed that undocumented workers were a benefit rather than a burden to the U.S. economy: they created jobs, paid their fair share of taxes and were often afraid to apply for or were misinformed abut their eligibility for benefit programs to which they were entitled. Instead of milking the American economy, as is often alleged, immigrants were shown to have been subsidizing it.

The passionate national debate on the subject climaxed with the passage of the Immigration Reform and Control Act of 1986 [hereinafter IRCA]. IRCA provided for the legalization of undocumented immigrants who could prove continuous residence in the U.S. since January 1982 and included penalties, commonly referred to as employer sanctions, for employers who either knowingly or unknowingly hired undocumented workers. The measure was designed as a cure-all, intended to stop both the exploitation of immigrants and the entry of any further waves of immigration into the United States.

Unfortunately, however, the January 1982 cut-off date excluded from eligibility in the legalization program a substantial number of asylum seekers, especially Central Americans, who entered the United States after that date. IRCA has also failed to deter people who, having nothing to lose by emigrating, continue to flee to the United States in search of safe haven. With the passage of the 1990 Act, law-makers finally seemed to acknowledge the fact that for many of these immigrants, more was at stake than their economic well being.

CURRENT LEGAL REMEDIES

Before examining the provisions of the 1990 Act, it is useful to take a cursory glance at current laws which apply to individuals in search of safe haven in the U.S. current legal remedies include both statutory-based relief (the granting of refugee status, the granting of asylum status and the withholding of deportation) and non-statutory relief (extended voluntary departure). These remedies permit aliens who have been determined to have been subject to persecution in their native countries to enter into and/or to remain in the United States. The legal prerequisites governing the granting of each form of relief are distinct.

Both asylees and refugees are covered by customary international law and international treaty, with the *Handbook on the Procedures and Criteria for Determining Status Under the 1951 Convention and the 1967 Protocol Relating to the Status of Refugees* [UN Handbook] serving as a guide to interpreting and giving effect to international treaties. While the relevant international law is intended to provide protection for refugees, asylum applicants must, in fact, rely on both statutory and non-statutory domestic law.

U.S. Statutory Law

In keeping with the definition of a refugee as provided in the *1967 United Nations Protocol Relating to the Status of Refugees,* the Immigration and Nationality Act, as amended by the Refugee Act of 1980, currently vests the Attorney General (AG) with discretionary power to grant asylum to individuals in the U.S. who have been persecuted or who have a well-founded fear of persecution on account of their race, religion, nationality, membership in a particular social group, or political opinion. This law was intended to adopt an approach in harmony with international legal standards, thus eliminating any former geographical or ideological bias operating in favor of individuals fleeing from Communist countries and against virtually all other refugees.

The statutory criteria for asylum applicants include the requirement that they prove that they are either unwilling or unable to return to the countries from which they have fled or to avail themselves of the protection of that country. This proof must include evidence that the applicants fled on account of either persecution or a reasonable fear of persecution, and, also that there would be "a reasonable possibility of actually suffering such persecution" should they return. This "reasonable possibility" test was established by the Supreme Court to replace the unduly restrictive "clear probability" test formerly employed by the Executive Office of Immigration Review (EOIR), the Board of Immigration Appeals (BIA) and some circuit courts of appeal. The Court held that the standard of a well-founded fear of persecution could be met if individuals could demonstrate that there was even a ten percent probability that they would be subject to persecution if forced to return to the countries from which they had fled. Applicants could meet their burden if they showed, by a preponderance of the evidence, that there existed in their native countries a pattern or practice of "persecution of groups of persons similarly situated" as the applicants, and that the applicants' inclusion or identification with such group of persons makes "their fear of persecution reasonable." The applicants need not prove that they "would be singled out individually for persecution." If granted asylum, these individuals would have the right to remain in the U.S. and, after one year, would obtain the right to apply to become permanent residents.

Unfortunately, thousands of individuals fleeing from civil strife and widespread violence in their native countries find it impossible to meet even this seemingly relaxed standard in proving a well-founded fear of persecution. Particular applicants from certain countries are still called upon to meet what amounts to a stricter standard of proof:

> Haitians, Salvadorans and Guatemalans have been special targets of negative presumptions. According to the experience of numerous immigration attorneys, asylum applicants from these countries face enormous difficulties when seeking to demonstrate a well-founded fear of persecution. Many [INS]

district directors and immigration judges with an INS background, presume that aliens from these countries are economic migrants in search of a better life, while considering those from communist-dominated countries to be subject to persecution due to the nature of the political system.

The holdings in a number of cases highlight the inequities in the application of the standard as it has been applied to Salvadoran asylum applicants.

In one case the BIA found that evidence presented by a Salvadoran showing that he had been imprisoned for eight days, interrogated, beaten and threatened with death was insufficient to support a successful asylum application. According to the BIA, such an occurrence was representative of the general level of violence in El Salvador and, therefore, did not support a finding that the applicant qualified for membership in one of the protected classes. The BIA also initially refused to grant asylum to Salvadorans who, because of their neutrality, had been threatened by members of more than one party to the conflict in El Salvador. The Ninth Circuit overruled this practice, however, holding that neutrality does constitute political opinion.

The BIA placed an enormous burden on asylum applicants in other cases by requiring that they prove that the threat of persecution existed country-wide, not just in one particular section of the country. Thus, a taxi driver who received notes threatening his life if he refused to participate in work stoppages was held ineligible for asylum although three of his co-workers had been murdered after receiving similar threats. "It may be," held the BIA, that "the respondent could have avoided persecution by moving to another city in that country."

The standards as they have been applied to Salvadoran applicants are interpreted much more strictly than when they are applied to similarly situated applicants from countries towards which the United States has established different foreign policy objectives. In *Sanchez-Trujillo v. INS,* for example, the Salvadoran petitioners presented evidence that members of the social group consisting of young, urban, working class males of military age were targeted for persecution if they failed to serve in the military. Witnesses, including former members of the Salvadoran military, testified that young males were more likely to be suspected of disloyalty and, therefore, were subject to a greater risk of persecution. While the BIA acknowledged that a substantial number of the victims of military and paramilitary reprisals in El Salvador had been young males, it refused to grant the petitioners asylum noting that the danger would hardly be unusual during any violent conflict.

A stark difference exists between that holding and the holding in *Matter of Salim* in which the BIA found that an asylum applicant from Afghanistan had established a well-founded fear of persecution based upon his refusal to join the Soviet controlled Afghan army. Here, the BIA attached "significant weight" to a report issued by the Bureau for Human Rights and Humanitarian Affairs [BHRHA] at the U.S. State Department which confirmed the petitioner's claims regarding forced recruitment. Unfortunately, in asylum matters immigration judges rely heavily, and INS interviewers rely virtually exclusively, on advisory opinions from BHRHA. Such decisions, usually distributed as preprinted form letters, are influenced by current U.S. relations with the country from which the asylum seeker has fled. Because of the ideological bias inherent in BHRHA findings, it has become widely accepted by U.S. immigration officials that individuals who flee from communist states are more deserving of the granting of asylum than are those refugees fleeing from persecution engaged in by governments considered to be friendly to the United States. As one commentator points out, "[i]t is easier for a Russian dancer forbidden to practice his art to gain refuge in America than for a Salvadoran likely to be shot in crossfire to find safety here." In its review of asylum approval rates, the General Accounting Office established in January 1987 that the approval rate for refugees from El Salvador was 2%, whereas the approval rate for Polish refugees was 49% and for Iranians 66%. This bias continues to operate. In 1989, 91% of the Soviet applicants (109 out of 120) received asylum, while the rate for Salvadorans remained at 2% (337 out of 14,198). Reviewing the implementation of the Refugee Act over the past decade, the Lawyers Committee for Human Rights has concluded that "[i]mmigration enforcement priorities and foreign policy considerations have overwhelmed humanitarian responsibilities in refugee status determination."

Non-Statutory Law—Extended Voluntary Departure

Extended Voluntary Departure [EVD] is a form of nonstatutory, ad hoc relief granted to either groups of people or to individuals whose deportation the INS is willing to postpone in "exceptional cases." The decision to grant EVD is made by the Department of State (which is responsible for initiating and then terminating the procedure) and by the Department of Justice. When applied to groups, EVD is granted to nationals of certain countries which are characterized by unsettled, unstable and dangerous conditions. EVD provides temporary relief for individuals of designated nationalities who fail to qualify for asylum but whose lives would be in danger should they return to their native countries. In the past, EVD has been granted to nationals from Poland, Uganda and Afghanistan. Those qualifying for EVD receive employment authorization but few other benefits. They cannot easily obtain documents which would make it possible for them to travel outside the United States, nor can they make arrangements to have their families join them. Most importantly, unless individual members of these groups meet some other statutory criteria, they are not entitled to apply for any adjustment in their immigration status.

The major problem with the EVD program is that, like asylum, it is a discretionary measure, and, as such, no individual can claim a right to the relief regardless of how unsettled, unstable or dangerous the conditions in their native countries. The problem is also complicated, as it is in asylum cases, by the U.S. government's unwillingness to offend friendly governments. Thus, although the danger to nationals of certain countries in Central America has been widely accepted, the State Department has been unwilling to extend the benefits of EVD to refugees from that region. Ironically, the mechanisms involved in granting EVD have never been subject to the kind of public involvement and debate that might be expected considering the wide discretion afforded the State and Justice Departments in granting EVD relief. Instead, the administration has chosen to ignore all calls from refugee advocates for the granting of EVD to refugees from Central America, where, it is often argued, the U.S. government owes the people some kind of protection from the havoc wrought, at least partly, by its own policies and practices in the region.

The judiciary, deferring to the plenary power of Congress in immigration matters, has thus far refused to overturn denials of EVD. When a union, comprised primarily of Salvadorans, challenged the Attorney General for denying EVD to its members, the Court of Appeals for the District of Columbia held that "EVD is an extra-statutory remedy and . . . the decision to award or to withhold it for citizens of a particular nation lies squarely within the discretion of the Attorney General."

Thus EVD does not protect many Central American or other refugees who make it to the U.S. seeking a safe haven from armed conflicts and generalized violence at home. Immigrant's rights groups and some legislators, notably Representative Moakley and Senator DeConcini, have long argued that there was a necessity for some measure that would afford protection to individuals who were not covered by existing laws but who had valid concerns about their personal security due to perilous conditions in their home countries. The Temporary Protected Status provisions of the Immigration Act of 1990 were enacted in an attempt to relieve some of these problems.

TEMPORARY PROTECTED STATUS FOR NATIONALS OF DESIGNATED STATES

Under the new law, nationals of certain countries or residents of certain parts of countries are eligible for Temporary Protected Status [TPS] if their country is designated by the Attorney General [AG] and if the applicants themselves meet certain criteria. Countries may be designated as a result of ongoing armed conflicts, natural disasters (such as earthquakes, floods, droughts, epidemics or other environmental disasters), or any other extraordinary and temporary condition which prevents the safe return of residents to the designated area. The Department of Justice has approved the designation of Liberia, Lebanon and Kuwait as countries whose citizens are eligible for TPS under these criteria.

In addition, applicants for TPS from the designated countries must meet certain eligibility requirements. They must have been continuously physically present in the U.S. since the date of the most recent designation, they must have registered within the 180-day period established by the AG, and they must be otherwise admissible as immigrants. Certain grounds of exclusion enacted in earlier statutes are inapplicable under this statute, while certain others are waivable to achieve humanitarian purposes, to ensure family unity, or to accomplish what is otherwise in the public interest. (302(a)). The provisions providing for the exclusion of applicants convicted of the commission of serious crimes or of any drug related offenses, however, remain non-waivable. (302(c)(2)). The initial period of designation, to be specified by the AG, will range from six months to eighteen months. (302(b)(2)(B)). After reviewing conditions in the country, the AG has the discretion to renew the designation for an additional eighteen months. It is important to note that TPS will not be granted to those seeking to enter the United States. Thus, unless applicants have already found their way into this country, they would not be eligible for protection under the law—a law designed to deter further illegal immigration, despite recognition of the need for those nationals already out of the country to receive protection against being forced back into life-threatening situations.

The Limited Benefits Afforded by Temporary Protected Status

Limited immigration-related benefits are available to aliens from designated countries while their TPS is in effect. They may not be detained or deported, for example, as long as they continue to meet the statutory criteria. (302(a)(1)(A) and 302(d)(4)). Furthermore, if they are placed in deportation proceedings the AG has an affirmative obligation to give them prompt notification, in their native language, regarding the provisions of the legislation. (302(a)(3)). Denials of applications are reviewable by the INS Administrative Appeals Unit. (302(b)(5)(B)). The most important benefit granted to those who qualify for TPS, however, is work authorization which is valid during the period the status is in effect. (302(a)(1)(B)). This benefit is particularly valuable since employers are subject to sanctions for hiring employees who do not possess documents satisfying INS requirements.

The legislation provides other key advantages for qualified aliens. They are free to travel outside the U.S. as long as they have the prior consent of the AG. (302(f)(3)). They are also considered by the INS to be in lawful status and therefore do not have to relinquish any other rights and privileges to which they may be entitled. (302(a)(5)).

The Potential for Continued Inequities in the Application of TPS Standards

TPS was enacted to protect aliens who, in spite of any legitimate claims they may have concerning dangers to their safety should they return to their native lands, might find it difficult to assert affirmative asylum claims. Unfortunately, as is the case with so much immigration legislation, the program is fraught with pitfalls for undocumented applicants.

The section of the law that outlines the procedures to be used in designating countries for the purpose of granting TPS (302(b)) is fraught with uncertainties and ambiguities. While all decisions by the AG regarding designation, extension and termination will become effective only after they are published in the Federal Register (thus making possible wider public awareness concerning the implementation of the program), the law vests the AG with virtually complete discretion concerning the decision regarding designation as long as he consults with "appropriate agencies of the government." (302(b)(1)). The specific agencies with whom the AG must consult, the roles they might play in the decisions to designate, and the procedures to be followed in making the designations remain unclear, thereby inviting the same kinds of problems associated with the implementation of the Refugee Act. If the AG depends upon the determinations of the State Department or BHRHA (whose reports often depart from the findings of independent organizations), it is distinctly possible that the intent of TPS legislation will be frustrated by the weight given to extraneous foreign policy considerations.

The fact that there is no provision in the law affording judicial review of the AG's determinations also invites abuses of discretion. This danger is relieved to some degree, however, because, beginning in 1992, the AG must submit reports explaining the reasons why specific countries were designated, terminated or extended. Unfortunately, these provisions afford no affirmative relief for nationals of countries that are not chosen, or even considered, by the AG for designation in the first instance.

The actual criteria to be employed by the AG in designation are also dangerously nebulous. For example, a country may be designated if the AG finds that there is "an ongoing armed conflict within the state and, due to such conflict, requiring the return of aliens who are nationals of that state . . . would *pose a serious threat to their personal safety.*" (302(b)(1)(A), emphasis added.) Interpretation of this phrase could easily hinge on U.S. relations with the specific country.

The other basis for designation involves countries where, due to "earthquake, flood, drought, epidemic, or other environmental disaster in the state [there exists] a substantial, but temporary, disruption of living conditions in the area affected." (302(b)(1)(B)). Under this section, the designated country must be both "unable to *handle adequately the return to the state of aliens* who are nationals of the state" and must officially request designation, or must be found by the AG to suffer *extraordinary and temporary conditions* that prevent the return of its nationals. None of these provisions, however, permit granting TPS if it would be *"contrary to the national interest of the United States."* (302A(b)(1)(B), emphasis added).

Vague phraseology such as that highlighted above lends itself to the kind of flexibility in interpretation that could easily result in too much weight being given to considerations having little to do with the goals of the TPS program. The phrase "national interest," for example, could be brandished freely depending upon the official attitude of the United States towards the country under consideration for designation. In addition, while the clause providing for a country to officially request designation may assist the United States in designating a country without offending the national pride of a reliable ally, it seems just as likely that, if undue weight were afforded that provision, concerns might arise that would run counter to the original need for statutory-based relief.

The Dilemmas Presented for Applicants by Temporary Protected Status

Because the relief granted by TPS is only temporary, it presents a series of problems for undocumented individuals whose countries have been designated. If individuals fail to register during the designated period or if they should fail to renew that registration annually as required, they become immediately deportable. If they do decide to register, however, they risk deportation when the program ends. Also, aside from the benefits of work authorization and temporary legal status described above, they would enjoy no significant long term benefits. They would not, for example, be considered to be "permanently residing in the United States under color of law [PRUCOL]," and, thus, would be ineligible to receive public assistance. (302(f)(1) and (2)). There is also no provision whereby applicants under TPS could arrange for their families (spouses or children) to join them.

Another complication for TPS recipients involves the seven years of continuous physical residence they must be able to document in order to be eligible for suspension of deportation. Under the statute, the protected status period would be counted in computing the seven year residency requirements but only if the AG finds that extreme hardship exists. (302(e)). The adverse effects of these rules are exacerbated by a provision in the legislation whereby the Senate may not enact any legislation permitting aliens under TPS to adjust their status unless that legislation is approved by a three-fifths majority. (302(h)).

More troubling yet is the issue of confidentiality. Although §302(c)(6) provides that the AG "shall establish procedures to protect the confidentiality of information provided by the aliens," the interim regulations make it clear that the Department of Justice (including the INS and federal and, by extension, state law enforcement agencies) may have access to any information provided by applicants. Under the IRCA, applicants for the legalization program were protected from INS enforcement efforts because none of the information they provided could be used to initiate deportation proceedings unless the applicant had committed either fraud or perjury. That assurance was vital to the success of the program.

Immigration practitioners have called for a similar provision assuring confidentiality to be added to the TPS program. A clear example of the dangers threatened by the lack of such a provision was provided by the Law Offices of Hogan & Hartson in representing the National Immigration Refugee & Citizenship Forum:

> Under the Interim Regulations, information provided by employers on behalf of their employees could be used against the employers in an IRCA-based enforcement action. We submit that an employer should not be sanctioned for IRCA violations on the basis of information provided to the Service on behalf of a TPS registrant. . . ."

Applicants who lack adequate documentation to meet the eligibility requirements, therefore, would be deterred from applying for TPS because they would be unable to rely on their employers for documentation.

Applicants are also threatened by the possibility that, at the termination of designation, registered aliens could be placed in deportation proceedings based on information taken from their TPS applications and turned over to INS enforcement officials. Even though the statute and the regulations are silent on the issuance of Orders to Show Cause, this possibility will undoubtedly deter many potentially qualified applicants from applying for TPS.

Given all the disadvantages, both in terms of the complete deference granted the AG in making determinations and in terms of the limited incentives provided to encourage individual participation, the success of the TPS program seems doubtful. Instead of applying under the program, many aliens from designated countries will most likely weigh the risks and continue to cross our borders and reside in the United States without documentation and in spite of the threats of detention and deportation. Apprehension among refugees was evident as Salvadorans wrestled with the issue before the end of their registration period.

SPECIAL TEMPORARY PROTECTED STATUS FOR SALVADORANS

Official treatment of Salvadorans by the U.S. government has exemplified all the worst aspects of the application of our laws and principles to foreign nationals. For over a decade, human rights advocates have attempted to bring to the attention of the American public the plight of Salvadorans who, fleeing in desperation from the chaos in El Salvador, have found their way into the United States seeking safe haven.

Most immigrant's rights groups have proposed that these individuals have an unparalleled claim to asylum in the U.S., a nation that, at least theoretically, boasts of humanitarian instincts. To the Executive branch, the State Department and some legislators, however, Salvadorans are considered to be merely economic refugees who bypass several countries of "safe haven" in order to find their fortunes in the United States. In their view, granting safe haven in Salvadorans would send an unacceptable message both to other Salvadorans who would then be encouraged to emigrate to the U.S. and to "friendly" governments which depend on U.S. support. Those Salvadorans who have dared to apply for political asylum have met with an equally intransigent judicial system, fiercely resistant to the proposition that Salvadorans be considered eligible for asylum under present statutory criteria.

Thus, the provision designating El Salvador as a foreign state whose nationals residing in the United States would be granted TPS appears, at first glance, to provide a solution to several intractable problems. Under this measure, Salvadorans eligible for TPS must meet the following criteria: they must demonstrate that they are Salvadoran nationals, that they have been "continually physically present" in the U.S. since September 19, 1990, they must register for TPS during the period from January 1, 1991 to June 30, 1991, and, like those aliens eligible to participate in the general program, they must be otherwise admissible as immigrants. (303(b)).

Similar Benefits for Those in Special Temporary Protected Status

Many, but not all, of the benefits available to registrants under the general program are also available to Salvadorans. Once Salvadorans present in the U.S. prove eligibility, they become entitled to protected status which shields them from detention and deportation and qualifies them for work authorization. Although there is no provision for renewal under this section of the statute, on June 30, 1992, when El Salvador's statutory designation terminates, the Attorney General can subsequently redesignate that country under the general TPS provisions and continue to grant Salvadorans protection.

At first glance, registering under this program would seem preferable to applying for asylum because registrants stand an almost certain chance of being granted TPS, unless they are excludable. An asylum claim, conversely, is almost never granted if the only argument available to the claimants involves the fear of returning to and becoming subject to violent conditions in their native countries. Thus, TPS takes away much of the worry associated with fighting against great odds to win on asylum claims which have a notoriously low approval rate for Central Americans.

Among the considerations to be weighed by anyone considering applying for TPS is the recent stipulated settlement of *American Baptist Churches et al. v. Thornburgh* [ABC], a class action suit contending that Salvadorans and Guatemalans are routinely discriminated against in the asylum process. Commenced in 1985, the suit challenged the way in which INS and the Executive Office of Immigration Review (EOIR) adjudicated asylum applications. The preamble to the settlement reaffirms the principle that neither foreign policy concerns nor border enforcement problems should be factors in decisions determining the eligibility of asylum applicants. It also reiterates the policy that the "same standard for determining whether an applicant has a well-founded fear of persecution applies to Salvadorans and Guatemalans as applies to all other nationalities." One important term of the settlement requires that all Salvadorans who were in the U.S. as of September 19, 1990, and all Guatemalans who were in the U.S. as of October 1, 1990 and whose asylum applications were denied be afforded *de novo* affirmative asylum interviews under new guidelines intended to insure greater fairness.

The greatest benefit offered to Salvadorans under the settlement is that they may take advantage of the *de novo* interview when their TPS terminates. Thus, instead of being threatened with deportation in June of 1992, Salvadorans with asylum claims may choose to pursue their applications while continuing to receive employment authorization. Those interested in participating in the ABC settlement must apply by June 30, 1991. If they apply for TPS, however, they are automatically considered to be candidates for relief under ABC. Eligible applicants also have the option of choosing to apply directly for relief under the provisions of ABC without applying for TPS. Those who do not intend to file asylum claims, however, face greater risks when their protected status ends.

Problems Inherent in Special Temporary Protected Status

The provisions granting Salvadorans temporary protection are far more stringent than are those that apply to nationals from countries designated by the AG. Under the general program, for example, Congress provided that a reasonable fee not exceeding $50.00 be charged for both registration and employment authorization. (302(c)(1)(B)). Although Congress did not repeat the fee cap in the provisions relating to the Salvadoran program, it did repeat the requirement that the fee be reasonable and it did not provide for additional fees for renewals. INS final regulations, however, have imposed a much larger fee on these registrants totalling $110.00 per person exclusive of renewal costs which the INS wants to charge. There is also no family cap on fees. Many consider the excessive fee as a major threat to the viability of the program since many eligible Salvadorans would find it unaffordable. Salvadorans will also suffer under the burden of reregistering and renewing work authorization every six months (as opposed to once a year under the provisions of the general program).

In addition, the "brief, innocent and casual" departure exception to the continuous residence requirement does not apply to Salvadorans. (303(b)(1)(A)). Thus, if a Salvadoran left the U.S. for even a few days after September 19, 1990, she would be ineligible to participate in the program, even though she may have resided in the U.S. for years prior to that brief departure. Upon returning to the United States, she could be apprehended by the INS at the border in which case she would be treated under the exclusion rather than the deportation provisions of immigration laws and she would be forced into the precarious position of arguing that she remained eligible for TPS. Travel restrictions are also more stringent for Salvadorans: in order to obtain advance parole to re-enter after a short trip abroad, the would have to establish that the trip was necessary due to emergency conditions beyond their control. (303(c)(4)). Also, as is the case under the general program, Salvadorans cannot bring to the U.S. family members already in the country who are ineligible for the program.

The most threatening aspect of the Salvadoran program, however, is that when the designation of El Salvador ends, it becomes mandatory that the INS place registered Salvadorans in deportation proceedings. (303(d)(1)). Unless they can show "exceptional circumstances," those who fail to appear at those proceedings may be deported in absentia (303(d)(2)), and, therefore, would be barred from most other forms of discretionary relief including voluntary departure, suspension of deportation and adjustment of status.

Salvadorans who are not presently in deportation proceedings, therefore, are put in the difficult position of deciding whether it is worthwhile for them to apply for TPS. Only if their need for employment authorization clearly outweighs all the risks cited above will the decision to register under the program be a simple one. Also, given the fact that it took a decade to pass this legislation, the prospect that El Salvador will be redesignated might also seem grim, in which case short-term protection will prove an insignificant incentive in the face of imminent deportation.

Some advocates for Central American refugees, however, believe that with an active campaign aimed at exposing current conditions in El Salvador, they may be able to instigate a redesignation:

> After witnessing more than 10 years of armed civil war and horrible human rights violations in El Salvador, we know that a significant and long-lasting improvement in the situation is not at all likely to occur over the next year and a half. Just as we finally convinced Congress that the situation there is too dangerous now for Salvadoran refugees to be forced back, we need to convince them that the conditions in El Salvador will not be safe for Salvadoran refugees in June 1992.

Describing the legislation as a "tremendous victory," the Central American Refugee Center [CARECEN] feels that with it comes the hope for "raising demands for respect of human rights in Central America and for peaceful negotiations in the conflicts there."

Unfortunately, after the registration period is over, many Salvadorans will remain underground, easy targets for exploitation. One month after registration began, only 26,395 Salvadorans had applied for the program and since individuals cannot take advantage of the program once the registration deadline has passed, many more Salvadorans seem doomed to be deported if apprehended by the INS, though El Salvador remains a designated country. Moreover, Salvadorans who arrived in the U.S. after September 19, 1990 are unprotected even though the conditions in their country that led to its designation have not changed at all. It appears that we have come full circle.

CONCLUSION

While it is refreshing to see Congress take any action at all on refugee matters, the success of this program seems doubtful. At the end of 1990, the INS border patrol reported a fresh increase in the number of people trying to cross the border illegally. This is the first increase since the passage of IRCA in 1986 led to a decrease in 1987. The reality is that as long as conditions at home remain hopeless and as long as immigrants find the means to survive in the United States while avoiding employer sanctions, millions of immigrants will continue to scale the golden gates.

What is needed, it seems, is not an ad hoc system of treating symptoms but, rather, a system embodying an honest approach to finding a cure for the disease which usually incubates in the refugee's home country. Implementing "band-aid" solutions encourages us all to continue to ignore the clear relationship between U.S. foreign policy and surges of refugees. As one commentator has written, "The root causes of contemporary refugee situations require political intervention with governmental violators of human rights, preferably before refugees begin to flee." Meanwhile, until long term solutions can be formulated, the United States should honor the invitation engraved on the base of the Statue of Liberty in New York harbor and open its arms to all "the tired, the poor and the huddled masses yearning to breathe free."

Editor's Note: This article has been edited for publication.

Immigration Policy

Austin T. Fragomen, Jr.
Fragomen Del Rey and Bernsen, P.C.

What is U.S. immigration policy, or perhaps more appropriately, does the United States have an immigration policy? I have pondered this question intermittently since first starting my career as staff counsel to the Subcommittee on International Law, Refugees and Immigration of the House Judiciary Committee.

It is common knowledge that there is no overriding policy which was planned and implemented at a single point in time. However, I would suggest that a policy may be extrapolated from the law. This deductive process results in what at a minimum must be regarded as a de facto policy. I am suggesting that even if there is no comprehensive policy there is a body of law which, taken as a whole, is "the policy."

The problem of defining policy lies in the legislative process, balancing competing interests while reflecting concerns and mores of a particular era and adopting amendments through a quiltwork approach where the entire law is never rewritten at once but rather as a succession of disassociated events.

To gain an insight into policy, let us dissect the law into a few basic categories which I would define as follows: 1) admission of foreign nationals either temporarily or permanently; 2) refugees; and 3) enforcement (IRCA, inspection/border control, deportation and discretionary enforcement).

Policy in the admission of foreign workers is undoubtedly the most developed and logically consistent of the various areas of concern. We start with a presumption that any foreign national seeking entry into the United States desires to come permanently and, if so, must meet the documentary requirements for permanent admission. The nonimmigrant categories create an exception to this general proposition. Each is carefully crafted to assure that the foreign national will have minimal adverse impact upon the labor market. The interface between the needs of the employer and the protection of the domestic labor force may be explicitly recognized, as in the case of the H-1, H-2, O or P, or more subtly imposed. Specifically, the H-2 category contains the dual restrictions of limiting eligibility to temporary job needs and certification from the Department of Labor. By definition, a temporary job is

In Defense of the Alien, Lydio F. Tomasi, ed., (1993: The Center for Migration Studies, New York, NY).

seasonal, intermittent or lasts no more than one year (note that the criteria does not pertain to the need of the specific employers or the intent of the alien, but solely to the duration of the job). Labor certification requires either evidence of specific recruitment or concurrent of the union. The H-1 category was amended, effective October 1, 1991 to require an attestation from the employer that the foreign worker would be paid the higher of the prevailing pay rate or the actual pay rate, that there is no labor dispute in progress, that the bargaining representative or the other workers at the place of employment have been properly advised, and that the employer guarantees similar working conditions as those enjoyed by domestic workers. Of course, the H-1 category is limited to professionals. Significantly, where the H-2 requires a finding by the Department of Labor that there are no U.S. workers available, the H-1 only requires fair wages and working conditions. A policy differentiation between professional and nonprofessional workers reflects a heightened concern for protection of the latter. Other nonimmigrant categories are more limited in scope, such as I visas for members of the foreign information media, L visas for international transferees, E visas for treaty traders and investors, and F visas for foreign students. In each of these categories, where the role of the alien impinges upon the concerns of U.S. workers, nuances of interpretation effectuate the Congressional intent to protect the U.S. labor force. For instance, to engage in summer employment, foreign students holding F visas must either work for an employer who has attested to the Department of Labor that U.S. workers are not available, notwithstanding the employer's promise to pay prevailing or actual wages and to assure comparable working conditions. I visas are limited to persons involved in newsgathering, but not the business functions of foreign-owned media organizations. Specialized knowledge for L purposes is restricted to persons having proprietary or specific knowledge of the products, processes, methodologies or services of the multinational company, thus assuring that U.S. workers could not perform these functions. Newly proposed E regulations require the employer to demonstrate that specialist personnel will be replaced eventually through the training of U.S. workers or to explain why this will not be possible. Occasionally, litigation, initiated by organized labor, such as the *Bricklayers* case, enlists the assistance of the judiciary in assuring adherence to policy objectives.

The criteria to qualify for permanent resident status is meticulously set forth in the law and clearly reflects our policy in who should be allowed this coveted privilege. Restrictions are both quantitative and qualitative, thus reflecting the policy that even among the most selective and desirable, limitations are appropriate. The United States elects an all or nothing approach as opposed to more flexible policies reflected in countries such as the United Kingdom that typically allow long-term temporary work permit holders to convert to resident status or to Canada which uses a point system. The applicant for resident alien status must fall squarely within the set system, either

by having a prescribed familial relationship or an employment-based quali-
fication. The degree of specificity is remarkable. For instance, intracompany
transferees in managerial or executive positions bypass recruitment-based
labor certification procedures, but specialized knowledge personnel do not.
Basically, the policy mandate is to accord greater protection to the U.S. worker
in the immigrant selection system than in the admission of temporary workers.

The law equally carefully specifies what grounds will bar the foreign
national from entry into the United States. Everything from the insidiousness
of previous totalitarian party membership through the nuances of the particular
mental disorders are specified and weighed; even waivers of the bar to admission are divided by significance, requisite familial relationship, passage
time and discretion. Policy reflected in this area is strikingly precise. For
instance, a single conviction for possession of less than 30 grams of marijuana
may be waived where the applicant has a U.S. citizen wife, but a conviction
involving traces of cocaine may never be forgiven.

Granted, the administration of the law may subject policy to political
manipulations and create the appearance of undesirable ambivalence as a
result. The 1990 Act bars admission of aliens with a dangerous contagious
disease of public health significance. An initial finding that aliens who tested
HIV positive would not fall within this classification since the disease is not
involuntarily communicable and, therefore, not contagious was withdrawn by
the Public Health Service following public outcry.

Policy ambivalence through political manipulation is even more evident
in the refugee and asylee area. Elaboration, particularly to this audience, is
unnecessary. The basic policy is clear enough. It is the execution that creates
the crisis. The law protects persons having a well-founded fear of persecution
based upon specified factors and envisions individualized determination.
Legitimate legal issues are created through the terminology. For instance, is
"well-founded" essentially an objective or subjective standard. However, it is
not the existence of such questions that undermines policy. When citizens of
one country are summarily granted asylum almost regardless of particular facts
and those from another land held to the highest burden of proof, it is not the
fault of the policy embodied in the law, but rather its implementation.

Enforcement at first blush seems straightforward. Foreign nationals who
engage in certain prescribed conduct are deportable from the United States.
Due process must be accorded to such aliens in deportation proceedings and
during the apprehension process culminating in the proceeding. We may
dispute the efficacy of a law that allows for hearings *in absentia* under
specified circumstances. The policy may be harsh, but it is clear. The high
percentage of abscondees provides an underlying logic.

Discretionary enforcement provides an outlet to too rigid a policy. The
law mandates that undocumented aliens be subject to deportation proceedings,
but proceedings may be held in abeyance for humanitarian reasons. We could

argue that the exercise of this prosecutorial discretion is not properly exercised when persons from certain countries are allowed to remain in the United States while others are forced to leave. Once again we must distinguish between proper implementation which defines policy and improper implementation which subverts policy. When the legislative process ends in the enactment of a law according special privilege to nationals of a particular country, such as Temporary Protected Status, we may cry discrimination, but it must be recognized as a manifestation of immigration policy.

The Immigration Control and Reform Act of 1986 is an example of policy so ill-conceived that regardless of your opinion of the objectives, it was doomed to failure from the outset. The law causes discrimination while not meaningfully impacting upon the influx of undocumented workers. Amnesty was granted to aliens long resident in the United States and, therefore, presumptively absorbed into the mainstream of society. Employers were mandated to verify immigration status of all prospective employees while not discriminating against protected classes. Stepped up border enforcement and entry point inspection were designed to curtail the influx of undocumented workers.

Superficially, this program appears to be standard fare for most industrialized nations. We all recognize the inexorable push and pull factors which cause illegal migration. The amnesty, which one might view as niggardly, is a straightforward expression of policy. But I am more concerned with the enforcement issue. No other industrialized country, with laws prohibiting the employment of undocumented aliens, places the entire onus of determining alienage and right to work upon the employer. I am not suggesting that our country adopt national identity cards, called by whatever name you wish, but I am suggesting that an employer verification program cannot possibly work without universally held work documents issued by the government.

Lack of national documentation also increases the incidence of discrimination. I would suggest that policy went astray at that point in the legislative process where the concerns of the civil libertarians rendered the conventional wisdom of the necessity of secure documents untenable.

Moreover, verification as a primary defense against employment of undocumented aliens assumes all employment is in compliance with the law generally. Of course, this is not the case. The "cash" economy is rampant and thrives on the undocumented.

Border endorsement is a "given" in the modern world. Every nation controls its borders with varying degrees of success. This would seem to be a noncontroversial policy; however, I would suggest that the United States has made a purposeful policy decision to inadequately regulate the flow of undocumented workers into the country. Allocation of adequate resources would address this issue were there a policy commitment. Stopping the influx across the Mexican border would not be difficult—albeit expensive. Traditionally, the policy has been to pay lip service to the severity of the issue but to expand minimal effort in its resolution. If we further analyze these various examples, we can reach certain conclusions about policy. In the immigration and refugee field, policy is usually expressed reasonably and even meticulously in the law. Perhaps the derivation is not a comprehensive study or white paper but the accretion of ideas over a period of time. At times specific policies may be controversial or, we may believe, dead wrong. But an identifiable policy exists. The matter is complicated by the role of the government, charged with effectuating policy. Ideally, in the implementation process, policy is honed and refined. Occasionally, however, a new agenda appears and policy is undermined. Finally, there are those few areas where policy is ill-conceived or possibly purposefully duplicitous. But to posit that there is no United States immigration policy is erroneous.

Editor's Note: This article has been edited for publication.

The Future of Refugee Policy

Priscilla Clapp
United States Department of State

We are in the midst of one of the most dramatic transitions in modern history, as we bring the era of the Cold War to an end. This transition has come upon us much more quickly and dramatically than any of our pundits could have predicted. Although the final scene of the drama is still unfolding, we can already see emerging the outlines of new opportunities and challenges that are likely to confront us in a world without the East-West conflict.

THE EMPHASIS ON REPATRIATION

Nowhere has the end of the Cold War had a more dramatic impact than on refugee and migration issues. There is both good news and bad news.

On the positive side of the ledger, the end of the Cold War has given us the opportunity to settle a number of long-standing conflicts. It is probably not unfair to say that the majority of the world's refugee populations, which our assistance sustains today, were spawned by East-West conflict and the expansion of communism throughout the world: in the Soviet Union and Eastern Europe, in Indochina and Afghanistan, the Horn of Africa, Angola and in Central America. The list is long. The number of refugees under international care is very high—some 16 million.

As political settlements have been forged, people have started to go home. Repatriation has now become a major durable solution, where it was only a hope in the past. In the preceding year, there have been large repatriations in Angola, Namibia, Nicaragua and Iraq. In the coming year, we hope to see large new repatriations in Cambodia, Afghanistan, Ethiopia and Eritrea, Southwest Africa and Vietnam. We have the opportunity before us to reduce the world's refugee population by one-third or more.

Another positive feature of the end of the Cold War has been the political empowerment of the United Nations to deal with humanitarian and refugee crises. One might say that the UN may have been the child of World War II, but it was the victim of the Cold War. During this period, it was nearly impossible to get the Security Council together on any significant issue. We were caught in what the United States and Soviet Union came to describe as

In Defense of the Alien, Lydio F. Tomasi, ed., (1993: The Center for Migration Studies, New York, NY).

a "zero sum game," in which a gain for one side was a loss for the other and vice versa. However, when it is added up, it always equals zero.

We are no longer living in a "zero sum" world, and we can now work productively with those who were formerly our rivals. This has revolutionized the role of the UN in dealing with humanitarian and political situations, including those involving refugees, potential refugees and large migrations. We have witnessed this already in the case of Iraq; we have witnessed it in the other cases I have just enumerated, and we are now beginning to witness it in Cambodia. There will be many more to come.

POST-COLD WAR ETHNIC CONFLICTS

Unfortunately, there is also a negative side to the ledger. Ethnic conflicts are breaking out not only in Europe, but also in many other parts of the world. Yugoslavia is suffering the vilest of ethnic battles, even beyond imagination. This kind of ethnic warfare threatens to spread throughout the territory of the former Soviet Union, where many different ethnic groups are comingled. We are seeing the tragic flight of a specific ethnic group from Burma into Bangladesh. Nasty tribal and religious rivalries are reigniting all over Africa, especially in the Horn.

The end of the Cold War also has brought us a new form of threat and new types of warfare. We saw that in the Persian Gulf last year. Let us hope this does not become a model for the future. It will be a challenge to the international community and the UN to hold in check the ambitions of regional strongmen and bullies now that the tension of the East-West conflict no longer serves that function. But we must expect that other regional strongmen will seek to test the limits of their power in their own regions and beyond. With each new conflict and each new power contest, there will continue to be more groups of displaced persons, migrants and refugees.

If the good news is that the end of the Cold War has empowered the UN politically to deal with these situations, the bad news is that the UN does not have the resources to meet all the challenges it will confront in this complex period. Thus we find ourselves scrambling to find the money for peacekeeping, in order to effectuate the repatriations and the resettlements that have been negotiated at the political level. Governments are learning that peacekeeping is extremely expensive and they are not yet ready to commit to the levels of expenditure that will be required.

Repatriation also is extremely expensive, especially for refugee populations who have been living in camps for many years and become accustomed to assistance. In some cases, repatriation may cost more on an annual basis than maintaining refugees under protection in camps. However, an investment in repatriation is an investment in the solution to a long-term problem and the end to annual payments for protection. However, it is difficult to convince governments to look at international contributions this way and to calculate the resources that will be saved by not having to make continuing contributions to protection.

Finally, there are also on the negative side of the ledger some disturbing long-term trends that do not augur well for refugee and migration problems. First, world population is growing very rapidly, some might argue it is out of control. By the year 2025, the population will have nearly doubled. Resources are already strained by this growth in the poorest parts of the world. Economic development is not keeping up with population growth. Ecological erosion is accelerating. And all these pressures together—population, poverty, ecological deterioration, human rights abuses and bad government—are causing migration on a larger and larger scale. There are not effective international strategies in sight to deal with the root causes of migration, and this is something that the international community, as well as individual governments, must focus on seriously and with urgency.

THE UNITED STATES AND REFUGEE ASSISTANCE

Let me begin with refugee assistance, focusing specifically on the account managed by the Bureau for Refugee Programs, called Migration and Refugee Assistance (MRA). Two-thirds of this assistance, some $400 million, goes to the protection and care of the 16 million refugees now under international protection. In the post-Cold War era, more of this assistance will be needed for repatriation projects and for humanitarian intervention designed to prevent or forestall large destabilizing migrations. There will be more investment in durable, permanent solutions to refugee problems. If we are prepared to make the investment, for example, we have the opportunity before us right now to repatriate some 3 million of the 16 million refugees under international care over the next two years. If repatriation to Afghanistan can be made tenable, that figure might even be 7 million. This would be a substantial reduction in the world's refugee population.

We also will see more attention devoted to treating root causes. By that, I have in mind measures that are taken to prevent refugee populations from being created in the first place. The movement by the United States into Northern Iraq last year to repatriate rapidly the Kurdish population who had fled into Turkey is a good example. Creating the conditions for a rapid repatriation under international protection saved these people from being herded into long-term refugee camps in Turkey (as happened with earlier groups fleeing poison gas attacks). They were returned in time to reclaim and rebuild the homes they had just left. The U.S. accomplished this repatriation with the use of military forces to make it safe for the Kurds to return in the first instance and then to secure their safety over time and to help them rebuild their homes. This was an enormous investment at the time, but it avoided a situation in Turkey that would have been far more costly and probably politically unsustainable.

Another preventive measure to which we must pay more attention in the future is calculating the potential for policy decisions to trigger large-scale migration. Before making decisions we must have a better understanding of what impact they will have on the people living in the area affected by the decisions. Many of the refugee or migration populations that we see today are the consequences of policy decisions, if not our own then those of other governments. Luckily, we saw the problem rising in northern Iraq and reacted quickly. In Haiti, there can be no question that using an embargo as a political tool has exacerbated migration pressures.

Turning back to the Migration and Refugee Assistance account, the remaining one-third is devoted to refugee resettlement in the United States. We bring some 120,000 to 130,000 refugees to the United States annually using the resources of this account and those of the Department of Health and Human Services. The end of the Cold War will also affect the nature of this program in several major respects.

First, the concepts by which we identify refugees for resettlement in the United States will inevitably evolve to meet the new situations before us. The International Refugee Convention of 1951 and its Protocol of 1967, which form the basis for U.S. refugee admissions law, were formulated in the conditions of the Cold War, especially for assisting those fleeing communism, as Michel Moussalli mentioned in his presentation. The asylum systems in Europe and North America that we know today are largely a reflection of the world that existed from the end of World War II until today. The assumption that resettlement was the only permanent solution for people fleeing communism has been a guiding principle. Today, the vast majority of people seeking asylum are not fleeing communism. In fact, there is very little communism left to flee.

U.S. refugee admissions law further provides that the annual admissions program will be based on national interest. For the period of the Cold War our struggle against communism has dominated our foreign policy, including the national interests that the U.S. body politic has used to determine the composition of refugee admissions to the United States. Most of our refugee resettlement has focused on groups fleeing communism: whether from the Soviet Union, from Eastern Europe, from Cuba, from Vietnam or from Ethiopia.

This year, for example, despite the end of the Cold War our admissions program is still very much a product of it. We are fulfilling what you might call an historical commitment. Of the 132,000 refugees that we are planning to admit to the United States this year, the vast majority come from Vietnam and the former Soviet Union. They represent the end—or perhaps more aptly, the last segment—of a refugee program that we have sustained for two decades. In the next three to four years, we hope that conditions will permit these very large Vietnamese and ex-Soviet programs to be brought to a close. Our definition of national interest as it affects refugee admissions will shift naturally to other types of refugees. For example, we are now beginning to resettle some of the refugees who cannot return to Iraq in the aftermath of the Persian Gulf War.

With the end of the Cold War, we also will see much greater complexity in refugee and migration problems. The causes of large-scale migration have become more diverse and the migrations have become larger. The economic causes are more widespread than they were before. Economic and political causes have become mixed together and difficult to separate. There is no neat dividing line between the two. Ultimately, national subjective judgments come into play.

The second wave of Vietnamese boat people in the late 1980s is a good example of this dilemma. It was clear that political fears were no longer the dominant factor pushing people to leave Vietnam, and national subjective judgments in the countries of first asylum began to define this as an economic migration that had to be stemmed. The situation demanded some sort of collective means of drawing the line between economic migrants and people seeking refuge from political persecution, in order to preserve the international principle of refugee protection and asylum. Thus was born the Comprehensive Plan of Action (CPA), which provided for the preservation of first asylum in return for a screening system under international supervision to distinguish economic from political migrants. Those determined to be refugees would be resettled in third countries; those determined to be economic migrants would be repatriated to Vietnam.

As we face more and more of these complex mass migrations, we will undoubtedly see additional efforts to organize comprehensive solutions embodying the principles that guided the CPA. Among these, I would enumerate: the principles of first asylum, internationally endorsed (UNHCR) screening for refugees, third country resettlement for refugees, and repatriation for nonrefugees. A comprehensive solution must by definition embrace the sending country, as well as the countries of first asylum and resettlement, so that repatriation can be carried out in safety and dignity, with adequate reception, monitoring and reintegration assistance.

Finally, let me return to the subject of "humanitarian intervention." This is perhaps the most revolutionary concept yet to emerge in the post-Cold War era, and it has come upon us very fast. Humanitarian intervention is compelled largely by a sense of responsibility in the international community for responding quickly and effectively to man-made humanitarian disasters that are producing large refugee migrations. The rules of humanitarian intervention are still being created and we have yet a lot to learn about what the most effective form of rapid response will be. This will vary from situation to situation, but it is important that it is now internationally acceptable to act decisively to meet humanitarian crises. We no longer have to stand aside and wait to treat the consequences.

Let me end with the hope that the international community will rise successfully to the challenges of the post-Cold War world and that we will find humane and effective responses to the ever increasing migration and refugee problems that lie ahead.

Editor's Note: This article has been edited for publication.

The Hidden Costs of American Immigration

Gerard Longspaugh

Most would agree that over the past two decades America has experienced a decline. The U.S. is a nation existing on borrowed resources, with an ever higher percentage of national income going each year toward paying the interest on the debt we are building up—a debt that is expected to increase by as much as $400 billion in 1993! Additionally, despite the huge sums spent on health, education and crime control, the U.S. has been losing ground in all those areas. America's decline has been so extensive and invasive that the causes of the decline must be errors of a very fundamental nature.

Approximately 7,000 of the most uneducated, unskilled and poorest people in the world take up residence in the United States *every single day*. Consequently, arguably the single most determinative of negative factors impacting on the American nation has been the prevailing policies on immigration.

There has been an almost universal unwillingness on the part of political parties and political aspirants to raise the topic of immigration policy in public forums. This reluctance is the result of several factors. First, arguments against the prevailing immigration policy face suppression and bias in the media, which generally favors even greater migration, legal and illegal, in collusion with pro-immigration interests. Second, many politicians now see immigrants as potential political supporters. Additionally, there appears to be a gross insufficiency of information on the true cost of immigration available to the media and the public. It is these issues which are addressed herein.

The cost of immigration to American citizens has essentially four components which may be cited as: 1) The Carrying Cost; 2) The Infrastructure Disbursement Cost; 3) The Cultural Degradation Cost; 4) The Ethnic Fragmentation Cost.

THE CARRYING COST

This financial cost is incurred if, over a substantial period, the arrival of immigrants causes the expenses of government services to increase more than the immigrants contribute in taxes. These government services include the cost

The Journal of Social, Political and Economic Studies, Volume 18, Number 1, Spring 1993, 79–84.

of providing health, educational, environmental, welfare and police services. This carrying cost is more likely to be greater if the immigrant is sick, uneducated, non-English speaking, unskilled, culturally dissimilar and has a criminal bias (as indicated by a willingness to violate American immigration laws). American immigration policy increasingly shows a preference for admitting people to these attributes. Accordingly, areas of the country most heavily impacted by recent immigration have experienced the greatest deterioration in quality of life and in financial and social stability.

THE INFRASTRUCTURE DISBURSEMENT COST

The approximate American population is presently 250,000,000. If the total value of the American infrastructure is roughly estimated to be $10,000,000,000,000, then each American's share of infrastructure is $40,000. Accordingly, every immigrant currently receives a free share of this infrastructure.

This $40,000 infrastructure endowment is one reason why immigrants want to come here and not to the "un-infrastructured" jungles of Brazil—where there is just as much space. Since there is no "free lunch," this $40,000 share of the U.S. infrastructure dispensed to each immigrant is necessarily a $40,000 cost to the American citizens, as the infrastructure is spread thinner. An excellent example of how this has impacted on other countries is Britain, where the Southeast is now so densely populated that despite constant high taxes and high spending to provide (amongst other things) drinking water, rivers are running dry, Ice Age aquifers are being sucked empty, and there are daily debates about how to solve the problem of the "drought." The "drought," of course, is caused by overpopulation. This extreme situation is also being replicated in California, where need for water for the immigrants crowding Southern California is leading to high costs in channelling water from the northern part of the state, where farmers have to share the water they need to operate their farms. Consider the endowment of infrastructure bestowed on a family of 5 who legally or illegally gains entrance into the United States: the value is $200,000. How much would such a $200,000 tax free gift help a struggling American family? How would an American family be treated if they didn't pay $200,000 allegedly owed in taxes? A $40,000 national loss in dispensed infrastructure per immigrant, multiplied by an estimated 3 million legal and illegal immigrants per year, means that the cost to the American people of the disbursement of infrastructure to immigrants is $120 billion per year.

What it took generations of Americans great sacrifice to build and accumulate, an immigrant receives free of charge in one instant! American citizens are continuously being required to pay "their fair share" in taxes.

Consequently it has been suggested that aspiring immigrants should be required to pay a tax equal to their share of the value of the infrastructure prior to their entrance. This would need to be extracted from immigrants as a condition of entry with the same intensity and zeal that taxes are extracted from American citizens by the IRA. For necessarily, if the immigrant doesn't pay, then the existing citizens have to pay!

An analogy might be made to an individual or a group of individuals purchasing shares in a company, or a new member paying an entrance fee when joining a club and acquiring, with membership, a share in the property of that club. But the immigrants are not currently required to pay even for the share of American infrastructure that they receive.

Doubtlessly, many politicians would cite their great compassion as a reason for their objection to a policy of taxing immigrants. To put such displaced compassion in proper perspective, consider that such self-righteously generous politicians virtually never generate compassion for those who must pay for their generosity. Rather, they regard responsible American citizens as contemptible beasts of burden whose proper function is mute submission to bearing any imposed cost or burden.

THE CULTURAL DISPLACEMENT COST

Depending on the immigrant, America can either experience cultural enhancement or cultural degradation. Recent immigration trends (which can be characterized as massive Third World immigration) have caused Western culture to be displaced and submerged in large areas of the country by the Third World cultures of the immigrants. As the rate of legal and illegal immigration rises cultural assimilation becomes more difficult, if full assimilation is even conceptually possible. Will the culture that produced unmatched affluence, put men on the moon and advanced literature, art, science and medicine to the greatest heights be displaced by cultures that only achieve poverty, ignorance and subsistence in place of wealth and beauty? We see what has happened to those parts of American cities that have become ghettoes: They have been almost literally demolished. Critics are asking whether unassimiliable waves of Third World immigration will bring America down to the level of corruption and decadence prevailing in so many of the countries they are leaving.

THE ETHNIC FRAGMENTATION COST

Ethnic fragmentation is often euphemistically referred to in recent times as ethnic diversity. A pseudo-truth, embodying sufficiently palatable and slippery verbalism to gain acceptance as a genuine truth, is the phrase: "America has become great *because* of ethnic diversity."

This phrase is often used in an attempt to validate current immigration policy. To understand the deception of this pseudo-truth, consider an automobile trip that was completed after sustaining several crashes. Would it be correct to say that: "the automobile trip was completed because of several crashes."? Hardly!

It would be more correct to say that: "the automobile trip was completed in spite of several crashes!"

Similarly, the phrase above should be: "America became great in spite of ethnic fragmentation."

Ethnic fragmentation, often euphemistically referred to as ethnic diversity, has always been predominantly a destructive force. It bestowed on America, for example—the Civil War, the Japanese internment camps, the race riots of the 60s, and more currently, the national subordination of the pursuit of excellence to the quest for "racial balance," and the imposition of major intractable racial conflicts on otherwise trivial issues.

In America, as in the rest of the world, there has always been a requirement for national survival. This requirement is that the cohesive forces of national unity be greater than the destructive force of ethnic fragmentation. Previously, America has had forces of national unity sufficiently strong and forces of ethnic fragmentation sufficiently weak for the nation to hold together. Now, however, the extensive and intensifying ethnic turmoil that prevails in America is an indication that immigration-propelled demographic trends are causing the destructive forces of ethnic fragmentation to prevail over the cohesive forces of national unity.

Historically and throughout the world (the Roman Empire, India/Pakistan, Yugoslavia, the Soviet Union, Lebanon), no political entity as ethnically fragmented as America is becoming has ever survived! The moral and intellectual imperative is that American immigration policy should be formulated with heedfulness of these harsh and often bloody lessons of history. The social guidelines of American immigration policy should be the achievement of national cohesiveness and ethnic compatibility, not the imposition of ethnic fragmentation.

Moreover, some of the political entities that had geographically-insulated ethnic factions and nevertheless could not withstand the ethnic fragmentation, merely broke up along common ethnic and geographic "dotted lines." Being an integrated society, however, the destruction of America as a result of excessively rapid immigration from the overcrowded countries of the world could possibly involve a Lebanon type ethnic blood bath. Noting the ever-mounting violence and polarization in its multiethnic cities, conflicts such as those already emerging between blacks and Hispanics and blacks and Vietnamese and Koreans is a possible indicator of future far greater conflicts.

COST SUMMARY

The reality of "cheap" immigrant labor is that it isn't "cheap"; to the contrary, it is highly expensive subsidized labor. For while politicians and healthy employers get "cheap" votes and "cheap" labor resulting from massive Third World immigration, American citizens pay the price by being victims of crime, unemployment, low wages, bad schools, inferior health care and by paying ever higher taxes in a futile attempt to support an increasingly Third World and a collapsing internal society unable to solve the problem of ethnic fragmentation on such an immense and rapidly escalating scale.

ALTERNATIVES

An interesting and informative comparison can be made between the use of labor in different regions of America. In the American mid-West, agricultural producers were confronted with the difficulty of physically tending large tracks of land without the availability of "cheap" labor. Necessity being the mother of invention, agricultural machinery was developed such that a small number of highly productive and well compensated workers were able to accomplish the task. By virtue of their great productivity and commensurate compensation, these workers, on balance, were able to provide for themselves, plus provide for others through their contribution to the tax system. The result of this arrangement has been a stable, prosperous, and productive society.

By contrast, in the far-West, the difficulty to producers of physically tending their agricultural interests was largely eliminated by immigration policies. These policies permitted vast numbers of unskilled legal and illegal immigrants to provide the required labor at a very low cost to the producers. There was no necessity for invention here, and consequently agriculture in these geographic areas is still mostly dependent on large numbers of unskilled, unproductive and consequently poorly paid labor. In earlier years, since the numbers were small, the cost to society of this arrangement was small, also, there is a lag between the time immigrants arrive and the time cost factors become manifest. Consequently, citizens and media failed to perceive the inherent flaws in the situation. Now, however, with the numbers much larger, and time having passed, the flaws are evident. California, for example, is collapsing socially and financially as a result of such immigration policies.

The fact is that multitudes—unskilled, under-productive and poorly paid—will import vast financial and cultural costs on society. Moreover, the situation is exacerbated if intrinsic to those multitudes is a dissimilar, under-achieving or hostile culture.

UNSKILLED LABOR IS NOT WHAT AMERICA NEEDS

Advocates of current immigration policies have informed us that America needs "cheap" unskilled immigrant labor for our low-paying jobs. Next we are informed that we need to spend vast amounts, since our labor pool is unskilled and needs to be upgraded to earn more and pay taxes. Then we are told again that we need more "cheap" unskilled immigrant labor for our low-paying jobs. The fact that America is on this immigration treadmill explains why the nation keeps losing ground.

The solution is to have a highly selective and restrictive immigration policy, as Japan does. This includes correctly regarding border integrity as a national security issue and committing adequate resources to keeping out illegal immigrants. Then necessity, the mother of invention, can provide the means to increase the productivity and the wages of currently low-paid citizens at no greater cost to employers and at considerable alleviation of the taxpayer burden. Again, this is the mechanism that brought prosperity and stability to agricultural areas in the American mid-West, and—more recently—increased productivity and prosperity to Japan.

Editor's Note: This article has been edited for publication.

Immigrants, Your Community, and U.S. Immigration Policy

The Study Circles Resource Center

This article was first published as a Public Talk Series discussion guide in November, 1963, and is reprinted by permission.

A GROWING BACKLASH AGAINST IMMIGRATION

America takes pride in being a land of immigrants. In comparison with other nations, we have welcomed a far greater number of people from outside our borders. Though there have been periodic waves of anti-immigrant sentiment, usually coinciding with difficult economic times, the American people have generally supported immigration in the belief that it makes our country unique and strong. "Immigrants built America" is a typical comment.

Now many Americans are becoming troubled about immigration. According to nationwide polls in the summer of 1993:

- 60 percent of Americans think that immigration is bad for the country;
- 62 percent agree that immigrants take the jobs of U.S. workers;
- 59 percent agree that "many immigrants wind up on welfare and raise taxes for Americans";
- more than 60 percent say that immigration should be decreased.

Anti-immigration sentiment is even stronger in the seven states in which more than three-quarters of all immigrants settle. In California, which absorbs more than one-third of all legal immigrants and about 40–50 percent of illegal immigrants, a powerful grassroots political movement is working to change U.S. immigration policy.

Some see the changes in attitude as due to a combination of prejudice, misinformation, and high-profile events involving foreigners, such as Haitian

The Journal of Intergroup Relations, Volume XXI, No. 1, Spring 1994, 32–39.

immigrants with AIDS and the World Trade Center bombing. Others, however, believe that a slow economy, widespread job losses, and cuts in government services have led many Americans to conclude that competition from immigrants hurts their own financial situation and is especially negative in its impact on the poor and on minorities.

The current wave of immigration is unprecedented except for the decades of 1900–1920, when 14.5 million immigrants came to America. By comparison, between 1971 and 1990, 10.5 million legal immigrants and an estimated three million illegal immigrants arrived. (Recent immigrants, it should be noted, represent a much smaller percentage of our country's *total* population, which is three to four times as large as it was near the turn of the century.) If the U.S. continues to absorb the same number of legal immigrants as in 1991 and 1992, more immigrants will come to the U.S. in the 1990s than in any previous decade.

The wave of immigration at the beginning of the century ended when Congress and President Harding passed a law that dramatically cut the number of immigrants, particularly those from the so-called "less desirable" countries of Eastern and Southern Europe. The quota system then adopted by the U.S. was abandoned in 1965. Since then there have been no laws to reduce legal immigration; in fact, the trend has been in the opposite direction. As recently as 1990, President Bush signed a law that increased legal immigration quotas by 40 percent.

In 1986, Congress did attempt to stem *illegal* immigration by passing the Immigration Reform and Control Act (IRCA), which granted amnesty to three million illegal aliens and barred employers from hiring undocumented immigrants. Virtually everyone agrees that IRCA has not worked well. This is partly because employer sanctions have been largely ineffective due to (1) the ease with which illegal immigrants can obtain counterfeit documents; (2) the willingness of some employers to risk hiring undocumented workers because they can pay them such low wages; and (3) the low risk of getting caught. Furthermore, IRCA has had an unintended consequence: some businesses have become hesitant to hire *legal* Asian and Latino immigrants, because of employers' unwillingness to deal with the paperwork and their fear that workers' papers will be forgeries.

The laws regulating *legal* immigration are complicated. Each year the Immigration and Naturalization Service (INS) issues visas in several categories that entitle people to come here as lawful, permanent residents. The President together with the Congress establish the numbers. Most legal immigrants are admitted under one of these categories: (1) "family reunification"—they are relatives of U.S. citizens or of permanent U.S. residents; (2) skilled workers, who can bring their families; (3) political refugees, who are granted asylum under U.S. law, or who are applying for asylum. It is not uncommon for people in the family reunification category to be on a waiting list for several years before they can reside in the U.S.

Each year illegal immigration adds another 20 to 30 percent to the number of immigrants. The INS, in charge of controlling illegal as well as legal immigration, is generally acknowledged to be underfunded and overburdened—and, many would say, ill-managed.

There is a consensus that the U.S. must regain control of its borders and reduce illegal immigration. When it comes to how many *legal* immigrants we should accept, however, there is intense disagreement.

KEY ISSUES IN THE PUBLIC DEBATE

The following key issues appear in the national public debate on immigration, but they are most starkly represented in communities that deal with the immigration question on a daily basis.

Economic issues. Many people who live in areas heavily settled by immigrants stress the financial burden on local and state budgets, which must carry most of the cost of medical care and other public services that immigrants receive. School systems in Los Angeles and other cities, for example, have been overwhelmed by immigrants. The result of these burdens, some say, is higher taxes, poorer education, and less government assistance for the needy who are already here.

The data about whether immigrants are a net economic cost or benefit are inconclusive. Over the years, almost all studies have concluded that immigrants pay as much or more in taxes than the cost of the services which government provides to them. However, a couple of recent studies have challenged this conclusion, arguing that recent immigrants are less educated, have fewer job skills, earn less, and are more likely to need government assistance than those who came before 1980.

The truth is, it's hard to know, partly because it depends on how we ask the question—for example, immigrants who may use more local services than they pay for when they first arrive may more than compensate for that over the long run. Also, accurate information—particularly about illegal immigrants—is hard to find. What is clear is that roughly two-thirds of the taxes immigrants pay go to the federal government, while most of the services they use are supplied by local and state governments. Many recent immigrants are poor, and like most poor people they tend to pay less in property and sales taxes and more in employment and income taxes. Another important factor is that the federal government, which once funded programs to help states resettle immigrants, has cut such programs over the past decade.

Another major economic concern is competition for jobs. Supporters of reduced immigration argue that our economy is not creating enough new jobs for the workers we already have, much less for all the new immigrants. They argue that though immigrants are taking jobs that native-born Americans are unwilling to do, the fact that immigrants will take these jobs and that they form a large pool of unskilled workers in some areas is depressing wages for low-skill jobs. They go on to argue that that is what keeps those jobs unattractive for native-born Americans with higher wage expectations.

Some Basic Facts About Immigration

How many immigrants are coming to the U.S.? Currently, total immigration is estimated to be about 1.1 million a year. About 700,000 legal immigrants come under policies for family reunification or skilled workers. Approximately 100–200,000 more legal refugees come because they are classified as "political refugees" or because they want that classification—that is, they are seeking asylum from political persecution. The annual net influx of illegal immigrants is thought to be 200–300,000.

Where do they come from? The origin of refugees to the U.S. has changed radically in the past decade. In the 1950s, 66% of all legal immigrants came from Europe and Canada. In the 1960s, this figure was 46%. In the 1980s, only 14% came from Europe and Canada, while 44% came from Asia, and 40% from Latin America. Today, 80% of immigrants are people of color.

What portion of the U.S. is foreign-born? About 1 in 12 U.S. residents is foreign-born, up from 1 in 20 in 1970, but far less than the 1 in 7 for the years from 1860 to 1920.

Where in the U.S. do most immigrants live? In recent years, more than three-quarters of legal immigrants have settled in just seven states: 40% of immigrants have settled in California, 12% in Texas, 10% in New York, 8% in Florida, 4% in Illinois, 3% in New Jersey, and 2% in Arizona.

Others say the argument that immigrants pose a financial burden is an exaggerated one. They say that immigrants help communities and provide a boost to our sagging economy—by creating new businesses and jobs, doing work that native-born Americans will not do, working hard for low wages, paying taxes on their wages, and reviving run-down neighborhoods. In fact, they argue, immigrants—both illegal and legal—use few services. Illegal immigrants use few services because they are trying to avoid the authorities. Some legal immigrants hesitate to seek out and accept services because they fear that it will hurt their chances of becoming a citizen, feel intimidated, or are simply afraid of government authorities.

Quality-of-life issues. In some communities, social and cultural concerns about immigration are those most loudly voiced. Immigrants tend to live close together, changing neighborhoods dramatically. Some Americans are disturbed by the different cultures and traditions of newcomers, especially those from Latin American and Asian cultures. Some resent the fact that immigrants want to use their own language and don't learn English, or don't learn it quickly. Some allege that immigrants have contributed to a breakdown in social order and to increasing crime rates. They say that immigrants hurt communities because they crowd several families into one home, are noisy and dirty, and hang out on the street.

These Americans fear that the national character, identity, and political values of the U.S. will change for the worse as the population becomes less European. They say that immigrants create social friction and may slowly erode the English-speaking hybrid European culture we call "American." They argue that the America of 1993, vastly different from the America of 1900–1920—there is less space for people, and the economy isn't growing in the same way. Today there is less need for entry-level workers, and we are less able to absorb people into our economy—and, therefore, our culture. Others add that periods of low immigration in our history may always have been vital to the assimilation process, and that perhaps we need one of those low periods now.

Some Facts About Illegal Immigration

How many immigrants are in this country illegally? There is disagreement about how many of the total number of immigrants in the U.S. (approximately 20 million) are illegal. Figures range from 3.2 million to 4.8 million, or 16–24 percent. Each year there are 2–3 million illegal entries into the U.S., but many of these people return to their country of origin. The number of undocumented immigrants in the U.S. is thought to increase by about 200,000 to 300,000 each year.

How do illegal immigrants get here? More than half of new illegal immigrants each year enter as visitors—students or tourists—and become illegal only when they overstay their visas. Most of the rest enter the U.S. by crossing the border from Mexico.

Where do illegal immigrants come from? The top 10 percent of origin for illegal immigrants are Mexico, El Salvador, Guatemala, Canada, Poland, the Philippines, Haiti, Nicaragua, Columbia, and the Bahamas.

To what services are illegal immigrants entitled? In 1982 the Supreme Court ruled that all children, regardless of immigration status, are entitled to free public education. Illegal immigrants are not legally entitled to receive welfare, Social Security, or other government benefits, except for emergency medical services and education for their children. However, their children who are born in the U.S. are citizens.

Other Americans believe that opposition to immigration is based on prejudice against people who are different and especially against people of color, who make up a large proportion of the current wave of immigrants. They point out that most immigrants are hard-working, family-oriented, traditional people, many of whom have taken enormous risks and given up a great deal to come to the "land of opportunity." The last thing most immigrants want is a government handout. There are no statistics to indicate that immigrants are more likely to commit crimes than native-born Americans, they say. Newcomers bring vitality and diversity that strengthen and renew our communities and our nation.

Supporters of immigration believe that the increasing multicultural nature of our society is a big plus. Our society has gone through numerous transitions, and what it means to be an American has constantly changed, they claim. The same prejudices that people currently express against Asians and Latinos were expressed against German, Irish, Italian, Jewish, and Polish immigrants from Europe a century ago. They point out that the U.S. has been able to assimilate people who came from dramatically different cultures and political systems in the past.

OTHER ISSUES

Population growth, the environment, and resource use. Some people don't mind increasing our population. They believe the U.S. has more space and resources and better environmental controls than do the poor, crowded nations from which immigrants come. Others feel that, at the current rate of growth of 2.7 million people per year, the U.S. population is already growing too fast. This country is already too crowded, they say, and the land has a limited carrying capacity. Americans may not like the idea of limits, but it's time to accept some. Since population growth over the next 50 years will be mostly due to immigrants and their children, we should reduce immigration. By taking so many immigrants we worsen the world environment, they add, because the newcomers use more resources here than they would at home.

Political asylum. Debates about which political refugees should be allowed to enter the U.S. continue. How do we allocate the roughly 125,000 U.S. visas among millions of political refugees? Are Haitian boat people economic refugees fleeing poverty, or political refugees who should be granted asylum? What about Chinese? Cubans? Currently there is a backlog of 300,000 people who are waiting in the U.S. to have their asylum cases heard. Some of them will simply fail to show up for their hearings, disappear into this vast country, and become illegal immigrants.

Our moral obligation to help people in other nations. What obligation, if any, does the U.S. have to help poor and oppressed people in the world? How do we go about fulfilling the obligation? Do we still have this obligation if other wealthy countries don't do their share? Should we continue to accept more immigrants than do all other countries combined? Should we focus more on assisting the poor and oppressed in their homelands and try to diminish the pressure for immigration? What if this means spending a lot more money to help other countries develop their economies?

KEY VALUES AND CONCERNS

Below are some of the most common conflicts among values and concerns that underlie discussions and debates about immigration. In many cases, these conflicts frequently exist within an individual's thinking as well as among people.

1. The desire to welcome strangers who have been poor and oppressed and give them a better chance, but not wanting to pay more taxes and make one's own life more insecure financially.

2. Valuing and admiring the hard work, courage, and persistence of many immigrants, but fearing them as competitors in business, for jobs, and for public services.

3. The desire to maintain the cultural integrity, comfort, and familiarity of one's neighborhood vs. valuing a more diverse neighborhood with the richness and excitement of people from different cultures.

4. The desire to welcome strangers, yet the fear that people who are different may not return that welcome by respecting (or giving deference to) one's own culture and traditions.

5. The belief that it is important to provide the best education for every American-born child vs. the belief that we should educate all the children in the community.

6. The belief that children benefit from going to school with people who have a common cultural background vs. the belief that children need to learn alongside people from different cultures.

7. The concern that large numbers of immigrants with no experience with democracy will undermine our political culture, vs. the belief that newcomers will add vitality to our public life.

8. Wanting to maintain an "open door" to the poor and oppressed of the world vs. concern about the natural limits of our land.

9. For newcomers, the desire to assimilate and "belong" to the dominant culture vs. the wish to value and maintain one's distinct cultural identity and heritage.

10. For newcomers, the desire to "fit in" vs. the wish to have one's cultural experiences validated and valued by the dominant culture.

THE POLICY DEBATE

Some Americans support current U.S. immigration policy, although they want to reduce illegal immigration. They feel that the current level of legal immigration—about 1 million a year, or 0.4 percent of our population of 250 million—is not only justifiable on moral grounds, but economically, culturally, and politically beneficial. The following policies, many argue, will make *current levels of legal immigration* more workable and therefore more acceptable:

- Return some federal tax money to the local areas that are bearing the greatest burden of resettling newcomers.
- Enforce existing labor law to reduce exploitation of immigrants and, thereby, help American-born workers.

Many Americans, however, are troubled by current levels of immigration. The following proposals have been made by those who want to *reduce legal immigration:*

- Impose a three-year moratorium on legal immigration, followed by a cap on legal immigration at 300,000 a year;
- Amend the Constitution so that babies born in the U.S. to illegal immigrants do not automatically become citizens;
- Allow naturalized American citizens to bring only members of their immediate family—and not *extended* family—to the U.S.;
- Stop admitting so many legal immigrants from countries that don't share our Western cultural heritage.

People who hold a variety of beliefs regarding legal immigration have stated a desire to reduce *illegal immigration.* There are a range of proposals to address this goal:

- Deny illegal immigrants access to basic public services such as free public education and health care;
- Strengthen the INS and its patrols on the Mexican border so that it can catch and deport more illegal immigrants;
- Give every citizen and legal resident a national identity card that would be impossible to forge.

Editor's Note: This article has been edited for publication.

The Study Circles Resource Center is a project of the Topsfield Foundation, Inc., a private, nonprofit, nonpartisan foundation dedicated to advancing deliberative democracy and improving the quality of public life in the United States. The Center's address is P.O. Box 203, 697A Pomfret Rd., Pomfret, CT 06258.

Immigration
The Symbolic Crackdown
Charles Mahtesian

Last summer, a man brought his sister into the emergency room at the Milwaukee County medical center and told the staff that she had been recommended for emergency heart surgery by her personal physician. Doctors examined her and decided she didn't need the operation, just medical treatment for heart disease. They gave her the treatment, then sent her home.

The only complication was that her home was in Iran. She wasn't an American citizen, a refugee, or even an undocumented worker. She flew from Teheran to Milwaukee specifically for medical care, carrying a return plane ticket with her, and then flew home. She wasn't charged a cent. U.S. taxpayers covered the entire bill. Her brother, a Milwaukee County resident, handled the negotiations.

An isolated instance? County health care administrators say it wasn't. They believe this sort of thing has happened before in Milwaukee. But they don't really know, because they have never kept records on the use of the health care system by illegal immigrants or foreign visitors. They haven't tended to ask, and the patients haven't volunteered the information. What they are sure of is that it has been easy to beat the system.

That is changing. Steps are being taken to ensure that no one tries such a stunt again. Now, prospective clients at the Milwaukee County Medical Complex must reveal their immigration status so the county can make sure illegal customers aren't taking advantage of scant local resources. Though some immigrant advocates and community health care providers are complaining about the new requirements, they might as well accept them. In Milwaukee, as in the rest of the country, the practice of providing unquestioned service to illegal immigrants seems gradually to be fading away.

When it comes to emergency health care and public education, there is little choice. The courts have mandated that these be available to all, whether legal residents or not. But access to other government services—ranging from preventive health care to driver's licenses to welfare benefits—is very much a matter of discretion, depending mainly on the zeal with which a state or local government wants to monitor the status of the immigrant.

Governing, May 1994, 52–57.

Until recently, in many places, that monitoring has been practically nonexistent. No health care provider wants to turn away a person in need, even when there is not true emergency. It is easier to ignore a person's immigration status, or more commonly, not to ask. "Technically, it is a sticky situation," says Jane Preston, director of the Milwaukee County Health Care Finance Plan. "While our plan could effectively deny treatment, our county hospital could not turn them away."

But as states and localities begin to assess the impact of immigration on their budgets, a growing number of them are attempting to cut back on the menu of non-mandated services and benefits available to illegal immigrants. While the immigration debate at the federal level stalls over the questions of which and how many immigrants get in, at the state and local level the debate is over which immigrants get what.

Whether the illegal population is small, as in Minnesota, or moderate, as in Virginia, or all but unmanageable, as in Florida or California, the bottom line these days is the bottom line. In the search for budget savings, residents who are in the country illegally make an enticing target, especially when the other option is limiting services to those who reside here legally.

"You simply cannot provide first-class services without regulating immigration. Since states can't control immigration, they are doing the only thing they can rationally do," says Dan Stein, executive director of the Federation for American Immigration Reform, which advocates immigration limits. "There has to be some reasonable regulation over the numbers of people you provide services to."

In the long run, unless the federal mandates on education and emergency health care are lifted, it is not clear just how much the current state and local crackdown is going to accomplish. Some argue, for example, that illegal immigrants are infrequent users of all but emergency health care in the first place, and screening them out will be more trouble than it is worth. "Think about it," says Dr. Len Kirschner, former Arizona health care director. "How many undocumented aliens apply to get their annual physicals? Not many. I don't believe we'll see any cost savings." Others warn that a population of untreated illegal immigrants could become a costly threat to public health, as AIDS and tuberculosis cases increase.

Taken as a whole, says Michael Fix of the Urban Institute, a package of restrictions and cutbacks in the limited area open to discretion will do little to address the most important immigration issues. "I don't think A) it's going to solve the problem, B) it won't make the states solvent, and C) it won't make a statement as a political symbol," Fix insists.

Many experts, however, disagree with Fix on at least the last point—they concede the potency of the immigration crackdown as a political symbol. While budgetary concerns play the major role in the decisions to get tough on illegals, politics enters into nearly all of them as well. In California, where the legislature has been buried under an avalanche of immigration-related bills, immigration is shaping up as a major political issue in the 1994 campaign. Democrats insist that Republican Governor Pete Wilson's crusade against illegal immigrants is poll-driven and timed to coincide with his 1994 reelection campaign, but even within the state Democratic Party, immigration is surfacing as a wedge issue. Some Latinos have threatened to leave the party unless colleagues desist in supporting anti-immigrant bills.

Estimates of how many illegal immigrants are in this country range anywhere from 2 to 6 million. The Census Bureau puts the number at about 4 million, with the vast concentration in six states: California, Texas, New York, Illinois, Florida and New Jersey. Another handful of states—Arizona, Virginia, Maryland, Washington, Colorado, New Mexico and Massachusetts—are home to more than 25,000 each.

Illegal immigrants are legally entitled to such federal benefits as the Women, Infants and Children nutrition program and emergency medical care under Medicaid. They are guaranteed free education from kindergarten through grade 12. A few states allow illegal immigrants to receive benefits from state-funded welfare programs.

For all the noise surrounding the issue of illegal immigration and its effect on federal, state and local budgets, there is little evidence showing that illegals are abusing social services. Many do not even bother to claim them because of language or other cultural barriers. Others fear being reported to federal authorities. Either way, it is hard to know, since most states and localities have never tracked recipients by immigration status. The figures that states provide on the costs of providing services to illegal immigrants are only rough estimates.

Still, it does not take an economist to figure out that the cost of providing mandated elementary and secondary education, emergency medical care and prison space to illegals is a crushing burden. In California, the governor's office reports mandated state and local government expenses for illegals at $2.3 billion a year. According to a survey conducted by the Los Angeles County Department of Human Services, two-thirds of all mothers who gave birth in the county's four public hospitals in the 1990–91 fiscal year were illegal immigrants. In Miami, Jackson Memorial Hospital has admitted 26,000 illegals and treated 6,000 as outpatients at a cost of $300 million over the past three years.

In Santa Cruz County, Arizona, on the Mexican border, where the total population is only about 30,000, the per-capita burden is even more staggering. Last year, county officials had to boost property taxes by almost 9 percent to cover health care and corrections costs for illegals. "Seventy to 80 percent of the inmates in our jail are from another country," says County Manager Dennis Miller. "There is a tremendous impact on our criminal justice system. That's the one that's breaking us."

All this must be done at a time when the federal spigot has been all but turned off. Federal aid for legalized alien and refugee resettlement—never a substantial figure—has steadily declined. Federal cash, medical and social services assistance for refugee resettlement dropped from a high of $550 million in 1982 to an estimated $100 million in 1993, according to figures provided by the National Conference of State Legislatures.

In Florida, where the state spent an estimated $884 million on illegal immigrants in 1993, Governor Lawton Chiles is suing both the Immigration and Naturalization Service and the federal government for not reimbursing Florida for health, education and welfare benefits to illegal immigrants, an action that several other states are considering. Florida contends that it is the federal government's responsibility to set immigration policy and to enforce immigration laws, so the feds should pick up the tab to pay the cost of implementing the policies—or, as the case may be, the failure to enforce its own laws.

Most of the attention, however, has been focused on California, where more than half the country's illegal immigrants reside and where Governor Pete Wilson has mounted a high-profile effort to reduce what he and others refer to as the "magnet" of free services. Wilson is calling for a constitutional amendment denying birthright citizenship to the children of undocumented aliens and asking the feds to lift the federal mandate to provide health care. Wilson even took out ads in newspapers across the country calling on President Clinton to support the amendment.

State officials have worked up some dramatic statistics to try to bolster their case. California argues that five jobs are required to produce the revenue to fund services to one prison felon. Twenty-two jobs are needed to pay for one classroom. The state claims that the 1994–95 cost of services to illegal immigrants will be the equivalent of 750,000 tax-paying jobs.

Earlier this year, the California legislature passed a law requiring all first-time driver's license applicants to show proof of legal residency. It may not sound like much, but if New Jersey's experience is any indication, the restrictions will affect a highly sought-after commodity.

New Jersey used to be one of only two states—Colorado is the other one—where applicants had to divulge their citizenship when applying for a driver's license or permit. But after a legal challenge in 1991, the state agreed to rescind the policy. In the first weeks following the change, Department of Motor Vehicles offices were swamped with new customers. In the month prior to the decision, New Jersey officials reported that 39 people applied for driver's licenses or permits without Social Security numbers. In the three weeks after the decision, 6,500 such people did. For the record, California's illegal immigrant population is about 30 times that of New Jersey.

No one argues that restrictions on driver's licenses will do much to ease California's fiscal burden. Critics warn of a surge of unlicensed drivers, many of whom will have a strong incentive to leave the scene of an accident. It will, however, send a message. At the very least, it is one more reason for an illegal immigrant to go elsewhere.

Another new inconvenience is aimed at many of Southern California's day laborers, the job seekers who congregate on sidewalks and in commercial areas in hopes of picking up work. While most day laborers are not illegal immigrants, a significant number are. So the Los Angeles County board of supervisors recently responded to neighborhood complaints by considering criminalization of curbside job solicitation. Latino and immigrants-rights advocates protested, and in a compromise, the board agreed to limit the places where job seekers may look for work. Property owners may now ban day laborers from commercial parking areas if they post signs to that effect and provide other areas where laborers may congregate. Neighborhood activists were not mollified, but for illegal immigrants, it served notice that local official were keeping tabs.

In some cases, states are deliberately seizing on test cases to try to send the federal government a message. While Florida is suing the feds for relief, its Department of Health and Rehabilitative Services is attempting to deny foster care to two children who are living in the state illegally. The problem of illegal children is not exactly a budget-buster—only about 75 such children are in the state's foster system. But Florida contends that they are the responsibility of the Immigration and Naturalization Service. It is, for the most part, an ultimatum to the INS.

"I don't mind providing the service. God knows they need it," says Jim Towey, director of Florida HRS. "But there's no place in the state budget for providing for these children. We just could not say yes to them and then look all the other kids we're serving in the eye. The soup we're serving them is real, real thin."

The recent efforts against illegal immigrants mirror a shift in public attitude toward all immigrants, both legal and illegal. A decade ago, scores of cities and states declared themselves sanctuary for immigrants, where refugees from war-torn Central American countries could seek shelter without fear of deportation by the INS. Few localities actively encourage immigration anymore, outside the few seeking low-wage workers for industries such as meatpacking or poultry processing.

In California, the cities of San Francisco, Berkeley, Oakland, San Jose, West Hollywood and Sacramento all proclaimed themselves sanctuary cities in the 1980s. Last year, that support began to break down as the state prohibited any city from adopting ordinances against sharing the names of alleged felons with the INS.

It is breaking down on the East Coast as well. In Somerville, Massachusetts, where city officials declared their municipality a sanctuary back in 1987, a group of local residents qualified a 1993 ballot measure to repeal the ordinance. In the end, the measure was thrown out because of invalid signatures, but the tone of the debate made one point clear: Somerville was no longer an immigration sanctuary of any kind. "The climate," notes Duke Austin, senior spokesman for the INS, "has changed dramatically from what it was 10 years ago."

To many state and local governments, however, the logical way to save money on immigration is to do something they have been very reluctant to do in the past—ask people about their immigration status at the time they apply for benefits. It was this reluctance that led Milwaukee County into its heart patient case last summer. "If you don't ask the status question or verify status, by default you are giving those benefits," says Rosemary Jenks, senior analyst for the Center for Immigration Studies. "Unless you are taking active steps to prevent illegal aliens, you are in effect helping them to get benefits."

Until last summer, patients in one state-funded category of the Arizona Health Care Cost Containment System—the state's plan for indigent or low-income residents—were not required to prove citizenship to obtain services. Then the legislature figured it could squeeze $31 million in budget savings by closing that loophole to prohibit illegal immigrants from receiving medical care except in emergencies.

Before that change took effect in July, there were 48,000 individuals in the medically indigent/medically needy category. As of March 1994, there were 31,000. The drop was not attributed solely to the rule changes, but a good portion of those who left the program were in fact illegal.

Even in states with significantly smaller undocumented populations, there are moves afoot to limit access to benefits. Minnesota, for example, has been one of the few states to allow illegal immigrants access to state-funded welfare programs. Last year, however, a new law took effect eliminating those cash and non-emergency health benefits. Minnesota expects to save about $5 million by excluding illegal immigrants from the programs.

Challenging illegal immigrants in Minnesota is a relatively easy political undertaking. The number of illegal aliens is minimal and the voice of local immigrant-rights groups muted. But cracking down on illegal immigrants is not a politically free move in every state, as Virginia's legislature learned in March.

Growing concern over the size and cost of the state's illegal population—estimated to be about 46,000—generated a bill in the legislature to require an attempt to identify illegal immigrants who use publicly funded social services. Once identified, they would be reported to federal authorities. While the bill's sponsor, Senator Warren E. Barry, said his main concern was getting an accurate accounting of the costs of social services for illegal immigrants, Latino activists attacked the bill, complaining that it would lead to discrimination against legal immigrants as well. Besides, they noted, it would serve to discourage immigrants from claiming services to which they are legally entitled—a possibly unconstitutional move. Opposition to the measure proved so fierce that legislators backed off from the provisions to report illegals to the INS. And in the end, the legislature shelved the whole measure until next year.

If California and Florida are any indication, though, the bill stands a good chance of passage the next time around. Once it is stripped of its purely punitive provision—that is, reporting illegal immigrants to the INS for deportation—there will be a strong temptation to vote yes, especially for legislators outside the Northern Virginia region where most of the illegal immigrants reside.

But if the measure does pass, what will it accomplish? Not much, other than to confirm what states like California and Florida already know: that the costs of educating and treating illegal immigrants are considerable, and that there is little they can do about it. Except, perhaps, make the state a little less attractive to potential newcomers.

Editor's Note: This article has been edited for publication.

Immigration Dilemmas
Richard Rothstein

During the presidential campaign, Bill Clinton delivered a foreign policy speech in Los Angeles; the first question from the audience was a predictable. "Who are your foreign policy advisers going to be?" Clinton demurred, calling such considerations premature. Next, a questioner asked the candidate what he proposed to do about illegal immigration. Clinton said he didn't know what to do, since immigration was the most complex issue facing the nation. "If you have an answer," Clinton told the questioner, "*you* can be my foreign policy adviser!" It may have been the first time the "policy-wonk" candidate couldn't come up with a ready solution.

The impossibility of border control is the most obvious difficulty. The Coast Guard can't effectively police every mile of our coastline; the occasional interception of a Chinese human cargo ship is only token. We now have over three thousand federal agents patrolling two thousand miles of the U.S.-Mexican land border, also with little success. Last year, the border patrol intercepted 1.2 million would-be immigrants from Mexico, but since there is no point to incarcerating them (or jail space to do so), nearly all are sent back to try again: 100,000 to 600,000 a year evade capture. So if the intercepted ones keep trying, the odds are increasingly in their favor.

Giving up on border control is no solution either. Open contempt for any important law engenders disrespect for law itself, so we owe it to our national integrity to make serious attempts at enforcement. Also, setting aside for the moment the complicated question of whether newcomers compete with native workers for jobs, it is indisputable that undocumented immigrants who take jobs in labor-short occupations deny places to would-be lawful immigrants who live in nations from which illegal entry is less practical. It is to these equally desperate and ambitious migrants that our ineffective border control is most unfair.

When we attempted to rescue respect for law by abandoning our 55 mph speed limit in rural areas because most people flouted it, we established a new limit of 65 mph, a level we thought drivers would respect. But for illegal immigration, there is no analogous solution, because the most sophisticated analysts can't make a reasonable guess at the level of immigration that must be allowed before control is practical. Even today's educated guess would

Dissent, Fall 1993, 455–462.

change tomorrow, based on political developments abroad (like the Tiananmen massacre or the overthrow of Aristide) or changes in economic growth rates and job creation in places like Mexico and the Dominican Republic. The reality would also change with job opportunities here. Fewer immigrants would come if they knew there was no work awaiting them; even in poor countries, people rarely want to leave their families and communities. It's not that the pressure for illegal immigration is so great that if we relaxed our barriers, we'd be inundated with hordes of immigrants. Though nobody knows how many Mexicans would actually immigrate if they could do so unimpeded, the number is smaller than most Americans think. Early in this century, after all, when Mexicans were even poorer relative to Americans than they are today, American railroads and farmers had to send recruiters to Mexico to beg laborers to come.

In Europe, experts feared there would be massive migration of poor Italians to high-wage countries like France and Germany when the European Community (EC) was established, so Italian emigration was restricted. When restrictions were finally abandoned in 1968, however, few Italians left home. The wage differential between Germany and Italy was still four to one, but for most Italians, the income difference wasn't great enough to make the upheaval worthwhile. Today, despite continuing income differences between countries like Ireland, Spain, Greece, and Italy, on the one hand, and France and Germany on the other, only 1.5 percent of the EC's population was born in a different EC country from the one in which they now reside. The EC has lots of immigrants—but most come from poorer countries in Africa, Eastern Europe, and the Middle East.

Americans who are frustrated with our country's inability to regulate immigration might reflect on the experience of other industrial nations, even those with less inclusive traditions. Japan, for example, with its aging workforce and declining fertility rate, also has a need for low-wage immigrants, even now in a stagnant economy. Since 1989 Japan has crafted a temporary, and racist, solution by recruiting some 200,000 (according to official government figures) South American workers who have partial Japanese ancestry. But professional smuggling rings are already at work importing South Americans with documents faking Japanese bloodlines. As immigration expert Wayne Cornelius points out, of the 30,000 Peruvians now in Japan, half may be illegal. In addition to those counted in official data, there may be as many as 250,000 Brazilians who came to Japan as "tourists" and then stayed on to work. Japan also has illegal immigrants from Malaysia, Thailand, Iran, Bangladesh, and Pakistan who overstayed tourist visas. And there are 700,000 Koreans living in Japan, many descended from laborers imported by force during Japan's prewar occupation of Korea, others who immigrated illegally in recent years. The sociologist Nathan Glazer remarked a few years ago that "one does not note in Japan, a country with very few immigrants, unmade hotel beds, unwashed dishes in restaurants, unmanned filing stations. it seems there is a way of managing even without immigrants." Glazer should look again. In 1992 alone, 280,000 foreigners came to Japan on short-term visas and then disappeared into the country.

And then there is France, whose new conservative government proclaims a goal of "zero immigration." It's a fantasy. There are already one million undocumented immigrants living in France, with another 4.5 million foreigners there legally—mostly Algerians, Moroccans, and Tunisians. All told, immigrants make up over 10 percent of France's population, and many have relatives and friends who are ready to join them, legally or illegally.

Last year, one thousand would-be immigrants drowned while trying to swim to Spain. Uncounted others made it, ferried to a point two hundred yards from shore by Moroccan smugglers. In return for a promise of $2 billion in aid from the EC, Morocco has now agreed to station 3,500 troops on its beaches to try to deter human smuggling, yet the illegal immigration continues. In Germany, there are nearly two million Turkish immigrants, brought into the country over a thirty-year period as "guest workers," who never went home. All told, there are probably five million undocumented immigrants in Western Europe, 1.5 percent of the population. In the United States, there are perhaps three and a half million undocumented, a slightly smaller share of our population, though we have another three million formerly undocumented persons who were "legalized" after the 1986 amnesty. Our self-image of America as a nation uniquely open to immigration is historically accurate but less true today. Although our immigration restrictionists are now more civilized than those in Germany, the 8.5 percent of our population that is foreign-born is not much greater than the 8.2 percent of German residents who came from elsewhere. In 1920, however, over 13 percent of Americans were foreign born. *Then* we were unique, not now, when throughout the world, one hundred million people are immigrants in one country or another.

PUSH AND PULL

All industrialized nations have an "immigration problem" for similar reasons. When labor markets are tight or we want agricultural or service work performed cheaply, we welcome immigrants, sometimes without restriction, sometimes through official "guest worker" programs. But bringing guest workers into a country is easier than sending them home. Once they arrive, it is virtually impossible to prevent them from leaving the jobs for which they were recruited and finding other work.

It used to be easier to send immigrants back when their work was done, because their wives were content to wait for them at home. But many Mexican women, for example, are no longer willing to stay home while their husbands travel back and forth to earn money in the United States. Now, women want to come north to work as well, either with their husbands or independently. Since 1987 alone, the number of Mexican women attempting to cross the border illegally has doubled, while the number of men has not changed. A consequence is declining return migration for men.

Once an immigrant group establishes a presence, networks linking immigrants with their home country become difficult to break. In the United States, we give priority for legal immigration to "family reunification," meaning that immigrants can bring their relatives here at the head of the line. For example, workers amnestied under the 1986 law will soon be eligible to bring in family members—several million additional legal residents.

Few immigrants leave home without some idea of how to find work in America. Once an immigrant community is established here, this becomes a lot easier. Immigrants recruit friends and relatives from back home when their employers need additional help. In the garment districts of Los Angeles, New York, or Miami, entire plants are staffed by immigrants from the same small village in Mexico, El Salvador, or China. Once such powerful networks are established, policy is impotent to break them.

When George Bush and Carlos Salinas first began promoting a North American Free Trade Agreement (NAFTA), one of their claims was that providing more jobs in Mexico would reduce the Mexicans' desire to emigrate. The claim is heard less frequently now, because it's become clear that the relationship is more complex. Emigration is expensive (the illegal kind often requires hiring a guide and buying false documents for as much as $2,000), and the poorest Mexicans can't afford it. If Mexico becomes more prosperous, more people will have money to pay for emigration.

Traditional societies send few emigrants, but the disruption of traditional ways spurs emigration. As countries industrialize, formerly rural workers, now more rootless, begin to think of the next step—emigration. Industrial workers aspire to better jobs, and when they reach the limit of their upward mobility at home, think of the next step—emigration. Undocumented Mexican immigrants are almost never those without jobs at home; they have above-average education and aspirations whetted by urban industrial employment. In the 1970s, South Korea's economy was the fastest growing in the world, and its emigration rate to the United States was also the fastest growing.

Today, the ratio of U.S. to Mexican wages is about seven to one, and the ratio of living standards, (measured purchasing power) is about three to one. As this gap narrows, economic growth and development in Mexico will initially stimulate *increased* emigration to the United States. At some point in the future, most experts believe, the gap will become small enough that emigration will slow. But nobody can hazard a guess about when that point might come—one U.S. government commission recently concluded it could take "several generations." Something short of full equality with U.S. incomes is necessary. Few Americans, after all, move from city to city in search of relatively small wage increases, so long as they have a job at home. Mexicans are even less likely to abandon their culture and homeland for small income differences. As noted earlier, a four-to-one ratio wasn't enough to spur Italian moves to Germany.

Immigration flows are even more immune to policy influences because the relationship between economic status at home and the propensity to migrate varies from society to society and from time to time. By 1980, one-third of working-age persons born in Puerto Rico had migrated to the mainland. The migrants were Puerto Ricans with below-average education levels, and they were more likely to be unemployed before leaving the island—just the opposite of today's Mexican immigrants. Why? According to economists Alida Castillo-Freeman and Richard Freeman, it's because Congress raised Puerto Rico's minimum wage so high that island unemployment increased; for the remaining jobs, employers were able to select only the most qualified workers, who then chose not to migrate and accepted relatively good pay at home. Those left on the streets migrated. By establishing a high minimum wage for Puerto Rico, Congress in effect determined that it was better to bring unskilled Puerto Rican migrants to New York than to send New York jobs to Puerto Rico. Had the Puerto Rican minimum wage been lower, fewer islanders would have migrated, but more factories would have left the mainland for the island's low wage haven. Can we conclude from the Puerto Rican experience that Mexican migration will slow if Mexican wages are kept low? No: too many other factors will intervene.

In reality, NAFTA and trade policy could become irrelevant to the volume of future immigration flows from Mexico, since, as Wayne Cornelius suggests, these factors are likely to be swamped by Mexico's domestic agriculture policy. Before President Salinas's policies of economic liberalization, Mexico subsidized peasants to remain in rural areas; the government, for example, bought corn from peasants at twice the world price and prohibited the sale of communal farm lands to private investors. But last year the Mexican Constitution was amended to permit these lands to be sold, and it is widely expected that corn and bean subsidies will decline. The purpose of these policies is to encourage investment in efficient cash crops for export, but if successful, they will result in many fewer peasants working the land: approximately one million peasants are expected to leave farming annually during the next ten to twenty years. The Mexican labor force is already growing at the rate of one million jobseekers per year, from three hundred thousand to half a million more than current economic growth can absorb. Emigration pressures will be irresistible, regardless of NAFTA or U.S border policies.

PAYING FOR OUR PENSIONS

Two claims fuel much of the recent debate about immigration. One is that immigrants draw more on public services (like welfare and public health) than they contribute in taxes. The second is that immigrants take jobs from the rest of us.

It is true that local government is burdened by immigrant services. Over 10 percent of California's immigrants are on welfare, and over 25 percent of southern California's jail populations are immigrants. But at the same time, our national budget is becoming more dependent on immigrant taxes. Fewer Americans will be working when the baby boom generation (born between 1946 and 1964) begins to reach retirement age in 2010. By that time, we will have spent the boomers' Social Security contributions to offset the federal budget deficit. So we'll need the taxes of younger working immigrants to pay Medicare and Social Security for the older generation. The services-taxes balance of which we now complain will become part of the solution, not the problem.

Today, 12 percent of Americans are over sixty-five years old, and their health and retirement benefits consume about one-third of all federal spending. When the baby-boom generation retires, 20 percent will be over sixty-five. No longer paying income or Social Security taxes, they will instead consume Social Security and Medicare. These benefits can be paid for only by large tax increases on those still working, by big jumps in productivity or by changes in the ratio of working to retired Americans.

We can improve the ratio if we make people work longer and raise their retirement age. Minor steps have already been taken, the normal retirement age for Social Security will be raised to sixty-seven in 2027, and further increases are inevitable. We can also improve the ratio with an increase in birth rates, so that more young workers are available to replace those who retire. This is also happening: the age fertility rate (children borne by the average woman) has jumped from 1.87 to 2.05 in the last five years. But this is not something we necessarily want to encourage; it contradicts, for example, our desire to reduce teen pregnancies.

Ultimately, we can't increase the working-to-retired ratio enough without a lot more immigration. While only 26 percent of the U.S. population is now in the prime working age of twenty to thirty-nine, 46 percent of immigrants are in that age group. Retiring baby boomers need people who contribute more in taxes than they consume in services. Immigration will have to be an increasing part of the solution, not only in the United States, but throughout the industrial world. Germans now retire at age sixty, but the sixty-and-over set, now 21 percent of Germany's population, will make up 30 percent by the year 2020. With fewer workers to pay that many pensions, Germany has increased its retirement age to sixty-five, effective in 2012. Germany needs more young Turks, not fewer. Japan's fertility rate is only 1.53 and, in thirteen years, Japan is expected to become the first country in the world where over 20 percent of the population is older than sixty-five, a point the United States can expect to reach by 2025, unless there is a lot more immigration.

COMPETITION FOR JOBS

Do immigrants take jobs from residents? In some cases they do and in others they provide labor no native group is willing to supply. It is impossible to design an immigration policy that bars the "takers" and welcomes the "providers."

Important industries (garment manufacturing, for example) could not exist without an immigrant labor supply; no native workers are available or willing to work in these industries even in periods of high unemployment. If natives were willing to work, they would demand wage-and-benefit packages that would certainly make the industries uncompetitive with companies based abroad. Our minimum wage is now so low, however, that lawful employers can survive by paying the minimum to immigrant workers, while sweatshop operators exploit immigrants; vulnerability and collect an additional premium. Because of immigrant seamstresses, an industry exists that supports not only its professional and managerial employees but a variety of upstream workers in computer software, machine tools, textiles, and petrochemicals. In Los Angeles, with mostly undocumented immigrant workers, the garment industry has grown in the last decade, while manufacturing as a whole, and especially garment manufacturing, has declined nationwide.

There is also no displacement of native workers in low-wage service jobs, in restaurant kitchens, say, or hotels. It is, of course, theoretically possible that restaurants and hotels could be forced to pay wages high enough to attract American high-school graduates, but if they did so, we'd have many fewer (because much more expensive) vacations and conventions, not to mention meals away from home.

American upper-middle-class life is dependent on immigrant workers performing tasks at wages no established resident would consider. Zoe Baird didn't need to hire an illegal immigrant to care for her child, she could have afforded to pay good wages. But most two-job families or single parents are not in Baird's income class. Immigrant wages for housecleaning, lawn mowing, child care, and even carwashing make work outside the home feasible for people who could otherwise not afford it. Those who dream of cities without poorly educated, low-wage immigrants should be required to describe what middle-class and even lower-middle-class life would be like without them. It can't be done, but the fantasy persists that a policy could be devised that welcomes the restaurant, hotel, and personal service workers on whom we obviously depend, but bans all others.

Another important industry that could not exist but for immigrants is horticulture. In a way, George Bush's inability to banish broccoli from health-conscious American diets is one cause of undocumented immigration. Harvest of corn, wheat, and other grains is mechanized, but fruit, vegetable, and nut horticulture, occupying only 1 percent of U.S. farmland, is labor intensive and consumes 40 percent of total farm wages. A broccoli crop, for example, requires fifty-two labor-hours per acre. According to agricultural economists Phil Martin and Edward Taylor, U.S. acreage devoted to broccoli increased by 50 percent in the 1980s as Americans' annual fresh broccoli consumption almost tripled to 4.5 pounds per person. Broccoli alone brought two thousand migrant farmworkers from rural Mexico to the United States. Other healthy fruits and vegetables had a similar impact; fresh tomato consumption jumped from thirteen to eighteen pounds per person, and U.S. production grew by 38 percent. Production of all vegetables combined rose by 33 percent, because even imports from countries like Mexico and Chile couldn't satiate Americans' hunger for more vitamins and roughage. Besides, Latin Americans also want to stay healthy. Carlos Salinas's goal of "exporting tomatoes, not tomato pickers" is frustrated by Mexicans' consumption of tomatoes at twice the per capita rate of Americans. Even rapid expansion of Mexican tomato acreage won't replace U.S. growers' demands for immigrant labor.

Bush did make something of a contribution to solving the problem. Since fresh vegetable consumption rises with upscale lifestyles, holding down personal income growth kept vegetable acreage from increasing even more than it did. Martin and Taylor report that fresh vegetables have high "elasticities"; in other words, a 1 percent increase in family income is associated with a 1 percent increase in broccoli and lettuce consumption and a 2.4 percent increase for cauliflower. So if the Clinton administration succeeds in reversing the trend of declining family income, Americans will eat even more veggies, requiring more rural immigrants, legal or not.

Factoring these kinds of variables into rational immigration rules is beyond the ability of any policy maker. We can let migrant workers in as the demand for vegetables expands, but how do we reduce the number of "guests" when demand contracts, and how can we require them to avoid enticing their brothers and cousins to join them? Communist governments were mostly successful at preventing workers from being employed without authorization, but no other governments have been able to do so.

There are also industries where immigrants do compete with natives, and this competition not only creates native unemployment but reduces wages for those who remain at work as well. Here's one example: fifteen years ago, residential drywallers—the people who erect plasterboard for interior home walls—were represented by the carpenters union in southern California. They averaged about $1,100 in weekly earnings, in today's dollars. Union drywall agreements required homebuilders to pay for full family health insurance. Each employer contributed to a vacation and pension fund for each hour worked. But in the late 1970s, contractors began to hire Mexican immigrants to work without union contract protection. Immigrant workers in turn recruited their friends and relatives, and by 1982 enough nonunion drywallers (many from just one town in rural Mexico) were available, and the contractors stopped hiring union labor altogether. With the carpenters union out of the picture, contractors also dropped their health insurance plans, stopped paying into vacation and pension funds, and cut wages. Contractors now dealt only with labor brokers who paid workers in cash and ignored income-tax withholding, Social Security, unemployment insurance, and minimum-wage laws. By 1992, drywallers worked nearly sixty hours a week to take home $300 in cash, with no benefits. In an atypical action, these undocumented immigrant construction workers went on strike to bring back the carpenters union. A clever union lawyer went after the contractors for minimum-wage violations and used the potential back-pay liability to leverage a strike settlement that included reinstatement of health insurance and a wage increase. Drywallers now earn about double what they got before the strike, and about half what nonimmigrant workers earned a decade earlier.

The construction industry where immigrants displaced native workers and the vegetable industry where no natives choose to work are extreme ends on a scale of displacement. Advocates of loosening border controls cite the former; advocates of tightening cite the latter. Some industries, like garment, can be cited by each. Fifteen years ago, undocumented immigrants fully displaced African-American garment workers in many cities, because the immigrants were willing to tolerate wages and conditions far below what legal workers were used to. In Los Angeles, for example, fifty-five thousand native garment workers were displaced by immigrants in the 1970s. But today, international competition in garment assembly has become so fierce that a domestic industry probably could not survive if it paid the wages of fifteen years ago. Can immigrants, therefore, be said to have displaced African-American workers in the garment industry? Yes and no.

It's probably the case that today, more immigrants are working in jobs natives don't want than in competitive occupations. But even though laid-off aerospace engineers don't normally seek work as gardeners or carwashers, this is a hard argument to make when unemployment is high and wages are declining. And the argument will become even harder if the proposals of some reformers—to increase the immigration of skilled workers—become law. Expanding legal immigration quotas for professional and technical workers will certainly increase competition for scarce jobs.

SOLUTIONS

Total border control is an unrealizable dream; it is impossible to calculate immigration flows to match domestic employment needs; and a variety of uncontrollable and unpredictable economic, political, and social developments in sending countries will, in any event, have a lot to do with the actual level of immigration. As candidate Clinton realized, we can't hope to design a coherent immigration policy. But there are piecemeal policies we can implement that address some of the problems, at least around the edges.

These reforms might, if we are lucky, combine with other political and economic developments to slow the "push" of immigrants from sending countries, provide some additional protection for native workers in those few industries where competition with immigrants is a reality, and encourage more honorable and responsible treatment of immigrants, who, in any event, will continue to arrive. It's not that stepped-up border patrols are entirely useless; it's just that we shouldn't delude ourselves into believing that massive national and international political and economic forces can be reversed by more vigilant policing.

One important reform would be a Mexican development program that goes beyond free trade. If we truly want less Mexican immigration, persuading the Mexican government to slow its agricultural liberalization would be one approach. Failing that, we could underwrite a targeted industrial policy in Mexico, which, in violation of free trade rules, would subsidize the development of small industries in rural areas where peasants are being displaced. Funds spent in this way might be more effective than hiring more border patrol agents.

Similarly, a more aggressive and earlier defense of Haiti's democratic government was, in retrospect, the only sensible (and morally decent) immigration policy we could have adopted with regard to that country's boat people. The civil wars in Central America and Indochina, whatever else they might have been, will ultimately have affected America most by raising immigration flows—as any tour through Salvadoran, Vietnamese, and Cambodian communities in California will attest. But these likely results are rarely considered when foreign policy is fashioned.

Better labor standards enforcement in this country would also address parts of the problem. If labor law had been reformed so it wasn't so easy for construction contractors to abandon their contractual relationships with trade unions, it might have been more difficult for immigrants to displace union members in California's homebuilding industry. Enforcement of minimum wage, health and safety, and other workplace rules could reduce, albeit only marginally, incentives for employers to substitute immigrants for natives in other industries where real competition takes place.

Higher labor standards in immigrant industries where native workers don't choose to work would also ameliorate political conflict over the unavoidable presence of undocumented workers. A national health insurance plan, for example, that covered all workers whether here legally or not, would relieve the burden of taxpayers to provide for immigrant health in public emergency rooms and hospitals. Minimum-wage enforcement in immigrant industries, along with a more hospitable climate for union organizing, would put more money into immigrant neighborhoods and increase their tax contributions to the broader community, while reducing immigrant use of welfare, food stamp, and similar benefits.

And also, of course, we could stop eating broccoli.

Editor's Note: This article has been edited for publication.

International Migration in the Nineties

Causes and Consequences

Gerald E. Dirks

Throughout the half-century that has elapsed since the end of World War II, governments, statesmen, academicians, and other informed observers of international politics have concentrated much of their attention on a comparatively short list of issues often described as matters of high politics. Among these issues were the search for military security, the prevention of nuclear proliferation, and the establishment of a dynamic, resilient international trading system. It was asserted that if these and other similar strategic issues of high politics could be resolved, global stability would be achieved as threats to state security diminished. The world thus witnessed what seemed to be an endless succession of multilateral and bilateral conferences which focused upon strategic arms limitation, international trade, Third World development, and other subjects thought to be germane to the over-riding question of achieving systemic stability and security. The pursuit of these activities absorbed world leaders and their officials, signifying the high priority such issue-areas had on the agendas of governments and international organizations alike.

But while attention was centered on these issues of high politics, other matters emerged and gradually assumed increased importance on these same agendas. New and unprecedented developments have come to be perceived as potential or even actual dangers to the attainment and maintenance of state security and systemic stability. Heading the current list of issues previously considered to be matters of low politics is the intensifying pressures arising from international migration which have especially captured the attention of the world's more affluent developed states.

Humanity has always migrated, whether from valley to neighbouring valley or from continent to continent. The practice of seeking out more commodious habitation sites, whether by nomadic peoples in ancient times or by white-collar professionals today, is a process well known to students of human behaviour. This article examines how contemporary migration across state

International Journal, XLVIII, Spring 1993, 191–214.

boundaries differs from traditional movements and thus poses new problems for the people migrating as well as for the governments both of their states of origin and of the countries to which they seek admission. After briefly describing the present global situation, the article will analyze the causes behind the present-day surge in the pressure for international migration and provide an overview of the consequences this phenomenon is expected to have for both sending and receiving states. Migrants in the context of this article include both appropriately documented persons, be they temporary contract workers or traditional permanent immigrants, and undocumented individuals who are categorized as illegal aliens.

I

At the outset, it is essential to recognize that neither the governments nor the citizens of developed states are especially surprised or alarmed by the migratory process itself. They are, however, astonished and dismayed by the intensity of current migratory pressures and the massive unregulated nature of the flow which is already apparent and is expected to grow. In fact, the flow of migrants across state boundaries in the 1980s was no greater than that during the late nineteenth and early twentieth centuries. Then, millions of Europeans formed a flood of humanity searching for more satisfying economic conditions in the enthusiastic immigrant-receiving countries of North and South America along with Australia and New Zealand. What has changed as the twentieth century draws to a close are the extent to which the profound desire to migrate has deepened, the enormous number of people exhibiting this desire, and the unprecedented erection of legislative and other barriers aimed at limiting or even preventing massive, unwanted, self-selected international migration. The seemingly insatiable urge to escape from undesirable economic, social, and political circumstances, primarily found in the less developed countries (LDCs), is today matched by the growing unwillingness of the developed countries to cope with a perceived potential tidal wave of unwanted newcomers. Rather than meaningfully addressing the multiple, complex causes giving rise to crossborder and intercontinental migration from the LDCs, developed states are establishing controls to regulate and even prohibit the entry of aliens. The actions of the 'have' governments seem to indicate that, in their view, the magnitude of illegal migration will substantially depend upon the ease with which it can occur.

Before identifying and analysing the causes of these migratory pressures, a brief overview of the contemporary global situation with respect to population mobility and growth would seem in order. There are no exact figures on the number of people annually departing, either temporarily or permanently, from their states of origin or habitual residence. One estimate considered to be reasonably accurate insists that between 70 and 80 million people were, by the late 1980s, on the move in one way or another. These millions can be placed into somewhat imprecise categories. For example, in recent years, somewhat in excess of 1 million persons annually immigrate legally into the world's traditional receiving countries where they are considered permanent residents. The principal countries of destination for this category of migrant are the United States which admits at least 70 per cent of them. Canada which accepts close to 20 per cent, and Australia and New Zealand which receive most of the remainder. Temporary residents form another category and include fixed-term skilled and unskilled contract labourers, transient professionals accepting short-term assignments, and a growing number of their dependents. A third category consists of political refugees, as defined in the 1951 United Nations Convention Relating to the Status of Refugees, and its 1967 protocol. Here again, estimates of the total number in this category vary, but experts believe there are between 12 and 15 million. The final category is composed of undocumented, and therefore illegal, migrants. Their number is unknown but certainly runs into the millions. The United States alone is presumed to have a minimum of 2 to 3 million illegal migrants, most of whom are Mexican nationals. It is widely believed that the already substantial world migration, originating largely in the LDCs and directed towards the comparatively affluent countries of the North, is just the bare tip of the iceberg. A number of factors support this conclusion including the current size and expected growth of the global population. A few current statistics and projections provide the justification for this view.

The world's human population, as of mid-1992, stood at approximately 5.5 billion and is increasing annually at a rate of 1.7 per cent or between 90 and 100 million persons. It is expected to reach 8.5 billion by 2025. Almost 95 per cent of this growth is occurring in the LDCs with Africa's rate of 3 per cent being the highest. While the annual population growth in all the LDCs, excluding China, stands at 2.3 per cent, the rate for developed countries approximates 0.5 per cent annually. The rate of population growth in the LDCs during the past generation has been substantially more than double that of the developed countries. Even should the LDC rate begin to level off or decline, the impact of the earlier growth will persist, especially as young people reach the age of employment. South Asia's population growth rate stands at 2.2 per cent, leading to the expectation that the region's population will double in the next forty years. At the same time, the population of the Gulf and Middle East region is growing annually at a rate exceeding 2.6 per cent while the rate in Latin America and the Caribbean area stands at 2.1 per cent. Another dimension of population growth in the in the LDCs is the movement from rural to urban settings. Between 1950 and 1985 urban centres in the LDCs increased in size fourfold, accommodating a combined population in the latter year of almost 1.2 billion. Needless to say, such enormous urban growth could not be matched by the development of an adequate service infrastructure.

Inhabitants of the LDCs do not see migration merely as a desirable option. Rather they regard it as an essential course of action in response not only to their burgeoning populations but also to what the demographic realities represent in terms of ever shrinking employment opportunities. To illustrate, in the countries of the European Community there are only 3 children not yet in their teens for every 10 adults over the age of sixty-five. The societies of Europe and the traditional immigration countries of North America and Australasia are aging, promising to place previously unknown strains on public pension and health care schemes. By contrast, in the countries of sub-Saharan Africa (admittedly the region of the world with the fastest growing population), there are an estimated 159 pre-teen children for every 10 adults at or above the age of sixty-five. Taking all the LDCs together, estimates suggest that up to 20 per cent of the present population is between the ages of fifteen and twenty-four, all anxious to find jobs where they simply do not exist today. Literally tens of millions of jobs would be needed in the LDCs to meet the mammoth demand for employment created by their exceedingly young populations. One consequence is that, as of 1989, an estimated 10 per cent of the population of sub-Saharan Africa was already residing either temporarily or permanently outside their country of birth in the hope of finding employment. While the migratory patterns are not exclusively from the LDCs to the industrialized states of the North—substantial migration does occur among countries of the South—the urge to resettle in a developed country nevertheless remains uppermost. In consequence, even Japan, usually considered to be a closed xenophobic community when it came to foreign labourers, has at least 100,000 to 150,000 illegal migrants. Some estimates, indeed, place the figure as high as 300,000.

The South's already large population, combined with the prevailing high birth rates in the LDCs, goes a long way towards explaining why pressures for international migration have noticeably intensified and will only mount still further. In the view of a Canadian foreign policy planner, 'rapid population growth together with poverty cripples economic development, environmental sustainability is menaced, political and social structures are corroded, and authoritarian reaction against feared unrest blocks progress in human rights.' The urge to migrate is thereby enhanced, and the likelihood of rising social tension threatening societal cohesion in the developed countries where many LDC migrants would prefer to reside is increased. There may even be the potential for increased danger to international peace and stability.

Additional statistical information about present and future population size could be cited. These data, however, clearly delineate one of the primary factors contributing to migratory pressures, for in many instances other causes of migration stem largely from the population issue.

II

The current size of the world's population and related factors in the LDCs undoubtedly account for a good deal of the migration fever at present being directed by nationals of poorer states to the more affluent, politically stable countries of the North. Yet it would be too simplistic and one-dimensional to suggest that its causes are exclusively related to the actual or expected population size of a country or region. The reasons for migration are complex and multidimensional. It is more usual for many causes to combine to create an irrepressible urge to migrate, whether temporarily or permanently. Trying to explain human motives—never an easy task—is particularly difficult when examining such a major personal decision as pulling up one's roots and moving, often to a distant and unfamiliar land.

In the most general sense, the causes behind human migration are deeply embedded in the economic, political, and social conditions of our times. It is by no means clear that governments and their publics, or even so-called experts for that matter, truly grasp the fundamental complexity of the multiple motives impelling societal migration. However, there is general agreement on the most common causes for human population movement which are conventionally divided, somewhat simplistically, into push and pull forces. It is believed that the decisions of actual or potential migrants are influenced by a combination of these repelling and attracting factors. Among the push factors, in addition to population pressure,are the absence or lack of employment opportunities, non-existent or inadequate public services such as health care and schools, and, increasingly, incidents of environmental degradation. In addition, the need to migrate continues to be felt by countless numbers of people experiencing traditional hardships arising out of the only too common phenomenon of state-directed or state-condoned political persecution and oppression in an era where a desire for the personal freedoms associated with liberal democracy is mounting. In some instances, one of these causes may be dominant, but it is more likely that several of these conditions combine to precipitate planned or even spontaneous migration. Literally millions of people are finding intractable conditions intolerable in the overcrowded and under-serviced cities of Africa, Asia, and Latin America where opportunities for employment are meagre or non-existent. Low wages blend with poor social conditions to create feelings of despair and hopelessness among vast numbers of people in the LDCs which fuel their desire to leave, even if conditions in the proposed destination are uncertain and possibly only marginally more attractive. Poverty, with its seemingly inescapable corollaries of hunger and inadequate public health and educational facilities, in an era where little probability of amelioration exists causes the young and the not so young to crave improvement. Conservative estimates indicate that in sub-Saharan Africa alone, 7.5

million new jobs need to be created before the close of this century to bring some hope of employment to the region's masses of young people. Another projection, this one still more alarming, estimates that as many at 730 million people world-wide will be entering the labour market by 2010.

Today, through the revolutionary changes in communications, the nationals of the LDCs know how poorly their lives stack up when compared with those of persons residing in the industrialized states of the North. People experiencing the many hardships of life in the LDCs now realize that there could be a better world in which they can live a more fulfilling existence and in which their own children might have a chance of acquiring more benefits. A frequent accompaniment to poverty, and all that goes with it, is social unrest resulting in many instances from ethnic tensions in diverse areas of the world. Internecine stress acts as a type of persistent 'white noise' which, over time, erodes the spirit and contributes another ingredient to the list of factors giving rise to population movement. Widespread economic and social instability within many LDCs constitutes the basis for a fear of emerging violence and encourages still more growth in migratory pressures.

Political oppression and persecution are persistent causes of population movement. When governments carry out or condone acts which threaten the physical, emotional, and economic well-being of specific segments of society, escape may appear the only option to persons in these situations. The twentieth century abounds in instances in which citizens of a state have felt compelled to flee from a government intent on pursuing programmes of imprisonment or worse against them for a variety of reasons. Frequently, the actual or well-founded fear of persecution, imprisonment, and even death is based upon religious, racial, or political intolerance. In such circumstances, substantial numbers of people may flee from their habitual country of residence in search of a temporary or permanent sanctuary in a neighbouring or more distant state. During the past decade alone, perceived threats to their safety have led millions of people to flee from Afghanistan, Cambodia, and Iran as well as from several countries in the Horn of Africa and sub-Saharan Africa. The vast majority of the world's political refugees over the past quarter-century have been produced by circumstances in the LDCs and have been granted shelter, often reluctantly by other LDCs, which are in no position to absorb such an influx of unwanted aliens.

Among the many and diverse causes for contemporary international migration, several are well known even to persons not especially knowledgable about the phenomenon. Over-population, under- or unemployment, and political oppression along with persecution and social unrest are issues repeatedly covered by the media in the developed countries of the North. Environmental degradation is a less widely recognized cause of migration, but it is already an important factor in explaining a growing proportion of internal and international migration and it is expected to become even more significant before the end of the century. This comparatively new condition is creating more and more environmental refugees, as they have come to be labelled. Since the dust bowl conditions on the North American plains gave rise to migration during the 1930s, environmental degradation has escalated world-wide and caused population movement on all continents.

Environmental refugees are, consequently, a growing category of dislocated persons in search of safe habitation. While the conditions that cause this type of migration may be of short duration—as in the case of such catastrophic events as earthquakes and floods—there are more and more long-term environmental factors compelling population shifts. There now are areas of the world, primarily but not exclusively in the LDCs, that can no longer support sustained human settlement. Data are still unavailable on how many people migrate primarily because of an inadequate water supply, spreading desertification, uncontrollable soil erosion, depletion of fuel for cooking and heating, or various forms of air pollution. Estimates in the late 1980s ranged as high as 10 million. By the early years of the next century, environmental refugees conceivably could outnumber the still enormous total figure of those traditionally defined political refugees. And for every environmental migrant or refugee, there are hundreds whose lives and daily existence are compromised because of unhealthy or hazardous conditions. To illustrate, should global warming lead to a rise in the world's oceans of as little as one metre, millions of people, primarily on the densely populated deltas of the Nile and Ganges rivers, will need to be permanently relocated. Desertification, a condition similar to the dust bowl of the 1930s in North America, is resulting in mass hunger. Again drawing upon Africa to illustrate, as is done so often when identifying many human tragedies and predicaments, an estimated 135 million people occupy lands that are well on their way to desertification.

One of the precursors of migration across state boundaries is the shift of sizable population groups from predominantly rural settings to urban centres, frequently though not always as a result of mounting environmental problems. In West Africa, for example, where uncontrolled deforestation has depleted the fuel available for cooking and the erosion of soil has curtailed agricultural pursuits, an estimated 20 per cent of Mauritania's population migrated into towns during the 1980s. Similar conditions triggered movements in Mali and Niger where 5 to 10 per cent of the total population has become dependent on food assistance from abroad. Often the overcrowding of inadequately serviced urban centres will lead to a further population shift, this time across boundaries to neighbouring states where conditions are thought to be better, or to more distant destinations in the affluent states of the North. Most migrants relocate in nearby countries usually because they lack the personal wealth and overall confidence to travel the vast intercontinental distances to the unfamiliar states of the North. Furthermore, the societies in neighbouring countries often have similar cultures and languages and their permeable borders facilitate relocation to these communities. Those nationals of LDCs who do make the journey to the industrialized Northern states tend to have at least a little personal wealth, a certain level of formal education, and possibly even a needed skill. These migrants thus constitute examples of the 'brain drain,' a segment of their populations developing states cannot afford to lose if they are to have any chance of closing the economic gap separating the South from the North. The majority of the migrants choosing to move among the LDCs are undocumented or illegal and no exact figure is therefore available but it is believed to be in the millions.

While the most intense migratory pressures today emanate from the states of the South, the phenomenon can also be detected in the countries of eastern Europe including several republics of the former Soviet Union. This has given rise to additional anxiety not only among the governments of the traditional states of immigration but also, indeed especially, among those of western Europe. With the recent demise of the closed authoritarian system in eastern and central Europe, obstacles to leaving the environmentally damaged and economically and ethnically troubled areas of this region disappeared. Prior to the collapse of the former regimes, ideological and philosophical factors had been the primary cause of whatever emigration did occur. These causes have now been replaced by the economic and ethnic anxieties of millions of the region's inhabitants. As the 1990s began, estimates of how many people might migrate from the former Soviet Union ranged as high as 8 million. It was assumed by many observers that the nearby affluence of western Europe would be too strong a magnet for the despairing people of eastern Europe to resist. In fact, a comparatively low number of 350,000 emigrated from the Soviet Union during 1990. Even though the movement has not become an uncontrollable flood, sizable migration from eastern Europe is expected during the next few years, especially if economic and ethnic turmoil remains unmanaged.

What have come to be the expected or traditional causes for population movements also continue to be relevant today. Among these are social motives including a desire for family reunification, a wish for social and political tranquility, and an unquenchable thirst for adventure, particularly among the young. Relationships leading to social networks develop and are maintained among persons who have temporarily migrated internationally and have returned, often with earnings, to tell others about their experiences—thus generating further migration. Different networks are formed over long distances between migrants who may not return home as quickly, or at all. Family members or friends still at home are encouraged to try their hand at seeking employment as contract labourers or in some other type of work abroad. During the 1980s an increasing number of women embarked as temporary or permanent migrants, either as the vanguard for other family members or as the suppliers of remittances that were sent home to support family members.

Social causes for migration can also include a search for better educational opportunities, a desire to remain with a loved one, or a need to explore beyond one's own land with peers in that time-honoured hunt for adventure and the better life.

The causes behind migration include pull factors as well push factors. The belief that a better way of life is possible surely is the broadest sort of pull force. Put more specifically, the heart-felt conviction that employment opportunities exist beyond one's immediate surroundings has a power comparable to magnetic attraction. Such a profound belief on the part of the would-be migrant frequently has its basis in the experiences of friends and family members who have found jobs abroad. They return, or write about their adventures, often describing their employment in somewhat exaggerated terms. Friends and kin, hearing about such glorious economic possibilities, are inexorably drawn by the chance not just of acquiring work but of earning in one day what it would take a month to obtain, if employment were available, at home.

Since the early 1960s in western Europe, and over a still longer time in the United States, there have been enough examples of available employment to fuel the aspirations of would-be migrants from the LDCs. Several countries in western Europe, led by Switzerland and what then was West Germany, embarked upon extensive 'guest worker' schemes under which hundreds of thousands of foreign labourers were welcomed, chiefly from Turkey and other poorer states around the Mediterranean. Even though guest worker contracts were for one- to two-year periods, many labourers remained and brought their dependents. Subsequently, migrants in search of work but without appropriate documentation reached these and other industrialized states of the North from South Asia, North Africa, and the Middle East. In the western hemisphere, hundreds of thousands of unskilled Mexicans seeking employment routinely entered the United States, often illegally and frequently only for temporary stays. In years when their economies were buoyant, governments of receiving countries took little if any action against illegal entrants, a signal which potential migrants from the LDCs interpreted as an open invitation to follow their peers and relatives. By the late 1980s, the movement of legal and illegal migrants to western Europe had become a flood and at the close of 1990, the number of foreigners residing in western and southern Europe exceeded 15.5 million. Among these foreigners were millions of asylum seekers who had made claims for refugee status. As many as 80 per cent of those whose claims were found to be fraudulent were never deported, in stark contradiction to the rhetoric emanating from government spokespersons.

Despite massive unprecedented immigration during the past decade, certain menial jobs, shunned by Europeans, still remain to be filled, a well-known fact among LDC nationals. These openings, not only in western Europe but in other industrialized countries of the North, are to be found in the agricultural, child care, custodial, and cleaning sectors. Many small enterprises eagerly employ illegal migrants at low, frequently exploitative wage rates. Even these types of jobs remain attractive to LDC migrants.

To be sure, for much of the past few decades, foreign labourers from the LDCs contributed significantly to the prosperity of the Northern industrial states. What may be less well known is that LDC migrant labourers were a significant factor helping the economic expansion and diversification of many petroleum-producing countries including Nigeria and those in the Gulf region. As much as 75 per cent of the work force in the Gulf states during the 1980s were composed of contractual foreign labour, primarily from Middle East countries but also from Bangladesh, Pakistan, and Indonesia. The sending states have in some instances welcomed the temporary emigration of a portion of their surplus labour force. First, exporting excess labour supplied a safety valve, lessening if not eliminating the basis for social unrest resulting from popular frustration provoked by chronic unemployment. Second, a substantial number of LDCs—as many as 60 by some accounts—depend on remittances as a meaningful component of annual national revenue.

The causes of transborder migration, both push and pull, are numerous and often inter-related. While economic factors head the list of motives explaining migration, political, social, and psychological reasons are also important. No matter what the cause, the extraordinary scope of the actual and potential population movement has and will continue to have considerable consequences for the governments and societies of sending and receiving states alike. It is to those issues this article now turns.

III

As with the causes of international migration, the consequences of this phenomenon are numerous, varied, and frequently interconnected. The impact of sizable population movements affects originating and receiving states differently. Moreover, the repercussions vary depending upon whether the migration is temporary or permanent.

To begin, it would seem appropriate to identify and examine some of the effects that temporary or permanent emigration may have on sending states. First, remittance, at least in the short term, may have the most positive implications for the originating state because nationals often send significant portions of their foreign earnings to their families. In most instances, these funds are used to purchase goods and services and thus soon enter the local economy. Second, the 'brain drain' may have a major negative bearing on the LDCs as citizens with potentially needed skills depart, possibly permanently, to earn in an industrialized state of the North what would be an unattainable income in their home country. Third, the lessening of social, political, and other forms of pressure within LDC societies through emigration may function as a type of safety valve which can eliminate a segment of the state's excess population. Finally, returnees, persons who choose to migrate only for a temporary period, have their own special impact on their home society and state.

While remittances do provide additional spending power for persons fortunate enough to receive them, thereby assisting segments of the local economy, their impact is nonetheless considered to be rather limited. For example, there is little if any evidence to support the view that remittances sent home by contract labourers or illegal immigrants act to forestall or retard additional migration or contribute to the economic development of LDCs. In the view of two American students of contemporary population movements: 'International migration for employment, whether officially organized or self motivated but facilitated by ethnic networks, is not a short cut to effective development, notwithstanding often substantial remittances. Instead, such migration often distorts a country's development in ways that guarantee continued migration pressures.' Labour migration may forge new links between originating and receiving countries but seldom closes the economic gaps which consequently continue to encourage persons to migrate. Originating countries complain that they 'get the glitter coins of remittances but little development.' Having remittances suddenly and unexpectedly terminated can nevertheless have a major negative impact on the local economy. This occurred during 1990 and 1991 when hundreds of thousands of foreign contract workers in the Gulf region who were providing remittances were expelled or required to leave the countries where they had been gainfully employed.

The term 'brain drain' brings to mind the image of vast numbers of highly trained and educated individuals emigrating from LDCs. While this stereotype has some validity, the concept as used here is more inclusive. The cream of an originating state's work force can be skimmed off by some or all the causes discussed previously. The best and brightest people, including manual workers, depart, leaving their homelands substantially worse off.

Rising emigration from the LDCs may provide a useful safety valve in certain circumstances. Societal stability may be preserved through short- or long-term emigration where unemployment among young adults entering the labour force is high, where the state's health and education infrastructure is inadequate to serve a rapidly growing population, or where the departure of large numbers of government opponents removes the likelihood of politically oppressive measures being introduced by the authorities. The ability to emigrate, whether or not it is exercised, may be just enough to avert destructive turmoil within many overpopulated countries.

The final consequence to be considered here is the effect returned migrants have on their states of origin. As with the causes for emigration, the reasons why persons return to their homelands are numerous and interconnected. Most who do return always intended to do so. They had only migrated to find employment, to earn more than they could at home, or to acquire an education or a particular skill. These returnees may not always be seen as providing any real material benefit to their country. Seldom have they enough capital to invest in any new enterprise that could create even a moderate number of jobs. Furthermore, only occasionally do returnees possess needed managerial and supervisory skills. At best, they may have returned with just enough financial resources to start a small retail business employing themselves and conceivably one or two other family members.

While mass migration undoubtedly has significant consequences, both positive and negative, for the LDCs, the attention of most Northern journalists, governments, and societies remains fixed on its effects on the North. Governments and their constituents in western, and to an increasing extent in southern, Europe, along with the few remaining traditional states of immigration have become genuinely alarmed over the consequences they experience as a result of intensifying South-North and growing East-West migration. The repercussions in these countries are profound and can be roughly arranged into economic, social, and political categories. Yet, no matter what particular class the consequence falls into, virtually all have provoked governmental efforts to increase the amount of control so as to restrict entry of unwanted, often undocumented, migrants. The implementation of increasingly illiberal regulations is driven by a desire to reassure the publics of receiving states. Although they have the appearance of hindering the entry of irregular migrants, experience shows that government moves to tighten entry requirements frequently do not halt the influx of refugee claimants, asylum seekers, and other undocumented migrants in search of jobs. Human ingenuity when combined with an urgent need to escape from impossible conditions merely leads to the use of hitherto untried channels by desperate migrants. The situation escalates as governments, seeing their efforts to control admissions circumvented, introduce ever more restrictive controls.

The economic consequences of contemporary international migration are as complex and interconnected as other aspects of this phenomenon. The primary economic implications resulting from interstate migration to the industrialized North are in the labour market. Among the member-countries of the Organization for Economic Co-operation and Development—the countries receiving the vast majority of all categories of migrants—liberalized international trade in goods and services has been a persistent objective since World War II. Migration, except among the member-states of the European Community, remains the major exception to this otherwise widespread economic liberalism. Whether immigrants are wanted by receiving countries temporarily or permanently, governments jealously cling to their belief, based on a rigid view of classical sovereignty, that they have the sole right to recruit and select necessary newcomers. Self-selection, the approach characteristic of many of today's interstate migrants, is condemned by the same governments that endlessly negotiate for the reduction or removal of trade barriers. These governments want to control the entry of foreign labourers who continue to be needed in unskilled occupations that remain unattractive to their indigenous populations. In some instances, the often unwelcome foreign workers are essential to maintaining high levels of employment among the native labour force. Thus, excluding all migrants is not in the best interest of receiving societies or their governments.

The economic impact of migration on the receiving states of western Europe extends well beyond the labour market. The costs to the community of providing basic services such as access to health care and education for dependents is seen as a major unwanted economic consequence of excessive migration. Moreover, because European receiving countries are still stubbornly refusing to conceive of themselves as immigration societies, they resist the expenditures associated with the public programmes aimed at trying to integrate foreigners that are commonplace in traditional immigration states such as Canada and Australia.

The social consequences of intensifying international migration in the receiving states of the North are somewhat less tangible than the economic ones. In countries with ethnically homogeneous populations and without any immigration tradition or experience, nativist and xenophobic tendencies are noticeable. In Germany, and to a lesser but still significant extent in France, Italy, and Spain, intolerance of migrants has manifested itself in the adoption of anti-alien policies by both mainstream and new extremist parties.

As routinely occurred in traditional states of immigration, contemporary newcomers to Europe have settled in close proximity to each other, creating ethnic ghettoes. Moreover, as the number of migrants from the LDCs increases, they constitute a burgeoning visible minority, fueling the intolerance only too close to the surface in many societies. Feelings of insecurity are exacerbated by the birth rate among the non-European migrants which tends to be markedly higher than that of receiving societies. For countries with comparatively small populations, any actual or potential influx of foreigners provokes anxiety in the indigenous society which believes its own culture to be endangered. Some European communities fear for the continued maintenance of a way of life with which they have grown comfortable. This perspective, drawing upon a variant of the overcrowded lifeboat analogy, asserts that the receiving society has no further capacity to absorb massive numbers of unneeded newcomers. Despite the inadequacy of the housing and health facilities in those European countries which do not perceive themselves as traditional states of immigration (such as Germany and France where sizable numbers of irregular migrants are being accommodated), however, they are still superior to those that foreigners have left behind.

The political consequences of migration in the receiving states arise in large part from the economic and social factors. The vital political issue of entitlements, one increasingly comprehensive political factor, is receiving increased attention in both traditional and non-traditional states of immigration. At its root, the fundamental question associated with entitlements is what distinctions if any should be made between the citizens of a country and migrants, whether legal or illegal, when it comes to the provision of basic political rights or access to such state services as unemployment insurance, health care, and welfare schemes. Should undocumented migrants be eligible for language or vocational training programmes without first having to pay a fee? Should the credentials of foreign professionals be automatically accepted by the receiving society? These and similar questions have become incendiary issues, especially within reluctant European accommodating societies. Some non-governmental and United Nations agencies, interested in human rights issues, have expressed concern over whether or not these frequently unwelcome migrants are being denied legal protection and excluded from programmes even though the governments of the states in question have been signatories to international conventions prohibiting such treatment. The inability of migrants to acquire citizenship in their adopted country even after many years of productive contributions to that society is held up as an example of how persons born elsewhere are discriminated against. Even in liberal democratic states, the matter of what constitutes basic rights for migrants may not be beyond controversy.

The escalating contemporary migration phenomenon has found its way onto the agendas of a growing number of multilateral conferences. Initially European governments but subsequently those of Canada, the United States, and Australia recognized that intensifying migration pressures could be most effectively managed through co-operative actions among receiving states. As western Europe was the first region to feel the impact of growing South-North and East-West migration, and as most of the states affected were members of the European Community, a multilateral approach to deal with the situation came quite naturally. By the mid-1980s, the Office of the United Nations High Commissioner for Refugees also had come to focus on the thousands of asylum seekers striving to enter and remain in western and southern Europe. The migrants often professed to be refugees but the status determination systems in the receiving states found the vast majority of these claims to be invalid although the numbers actually deported remained small. This migration issue did not comfortably fall within the purview of the high commissioner's office, yet 'first world' governments were resistant to the establishment of still another multilateral agency to deal with the matter. Ultimately, what has come to be known as the Informal Consultations Group was established, composed initially of European governments and joined, by the late 1980s, by Canada, the United States, and Australia. The group remains unstructured, functioning chiefly as a consultative body which attempts to ensure that receiving states are aware of each other's migration policies with the underlying expectation of formulating quite similar regulations for admissions. This harmonization, of course, was demanded within the European Community as, at the start of 1993, all twelve members had to implement common policies in a number of subject areas. It is too soon to determine whether this most recent form of migration policy co-ordination among Community members is having the desired effect.

IV

This article has identified and analysed the more significant causes for and consequences of intensifying contemporary migration. The array of factors motivating hundreds of thousands of persons to migrate annually, either temporarily or permanently, from one state to another is diverse and still expanding. There is no indication that the conditions which today result in major population movements are about to alter. If anything, the economic gap is widening between the comparatively affluent, stable countries and the less developed, precarious ones. At this time, governments of sending states have little if any incentive to adopt policies that might discourage short- or long-term emigration. In fact, a case can be made that such countries may even promote or at least not hinder population outflows.

At the same time, despite efforts to control arrivals, the governments of receiving states have not by any means succeeded in regulating the entry of undocumented aliens. A study appearing in a publication of the International Labour Office has gone so far as to state that 'policy makers appear to be waiting for some panacea that simply does not exist.' The measures that have been employed have not addressed the profound determination of would-be migrants to leave their undesirable circumstances and share in some of the benefits prevailing in the states of the North.

To the disappointment of observers, sending and receiving governments have done little to formulate a common or even a compatible approach to irregular migration. To date, multilateral consultation and co-operation, occurring exclusively among receiving governments, has been the dominant response pattern. The focus remains on preventing unmanaged migration rather than on alleviating the obvious causes in the LDCs which provoke it. Conventional wisdom has suggested the best approach, possibly the only acceptable approach, to unauthorized South-North migration is massive development in the LDCs to remove the economic incentives behind migration. This course of action conceivably could succeed, but experts assert that it would require a willingness on the part of industrialized states to accept the principles contained in the long-proposed New International Economic Order. Even then, it would be decades before the level of development reached the point where migratory pressures would decrease significantly. Unprecedented large-scale economic development nevertheless remains the only realistic solution to what may become an even greater exodus of migrants from the South as well as from eastern Europe and the republics of the former Soviet Union.

Editor's Note: This article has been edited for publication.

United States Policy Towards Asian Immigrants

Contemporary Developments in Historical Perspective

Roger Daniels

The publication of figures from the 1990 United States census showed that there had been a rapid increase in persons of Hispanic and Asian birth or ancestry living in the United States. When combined with a large but relatively static African American population, these statistics helped to set off a wave of confused press speculation and 'scare' stories about the country having a 'non-white' majority as early as the middle of the twenty-first century. What the data actually showed was that white persons made up some four-fifths of the population, blacks about an eighth, Hispanics abut an eleventh, and Asians less than a thirty-third (table 1). Some of the confusion stemmed from the way in which the Census Bureau listed its figures. Many journalists and others added up all of the non-white figures to get a false total of 28.6 per cent non-white. This was a flawed calculation. All the Hispanics had already been counted in other totals: as an often ignored Census Bureau footnote cryptically reminds us. Hispanics—an amalgam that includes persons of Mexican and Central and South American heritage as well as Cubans, Puerto Ricans, Dominicans, and some other Caribbean peoples—had already been classified as either black or white. In addition, the 9.8 million persons who were classified as 'other' were not of some strange race but persons who had either given 'wrong' ethnic information—that is, not using the bureau's criteria—or had left the ancestry part of their questionnaires blank. In previous censuses, procedures for what the bureau calls 'allocation and audit' have resulted in an eventual classification of more than 90 per cent of such persons as white, and there is no reason to believe that the final result in this census will be any different.

International Journal, Volume 48, Spring 1993, 310–334.

Table 1   Population of the United States by 'race,' 1990 census

Race	Percentage		Millions
White	80.3	ca	200.4
Black	12.1	ca	30.2
Asian/Pacific Islander	2.9	ca	7.3
American Indian, Eskimo, Aleut	0.8	ca	2.0
Other	3.9	ca	9.8
[Hispanic	8.9		22.4]

SOURCE: United States, Census, 1990 (preliminary).

Table 2   Asian American population of the United States, 1950–90

Year	Number
1950	599,091
1960	877,934
1970	1,429,562
1980	3,466,421
1990	7,272,662

SOURCE: United States, Census reports.

Nevertheless, the non-white and Hispanic elements of the population were clearly growing at a faster rate than the population of the United States as a whole. Between 1980 and 1990 the total population had increased about 10 per cent. For the same period the number of whites grew about 6 per cent, blacks more than 13 per cent, American Indians about 38 per cent, the Hispanic population some 53 per cent, and the Asian population more than doubled. The greater rates of increase were due largely to immigration and, in the case of some of the groups, to a higher rate of natural increase.

Although most of the 'scare' stories were evoked by the numbers on Hispanic elements in the population, the growth of the Asian population in recent years has been spectacular, as the figures in table 2 demonstrate. While some of this growth is illusory, resulting from the admission of Hawaii to statehood and the subsequent inclusion of its large Asian American population from 1960 on, the vast majority of this growth—more than 1,100 per cent in four decades—consists of recent immigrants and their descendants. Emigration from Asia, historically a minuscule portion of all immigration into the United States, began to grow in statistical significance after the end of World War II. In the 1950s Asians comprised 6 per cent of all legal immigrants: that percentage rose to 12 per cent between 1981 and 1989.

If one looks retrospectively at the data it would be only natural to conclude that, sometime after World War II, a conscious decision to increase the incidence of Asian immigrants had been taken at the highest levels of the American government. However, no such decision was taken, and it is all but certain that no one, either official or academic, had the slightest notion that the crucial changes effected in American immigration law between 1943 and 1965 would result in a large influx of Asians. While it would not be accurate to claim, as is often alleged about Britain's acquisition of its empire, that the changes in immigration policy were made 'in a fit of absence of mind,' it is nevertheless true that some of the results of those changes were undreamed of. To understand why these changes came about, we must, at least briefly, examine the evolution of American immigration policy.

IMMIGRATION POLICY TO 1952

Although Asians, almost all of whom were Chinese, were not very numerous in the United States in the late nineteenth century—constituting less than one-tenth of one per cent of the population—their presence was crucial in the formation of the nation's immigration policy. The first significant restriction of free immigration into the United States was the Chinese Exclusion Act of 1882 which forbade the entry of 'Chinese laborers' for a period of ten years. Renewed for another ten years in 1892, this ban was made permanent in 1902. Chinese were thus the first group to be excluded, and it can be argued that the 1882 act was the hinge on which all of American immigration policy turned. From that time until 1924, the once free and unrestricted immigration policy of the United States was repeatedly curtailed on economic, cultural, and political grounds.

Asians other than the Chinese were the second ethnic target. The rise of a Japanese immigrant population—72,00 by 1910, with more than 40,000 in California created a strong demand for a Japanese exclusion act, the first calls for which had come about 1892 when there were fewer than 5,000 Japanese in the whole country. Japan's growing military power caused the American government to negotiate an executive agreement—the so-called Gentlemen's Agreement of 1907–8—which slowed but did not totally stop the immigration of Japanese. In February 1917, on the eve of American entry into World War I, Congress excluded most Asians under a 'barred zone' provision which, because of the Gentlemen's Agreement, pointedly did not affect Japan. Nor, in the field of analysis, were Filipinos affected, as the federal courts ruled that as long as the Philippines was an American colony, its inhabitants—though not citizens—were 'American nationals' and could not be excluded. Although it is too much to argue, as E. P. Hutchinson has, that the 1917 law was 'an unmistakable declaration of a white immigration policy'—immigration from the Caribbean was not inhibited—it was a sign of things to come.

In addition, to these laws on immigration per se, the little-remarked American naturalization statutes had long discriminated against Asians. The original 1790 statute limited naturalization to 'free white persons,' but, in practice, dozens of Asians were naturalized in the nineteenth century. In 1868, during the first reconstruction period, the fourteenth amendment to the Constitution not only made the former slaves citizens but provided that all persons 'born . . . in the United States' were citizens: two years later, Congress passed a statute which expanded naturalization to 'white persons and persons of African descent.' An attempt at this time by the radical Republican senator, Charles Sumner of Massachusetts, to make naturalization colour blind failed as the majority in Congress wished to deny Chinese the right of naturalization. The 1882 Exclusion Act thus specified that 'no . . . court shall admit Chinese to citizenship,' and it was subsequently assumed that all Asians were 'aliens ineligible to citizenship.' The United States Supreme Court confirmed the bar in two cases in 1922 and 1923.

General immigration regulations had also begun in 1882 when a small head tax was levied on each incoming immigrant to 'defray the expense of regulating immigration . . . and for the care [and relief] of immigrants.' By 1917 American policy had created six different grounds for excluding non-Asian immigrants: certain criminals, contract labourers, persons who failed to meet certain moral standards, persons with various diseases, certain radicals, and illiterates. Congress and the nation were in a pronounced nativist, that is, anti-foreign, mood in the post-World War I years that John Higham has dubbed the 'tribal twenties.' The House of Representatives actually went so far as to vote a one-year ban on all immigration, but the Senate refused to go along. Congress did pass a one-year 'First Quota Act' in 1921 and eventually extended it until 1924, when the act 'To Limit the Immigration of Aliens into the United States' was passed. Both laws successfully sought to stem general immigration by imposing a relatively low cap on overall immigration and the immigration of southern and eastern Europeans—Italians, Greeks, Southern Slavs, Poles, and eastern European Jews—by assigning supposedly 'scientific' quotas based roughly on the ethnic mix prevailing in the census of 1890 before immigration from those groups had properly begun. Asian immigration, except for the judicially exempt Filipinos, was completely stopped by forbidding the immigration of any 'alien ineligible to citizenship.'

The 1924 act, which remained the basis for American immigration policy until 1965, seemed to some to bring emigration to the United States to a close. This was not only the reaction of politicians and publicists but also of the first two generations of American historians of immigration. In George M. Stephenson's *History of American Immigration, 1820–1924,* a pioneering text produced in 1926 before there was any considerable body of monographic scholarship, the narrative began by opining that the congressional curtailment of immigration had 'closed a momentous chapter in American and European

history,' and Marcus Lee Hansen opened his seminal 1927 *American Historical Review* essay, 'The History of American Immigration as a Field for
Research,' by speaking of the process of settlement 'from its beginnings in
1607 to its virtual close in 1914.' Similarly, John Higham, one of the premier
historians of the second generation of immigration scholars, closed his classic
Strangers in the Land (1955) by noting that, by 1924, 'although immigration
of some sort would continue, the vast folk movements that had formed one
of the most fundamental forces in American history had been brought to an
end.'

While these elegiac views—Higham speaks of an 'ebb tide' are understandable, the course of American history since these works were written has
meant that pronouncements about the demise of immigration are not unlike
the report of Mark Twain's death, an exaggeration. The 3.3 million legal
immigrants of the 1960s, the 4.5 million legal immigrants of the 1970s, and
the more than 6 million legal immigrants of the 1980s make it apparent that
immigration is again a major factor in American history and that the two or
three decades after 1924 were a mere aberration.

Nevertheless from 1924 until 1943 there were no significant changes in
American immigration legislation although, shortly after the Great Depression
began, President Herbert Hoover administratively changed the 'likely to become
a public charge' or LPC clause, instituted by Congress in 1882 to bar persons
unable to work, into a method to keep out people who were merely without
assets. His successor, Franklin Roosevelt, who changed so many aspects of
American life and government, never even considered instituting a New Deal
for immigration. The one significant legislative change effected during the
New Deal years closed the loophole that had allowed unlimited numbers of
Filipinos to enter. The 1934 law that promised independence to the Philippines
introduced a quota for Filipinos: the islanders were allowed fifty immigrant
entries per year, half the size of any other quota, and Filipinos remained
ineligible for naturalization.

We can now see that a small change instituted for reasons of international
politics in 1943 was, in fact, the hinge on which American immigration policy
again turned, and, as was the case in 1882, it was Chinese immigrants who
were at issue. To many internationalist-minded Americans the blatant discrimination of the Chinese Exclusion Act seemed an anomaly at a time when China
was an American ally in the war against Japan. Although Chinese Americans,
like other Asian Americans, deeply resented the discriminatory anti-Asian
statutes and provisions, the crucial impetus for the repeal of the act came not
from them but from members of what can be called the white establishment.
A Citizens Committee to Repeal Chinese Exclusion and Place Immigration
on a Quota Basis was spearheaded by the Asiaphile New York publishers,
Richard J. Walsh, the husband of the novelist, Pearl Buck. The more than 150
names on its letterhead spanned the ideological spectrum from Roger Baldwin

of the American Civil Liberties Union on the left to Henry Luce, publisher of *Time, Life* and *Fortune,* on the right. The committee's successful campaign was studied years ago as an example of 'pressures on Congress.' With bipartisan support in Congress led by Democrat Emanuel Celler and Republican Clare Booth Luce and a strong message from President Roosevelt, the fifteen separate statutes that had effected Chinese exclusion were repealed in December 1943. The new law was a simple one with three brief sections. Section one repealed the old laws. Section two awarded a quota to 'Chinese persons,' later set at 105 admissions per year. This was a global quota. A Chinese Canadian wanting to emigrate to the United States, for example, would have to find a slot within this quota. Other Asian Canadians were still inadmissible, whole non-Asian Canadians were non-quota immigrants. Section three amended the nationality act to make 'Chinese persons' eligible for naturalization on the same basis as other aliens.

Although President Roosevelt made it clear in two formal statements that the repeal of the acts was a good behaviour prize for the Chinese people because of 'their great contribution to the cause of decency and freedom' and although it did nothing at all for other Asian and Asian American groups, it was a major breakthrough and made a small hole in the dike of Asian exclusion. The hole soon helped destroy the dike. Within three years the alien Chinese wives of American citizens became eligible to enter as non-quota immigrants, the Filipino quota was doubled, and Filipinos and 'natives of India' were made eligible for naturalization and the latter were given a small quota. From 1945 to 1952, a period for which there were 840 Chinese quota spaces, 11,058 Chinese legally entered the United States as immigrants. Nearly 10,000 of these were women, which significantly changed the sex ratios in the hitherto heavily male Chinatowns of the United States. Another 20,000 Chinese women entered between 1952 and 1960. In addition, when Mao Zedong's forces triumphed in 1949, there were some 5,000 Chinese students studying in the United States. Many, perhaps most, of these 'stranded Chinese' were able to get immigrant visas and eventually became citizens. These students were the first sizeable increment of what came to be called the Asian 'brain drain.'

LIBERALIZING THE LAW 1952–65

If most of these accretional changes came about as a result of World War II politics, the general overhaul of American immigration policy in 1952 was strongly influenced by the Cold War. While the Immigration and Nationality Act of that year, also known as the McCarran-Walter Act, generally maintained the nativist quota system, it added anti-communist rhetoric and provisions including the infamous ban on issuing even temporary visitor visas to foreign scholars and artists who were even suspected of communism. The act was passed over the veto of President Harry Truman who denounced it and the quota system it perpetuated as 'false and unworthy in 1924 [and] even worse now . . . this quota system keeps out the very people we want to bring in.'

However in one special sense the 1952 act was an important liberalization of immigration and naturalization law: it dropped all of the remaining bars to the naturalization of Asians and made the naturalization process colour blind, as Charles Sumner had wished eight decades earlier. It also gave quotas of some kind to every nation on earth, although, to be sure, Asian quotas were still minuscule. But unlike Sumner, those who wrote the 1952 act were not devoted to racial equality, as can be seen by their treatment of black immigration from the colonial Caribbean. Although previously there had been no numerical cap on West Indian immigration, the 1952 act placed severe limits on those from islands, such as Jamaica, Martinique, and Aruba, which were European possessions.

The Cold War nature of the law can be seen in the discussion of the 'Asia-Pacific triangle' concept which resulted in granting each Asian nation then lacking a quota—and only China, the Philippines, India, and Pakistan had quotas in 1952—an annual quote of 100, plus an additional 100 for the entire triangle to take care of persons of mixed ancestry and residents of colonial dependencies. The quotas were racial as well as national: a Chinese citizen of Great Britain who entered as a quota immigrant would still be charged to the tiny and oversubscribed Chinese quota and not the large and undersubscribed British quota.

There was objection to the 'Asia-Pacific triangle' concept from both the racist right, which did not want Asians at all, and the anti-racist left, which objected to racial as opposed to national criteria. The concept's chief legislative backer, Walter Judd, a former missionary and now a Republican congressman from Minnesota who had been urging its adoption since 1947, made its Cold War context perfectly clear. He told his colleagues that proponents hoped that its adoption would 'influence greatly the battle for men's minds and hearts that is going on between the two philosophies of life and government that are locked in mortal struggle in our world' while assuring them that the small size of the quotas meant 'that there will not be any flooding of America with people of lower economic standards or other cultural patterns.'

But, as had been true of the Chinese admissions after 1943, many more Asians entered than the minimal quotas seemed to indicate was possible. Family reunification provisions in the 1952 act allowed Asians who had established citizenship or even residence in the United States to bring in certain family members without reference to any numerical limitation. Japanese Americans were the greatest users of the citizenship provisions of the law. Once naturalized, many Japanese immigrants, almost all of whom had come before 1924, began to bring in close relatives. In addition, a growing number of Japanese women who had married members of the American population forces entered the country. Thus, despite a minimal quota for Japan, more than 60,000 Japanese entered the United States as immigrants between 1952 and 1964. Members of other Asian American groups also used this process to bring in relatives, but in smaller numbers. Special provisions for refugee immigration, which had begun, belatedly, with the Displaced Persons Acts of 1948 and 1950, were extended in 1953 to some presumably anti-communist Asians. The result of these changes was that immigration from Asia began to grow both absolutely and relatively.

While that growth is often linked to the great liberalization that followed the 1965 Immigration Act—discussed below—it is important to note that the increase had already begun in the late 1940s and 1950s. Between 1951 and 1960 for example, Asian immigrants accounted for 6 per cent of all legal immigration to the United States, while in the years 1961–5, before the effects of the new law kicked in, it had risen to almost 8 per cent, and the trend surely would have continued even without any change in the law.

However the law did change. Calls for major changes had been fairly persistent since 1953 when a presidential commission, established by Truman in the wake of the override of his veto of the 1952 act, recommended replacing the national origins system with one which allocated visas not by nations but according to five principles: the right of asylum, family reunification, needs in the United States, needs in the 'Free World,' and general immigration. Whereas both the 1924 and 1952 acts had contained the same theoretical annual numerical caps—one-sixth of 1 per cent of the total population according to the 1920 census—the Truman commission proposed to keep the same percentage but base it on the most recent census: at that time this would have raised the theoretical cap from 154,000 to 251,000.

To be sure, not all of the growing volume of immigration could be attributed to the 1952 law: throughout the thirteen-year life of that statute both Congress and Presidents Eisenhower, Kennedy, and Johnson earmarked certain groups, mostly refugees from communism, for special treatment. The more generous treatment of refugees was facilitated in part by provisions of the McCarran-Walter Act, even though the word 'refugee'—anathema to extreme restrictions—appears nowhere in it. An obscure provision—section 212 (d) (5)—gave the executive branch, specifically the attorney general, discretionary parole power to grant temporary admission to unlimited numbers of aliens 'for emergent reasons or for reasons deemed strictly in the public interest.' This came to mean, in practice, that the executive branch could act— for Hungarians, for Cubans, for Tibetans, for Vietnamese—and Congress could later pass legislation regularizing that action. Congress itself, at the urging of the Eisenhower administration, passed a Refugee Relief Act in 1953 authorizing the admission of 205,000 visas over and above the quota system: 3,000 of these were earmarked for refugees 'indigenous to the Far East,' chiefly Koreans, and 2,000 for 'refugees of Chinese ethnic origin' as long as they were vouched for by the Nationalist Chinese government on Taiwan. These were the first Asian refugee admissions authorized by Congress. Of course, the 'stranded Chinese students' mentioned earlier were actually refugees who were granted asylum, but those terms were not applied to them.

During the Eisenhower years, despite many real changes in practice, immigration theoretically was still linked to the narrow, nativistic quota system initiated in 1921. The advent of John F. Kennedy to power raised great expectations among those interested in immigration reform. Not only did the 1960 platform of the Democratic party call for scrapping the national origins system but the nominee himself had written—or signed his name to—a book hailing the achievements of the immigrant experience. However, campaign remarks that Kennedy made to an audience of Japanese Americans denouncing the McCarran-Walter Act, which Japanese Americans cherished as the grantor of their right to naturalization, indicated a lack of sensitivity to Asian American issues. And, although the reforms of which Kennedy spoke and which his successor got through Congress were greatly to benefit Asian Americans, it is clear that the Democrats' attention was focused on redressing what they felt were wrongs. The party platform had denounced a post-World War I 'policy of deliberate discrimination by a Republic Administration and Congress.' The focus continued to be on immigration from Europe, a focus that became less relevant with every passing year (see table 4).

CHANGING THE RULES: THE 1965 ACT

Only in July 1963 did President Kennedy send an immigration message to Congress recommending a comprehensive series of amendments to the 1952 act concentrating 'primarily upon revision of our quota system.' Although the emphasis in the message was on the 'elimination of past discrimination' and focused on European immigration, it did propose abolition of the Asia-Pacific triangle and would have improved the position of Asian immigrants marginally. Despite this presidential leadership, no immigration legislation had emerged by the time of Kennedy's assassination and some supporters of immigration reform feared that it would be buried with the martyred president because his successor, Lyndon B. Johnson, unlike Kennedy, had voted to override Truman's veto of the McCarran-Walter Act in 1952. But of course President Johnson was not Senator Johnson, and the Texas quickly embraced immigration reform with an unequivocal statement in his 1964 State of the Union address.

Congress went to work on an immigration bill the following year. While it was clear that there was a majority for change, its opponents trotted out the same old arguments. The chief advocate for the status quo was Senator Sam Ervin, a Democrat from North Carolina who insisted that the McCarran-Walter Act was not discriminatory but was rather 'like a mirror reflecting the United

States, allowing the admission of immigrants according to a national and uniform mathematical formula recognizing the obvious and natural fact that those immigrants can best be assimilated into our society who have relatives, friends, or others of similar background already here.' What Ervin never admitted was that the 'mirror' was badly distorted, like those at amusement parks, and reflected not the population of the 1960s but that recorded in the 1920 census.

The legislative history of the 1965 act is complex and cannot be considered here. The meaningful debates were not about *whether* to change the old system, but about how and what degree to change it. The basic thrust of the 1965 law—which technically was not a new law but a series of amendments to the 1952 act—was to replace national quotas and origins with overall hemispheric limits on visas issued: 170,000 for persons from the eastern hemisphere, 129,000 for those from the western hemisphere. No country in the eastern hemisphere was to have more than 20,000 visas in any one year. (In a 1976 statute, hemispheric limits would be abandoned for a global ceiling of 290,000 visas, with the 20,000 per nation caps applying everywhere.) These provisions seemed to establish an annual limit of 290,000 immigrants, a little lower than immigration was actually running in the mid-1960s. Those 290,000 visas were to be distributed according to a system of preferences similar to those of the 1952 act. But, as had been the case during the life of the McCarran-Walter Act, two parallel systems were also adopted. The first, essentially a continuation from the 1924 and 1952 acts, exempted certain close relatives from both preference requirement and numerical limits. The second system added refugees of all kinds and, as it turned out, in unprecedented numbers, even though the 1965 act had set aside only 6 per cent of preference visas (17,400 annually) for refugees. The new land also abolished the Asia-Pacific triangle concept. The bill retained most of the barriers that Congress had been erecting to limit entry to the country since the 1880s, most significantly the LPC clause, the requirements for mental and physical health, and the various ideological and moral tests. The new law very much resembled its immediate predecessor but placed a much heavier emphasis on family reunification as table 3 comparing their preference provisions demonstrates.

Lyndon Johnson signed the bill into law in a ceremony on Liberty Island in New York Harbor with the then still dilapidated and unused buildings on Ellis Island in the background. 'This bill that we sign today is not a revolutionary bill. It does not affect the lives of millions. It will not reshape the structure of our daily lives, or really add importantly to either our wealth or our power.' Johnson was not indulging in uncharacteristic understatement. He was saying what his experts had told him. He and they saw the 1965 act as redressing the wrongs of 1924 and 1952, what he called the wrong done to those 'from southern and eastern Europe.' Members of his administration had testified before Congress that few Asians would enter under the new law, a misperception also held by the leading Asian American organization, the Japanese American Citizens League, which complained that for the foreseeable future Asians would continue to be discriminated against, even though post-1965 discrimination would be de facto rather than de jure.

Table 3   Preference systems: 1952 and 1965 Immigration Acts

Immigration and Nationality Act 1952

Exempt from preference requirements and numerical quotas: spouses and unmarried minor children of United States citizens.

1   Highly skilled immigrants whose services are urgently needed in the United States and their spouses and children: 50 per cent

2   Parents of United States citizens over age 21 and unmarried adult children of United States citizens: 30 per cent

3   Spouses and unmarried adult children of permanent resident aliens: 20 per cent

Any visas not allocated above distributed as follows:

4   Brothers, sisters, and married children of United States citizens and accompanying spouses and children: 50 per cent

5   Non-preference applicants: any remaining visas

Immigration Act of 1965

Exempt from preference and numerical requirements: spouses, unmarried minor children and parents of United States citizens.

1   Unmarried adult children of United States citizens: 20 per cent

2   Spouses and unmarried adult children of permanent resident aliens: 20 per cent

3   Members of the professions and scientists and artists of exceptional ability [requires Department of Labor certification]: 10 per cent

4   Married children of United States citizens: 10 per cent

5   Brothers and sisters of United States citizens over age 21: 24 per cent

6   Skilled and unskilled workers in occupations for which labour is in short supply [requires Department of Labor certification]: 10 per cent

7   Refugees from communist or communist-dominated countries, or the Middle East: 6 per cent

8   Non-preference: any remaining visas. [Since there are more preference applicants than can be accommodated, this has not been used].

SOURCE: Roger Daniels, *Coming to America: A History of Immigration and Ethnicity in American Life* (New York: HarperCollins 1990). 342.

In practice the law has worked quite differently than any of its sponsors expected. Looking backward and expecting the future to resemble the past, they ignored the evidence of the data available to them. As we have seen, despite the restrictions of the 1952 act, the incidence of Europeans among immigrants to the United States had dropped steadily even while the volume of total immigration had risen. Yet the experts continued to believe the great fallacy that there were large numbers of European immigrants ready, qualified, and able to come to America. Most seemed to think that 20,000 annual arrivals from many European countries would absorb most of the eastern hemisphere preference visa slots. Had the 1965 act, or something very much like it, been passed in 1952 when Truman recommended a full-scale revision of immigration law, such a result might well have obtained. But by 1965 most of those western Europeans who wished to come were not likely to meet LPC and other restrictions and, of course, eastern Europeans were not then free to come. Growing numbers of Latin Americans and Asians had been coming to the United States since the years of World War II and once such persons had permanent resident status a whole cohort of relatives became eligible to enter the country as second preference immigrants. And as soon as these immigrants became United States citizens—as unprecedented numbers of them did in the minimum five-year waiting period as Elliott Barkan's studies have shown— more persons became eligible as first, fourth, and fifth preference immigrants, while others could enter exempt from numerical preference. And, of course, those brought in could and did start the same procedure. Since the 1965 act went into effect this kind of chain migration, in which related immigrants follow one another as links in a chain, has accounted for a preponderance of all non-refugee migration. Such a process is likely to continue as long as the law stays essentially as it is and conditions in most of Asia and Latin America remain as they are.

Although the law speaks of a annual global ceiling of 290,000, that applies *only* to those subject to numerical limitation. Thus legal immigration, which averaged a quarter of a million annually in the 1950s, increased to a third of a million annually in the 1960, nearly 450,000 annually in the 1970s, and to more than half a million annually in the 1980s. Increasingly, this was immigration from Asia and Latin America as is clear from the data in table 4, which compares the percentage shares of the immigration which came from various regions in the 1950s with those for the 1980s, and table 5, which shows the Asian nations from which immigrants came in the period 1980–9.

The 1965 law, which remains the basis for immigration into the United States, has not worked out in the way that either its proponents or its opponents expected. Perhaps the most misleading aspect of the law involves the presumed 20,000 cap on entries from any one nation. That cap applies only to those entering subject to 'numerical limitation,' so that in a given year, for example 1985, there were 48,000 legal entries by Filipinos and 35,000 by Koreans, to cite only the two most numerous Asian groups that year. The cap has been a chimaera.

Table 4   Source of United States immigrants, 1950s and 1980s (%)

	1951–60	1981–9
Asia	6	42
Latin America	25	42
Europe	52	11
Africa & other	2	3
Canada	15	11

SOURCE: William P. O'Hare and Judy C. Felt, *Asian Americans: America's Fastest Growing Minority Group* (Washington 1991). 6.

Table 5   Asian immigrants to the United States by nation, 1980–9

Nation	Number	% Asian migrants*
Vietnam	679,378	24
Philippines	473,831	17
China†	433,031	15
Korea	338,891	12
Laos‡	256,727	9
India	253,781	9
Cambodia	210,721	7
Other	61,699	2
Thailand	59,638	2
Pakistan	55,900	2
Japan	41,739	1
TOTAL	2,865,339	100

SOURCE: William P. O'Hare and Judy C. Felt, *Asian Americans: America's Fastest Growing Minority Group* (Washington 1991). 2.

* Includes refugees.

† Includes Republic of China (Taiwan), Hong Kong, and Macao. In addition thousands of immigrants from Southeast Asia are ethnically Chinese and so identify themselves in United States census.

‡ Includes Hmong.

Although in the congressional debates over the 1965 law there was the usual restrictionist oratory about opening the floodgates, not even the most consistent restrictionist in Congress in 1965 predicted that in the 1980s some six million legal immigrants would enter the United States. Nor did anyone even hint that Latins and Asians would so completely dominate American immigration. By the 1980s more than four-fifths of all legal immigrants came from either Asia or Latin America: if there was a way of accurately including illegal immigrants in the calculation, this figure would undoubtedly exceed nine-tenths. The 1965 act, intended to redress past grievances of European ethnic groups and to give more than token representation to Asians, has, in one sense, turned traditional immigration patterns to the United States on their head.

In another sense, however, the patterns of immigration have remained consistent. People have tended to emigrate to the United States when a clear economic and/or social advantage could be gained from doing so. In the years after 1965 the average Briton, or German, or Scandinavian could see no such advantage in emigration; neither could the average Japanese. Most of those Europeans who wished to emigrate were in Eastern Europe. However, many Irish, the one western European group that sought entry in large numbers, were disadvantaged in their attempts to enter because there were too few recent legal Irish immigrants to provide the close blood kin to produce an effective chain migration. Many Irish therefore resorted, in fairly large but indeterminate numbers, to illegal immigration.

Under the 1965 law the golden door had swung open much wider but an entirely different mix of peoples was provided with legal access. The executive and legislative branches of the United States government had not only ended the blatant discrimination against Asians but also created a new system which could be used by Asians to make themselves the most favoured beneficiaries of the new law. The first result was intended, the second totally unintended. Had either branch understood the dynamics of immigration flows it would have insisted on a different law.

ASIAN AMERICA IN 1993: A SNAPSHOT

A discussion of changes in immigration law affecting Asians would be incomplete without a glance at the kinds of communities the changes have helped to create. To return to the 1990 census, table 6 lists the major components of the Asian American population it reported. It is misleading to speak about Asian Americans as if they were a homogenous groups; one only need think of the analogue, European Americans—a phrase that is almost never used—to see how inappropriate such terms really are. This is not to argue that the term should not be used at all: race—and Asian American is essentially a racial term—is still relevant in the United States. But those of us who use this term, for whatever reason, must be careful not to give to those it embraces a kind of false homogeneity. Asian Americans are diverse, and their diversities are significant both within and between ethnic groups. In the final analysis, in the years to come, it may well be that class rather than ethnicity will become more important in differentiating among Asian Americans.

We do not yet have detailed socio-economic data from the 1990 census, but that from the 1980 census showed us sharp disparities in age, gender, residence, education, and income between and within Asian American ethnic groups. Among the longer established groups, internal diversity can most easily be seen in the Chinese American community. While it contains many highly successful individuals, large numbers of Chinese Americans, some of whom are members of families that have been here for generations, live in poverty and deprivation and display the socio-economic profiles that usually accompany poverty.

Among the newer groups, I will mention only two: Asian Indians and Vietnamese. In purely economic terms, Asian Indians stood at the top of recent Asian immigrant groups, with the highest reported median income, an income that exceeds even that of whites. Asian Indians were the only large Asian American group under-represented in the Far West: only 19.2 per cent lived there—fewer than the 34.2 per cent in the northeast, the 23.4 per cent in the south, and the 23.1 per cent in the north central states. While in the northeast many are professionals and business executives—and thus part of the brain and capital drain from Asia—large numbers of other Asian Indians operate small businesses wherever they have settled. They have moved into one special economic niche: owning motels. For example, Asian Indians constitute some 40 per cent of motel owners along Interstate 75 which runs between Detroit and Atlanta. Many motels are owned by members of a numerous Gujarati clan named Patel so that a community ethnic joke speaks about 'hotel, motel, Patel.' Motels require relatively small amounts of capital and large amounts of unskilled labour, the latter often supplied by extended family or clan members. Continuing migration of these family members may well lower average income within the community.

Table 6   Asian Americans, 1990, by major ethnic group

Group	Number
Chinese	1,643,621
Filipino	1,403,624
Japanese	850,901
Asian Indians	814,538
Koreans	799,993
Vietnamese	610,904
Laotians (including Hmong)	239,000
Cambodians	210,724

SOURCE: United States, census reports. These figures are taken from listings which the Census Bureau provides under the rubric 'Asian and Pacific Islander.' It includes immigrants from East, Southeast, and South Asia and their descendants, and many Pacific Islanders, but not native Hawaiians. It is not used for Caucasians born in Soviet Asia—of whom there are very few in the United States—or for Iranians and other Asians from the region west of Pakistan generally known as the Middle East, or for most Australians and New Zealanders. As recently as 1970, Japanese and Chinese made up the lion's share— more than 70 per cent—of Asian Americans. In 1990 they were *only* just over a third. There are now very large Filipino, Southeast Asian, Korean, and Asian Indian ethnic groups in the United States, almost all of whom are the result of post-1965 immigration.

Unlike most of the other middle-class Asian Americans, few Asian Indians have adopted Christianity. Hindu temples have sprung up throughout America. Asian Indian family structure has remained highly traditional: in 1980, 92.7 per cent of all Asian Indian children under eighteen lived in two-parent families. Asian Indians, despite (because of) their middle-class status, have suffered increasing instances of anti-Asian racial violence. The worst examples were in Jersey City where a group of working-class white youths, calling themselves 'dot busters,' for the *bindi,* the small cosmetic dot that married Hindu women traditionally wear on their foreheads, assaulted a number of Indians on the streets, eventually killing one young man, a junior executive with Citicorp.

By contrast, Vietnamese and other Southeast Asian refugees and their children were, as a group, at the very bottom of the socio-economic indices in 1980. But, as is often true with refugee populations, the community's socio-economic range was tremendous. Many of the elite of the Republic of Vietnam eventually fled to the West. Former Air Marshal Nguyen Cao Ky, for example, is the proprietor of an upscale liquor store near Washington, DC. At the other end of the spectrum were Vietnamese fisherfolk and the Hmong, whose social and economic organization was essentially pre-modern.

Most Vietnamese have not been economically successful. More than a quarter (28.1 per cent) of all Vietnamese households received public assistance in 1979. While the media delight in reporting the success story—'Vietnamese Girl Wins Spelling Bee'—the reality is that a very large proportion of the Vietnamese American population has joined the under-class. Despite determined attempts by refugee resettlement groups to distribute Vietnamese refugees throughout the country, by 1980 significant clustering had already occurred in California where a third of them then lived. That percentage is undoubtedly much higher now. Within California the major concentration point is Orange County south of Los Angeles. Outside California, the major concentration point is Texas, where a tenth lived in 1980. Vietnamese were one of the few contemporary immigrant groups with no sizeable concentration in New York, which had, in 1980, only 2.5 per cent of them. Wherever most of them have gone in the United States they have faced a double disadvantage: not only are they foreigners from Asia, but most of them came without capital or the skills necessary to 'make it' in late twentieth century America.

Thus the conglomerate image of 'Asian Americans' is an illusion. Hmong and Japanese are no more alike than Albanians and Scots. Yet because Asian Americans are not Caucasians, the media, the Census Bureau, and almost everyone else will continue to speak of them as if they were one people. The category will almost certainly continue to grow, by immigration and natural increase, both absolutely and relatively. One educated estimate, made in 1985, predicted almost 10 million Asian Americans by 2000. If this prediction is correct—if I had to hazard a guess it would be that it will prove to be too low—Asian Americans will be about 4 per cent of the American population, or one person in twenty-five. As recently as 1980 they represented 1.5 per cent of the population, or one person in seventy-five, and in 1940 they had represented slightly less than two-tenths of one per cent, or one person in five hundred. Whatever the numbers, Asian Americans will surely play an increasingly important role in American life, but a varied one. A substantial percentage of the latest immigrants and their children will join the large number of Asian Americans who have already entered the middle and upper middle classes as their current presence in our elite institutions predicts. Others will, almost certainly, remain mired in poverty. No pan-ethnic appellation or set of attributes can possibly describe them all.

Editor's Note: This article has been edited for publication.

Stirring the Pot

Immigrant and Refugee Challenges to the United States and the World

Paul Burkhead, Rapporteur

Summary of a Symposium Held at the Council on Foreign Relations, New York, Monday, 18 October 1993

On 18 October 1993, during a symposium held by the Council on Foreign Relations in New York, experts from government and academia came together to discuss the challenges faced by the United States and the international community in the wake of increasing refugee and immigrant flows. The symposium addressed not only the specific issues that the United States must confront regarding immigration, but also broader issues on which it must cooperate with the international community to cope with exponential increases in global refugee flows. The symposium stressed the compelling need for leadership and decision making on both the national and international fronts.

The symposium, entitled "Stirring the Pot: Immigration and Refugee Challenges to the United States and the World," was presided over by Linda Chavez, John M. Olin Fellow at the Manhattan Institute for Policy Research, addressed two aspects of the refugee issue. Members of the first panel, Demetrios G. Papademetriou and Robert Bach, both senior associates at the Carnegie Endowment for International Peace, sought to answer the question "Immigration and the U.S.: Is America Still a Melting Pot?" Members of the second panel, Aristide Zolberg, University-in-Exile professor of Political Science at the New School for Social Research and Ambassador Warren Zimmerman, director of the Bureau of Refugee Programs at the U.S. Department of State, examined "The Refugee Crisis: Root Causes and Policy Issues." Both panels spoke to an audience of Council on Foreign Relations fellows, journalists and guests, whose questions and comments provided the panelists opportunities to elucidate their points.

A recurrent theme throughout each of the four presentations was the need for leaders to make policy decisions on issues they have thus far avoided. On the national level, Papademetriou identified a reluctance among political leaders in both Congress and the executive branch to address directly issues of

Journal of International Affairs, Volume 47, No. 2, Winter 1994, p. 579–588.

immigration policy, while Bach identified the need to redefine the national interest in the context of immigration and refugee issues. On a broader level of root causes and international responses to refugee and immigration flows, Zolberg also stressed the need for new policies and the rethinking of issues, and Zimmerman cited the necessity for a new philosophical approach to address the causes of refugee flows. World leaders must rethink problems, consider new options and reformulate policies to confront the dramatic escalation in population flows that has occurred in the last 20 years. Chavez concurred, noting that thus far few have taken the time to shape public perceptions about these issues.

DOMESTIC IMMIGRATION ISSUES

The first half of the symposium was devoted to discussing the challenges facing the United States specifically with regard to its immigration and refugee policies. Papademetriou cited a "current void in leadership" on immigration issues in the United States. Contradicting the popular concept of the melting pot, Papademetriou provided examples showing that the United States does not, in fact, have a history of openness to immigrants; the admission of individuals or groups to this country has always represented a policy choice based on a set of distinct issues. Controlled immigration in the United States developed over a period of 50 years, beginning in the 1870s, and gradually metamorphosed from qualitative to quantitative bases of control. The embryonic movement to open up immigration had its roots in the 1920s and eventually led to an erosion of immigration restrictions from the 1940s to 1965. In the 1980s, the U.S. government enacted legislation to restrict illegal immigration and expand legal immigration—in effect, closing the back door in order to open up the front.

American immigration policy historically has taken into account several key issues. First is the changing composition of immigrant groups. In the 1950s, 80 percent of those immigrating to the United States were of European ancestry; in the 1990s, 90 percent are of non-European origin. Second is the location where immigrants choose to settle. Whereas in the 1950s immigrants dispersed to all areas of the country, in the 1990s, only four or five states and several metropolitan areas account for the placement of most immigrants. Third is an issue that remains crucial to U.S. immigration policy: Who is accepted as immigrants? In this decade, 65 percent of immigrants to the United States are relatives of persons already living in this country; another 20 percent are admitted in the self-interest of the United States, that is, considered able to contribute to American business; and the rest, approximately 15 percent, are admitted largely for humanitarian reasons.

A simple question addresses the central political issue at stake in the formulation of immigration policy: What do immigrants contribute, and what do they take away? American political leaders have failed thus far to provide an adequate answer to this question. Of the leaders in the four countries that are considered primary receivers of immigrants—Australia, Canada, New Zealand, and the United States—only Australian and Canadian politicians have attempted to answer the question, and in so doing have presented opposite views. Canadian leaders tie the immigration issue to economic and population goals, and assert that immigrants strengthen the economy. Australian leaders, on the other hand, attempt to curb immigration, considering it a drain on the economy. Both, however, apply self-interested motives in their selection of the best immigrants from among those who apply.

Papademetriou argued that the United States must carefully chart its future course along two avenues. First, in order to maintain an open immigration policy, the United States must learn to integrate immigrants more effectively into American society. Second, U.S. leaders must articulate more effectively their immigration policy. No political leader in the United States in the last 20 years has attempted to address the reasons behind the adoption of a particular policy, nor has any attempted to shape public perceptions of the integration of immigrants into U.S. society. The United States must change this trend and begin to address this lack of leadership.

Bach explained the effects on immigration of the links between domestic and foreign policies, contending that such links are not always clear. For example, an isolationist foreign policy does not always imply a restrictionist immigration policy, although some connection undoubtedly exists. In keeping with the theme developed by each of the symposium participants, Bach cited the need to redefine the core interests of the United States. He concluded that U.S. leaders must work together to define the country's interests and address its problems.

The existing U.S. foreign policy, greatly influenced by domestic groups, is coupled with a stringent immigration policy. Both policies pose a variety of problems. First, transnational integration of labor requires an open immigration policy and a more open foreign policy. Moreover, immigration historically has helped the economy of the United States, at both the low- and high-wage ends. Second, immigration serves as an informal foreign policy. Remittances from immigrants to their home countries are considered a key form of foreign aid, with so important an impact that the World Bank has recognized this as a major development strategy. Finally, the allocation of refugee aid can serve as a major component of foreign policy.

Burden sharing, both at home and abroad, is of particular concern for the United States. Domestic relations among Americans have deteriorated in many ways, including the misrepresentation, or slandering, of immigrants. In the wake of such incidents as the 1992 Los Angeles riots, however, it must be noted that much of the violence has not been directed towards immigrants. Bach contended that Americans have now stretched their "caring capacity" to the limit, tearing the general social fabric of the nation. These are conditions that impose serious risks to immigrants, despite their underestimated ability to assimilate. The domestic goal of achieving more effective means to assimilation is linked with the American foreign policy goal of burden sharing.

A redefinition and statement of U.S. interests in both the foreign and domestic arena must occur if progress is to be made on immigration. National Security Advisor Anthony Lake recently called for "enlargement" of foreign policy, and President Clinton has spoken of an "inclusive" domestic policy. For immigration policy, these goals require that recrafting of the national interest with regard to immigrants. Policy makers must determine where in the national agenda to fit diversity.

During the discussion, the participants agreed on several issues introduced by the audience. Papademetriou indicated that immigration policy is not solely a responsive policy but often is controlled by domestic policy through, for example, reunification visas and employer needs. Demand for employment plays a key role in the influx of illegal immigrants, refugees and asylum-seekers. Bach cited the example of the improvement of European economies as a reason for the decline in emigration from Europe. Further, a large number of reunification visas (the largest group in the 1980s) may be attributed to American "projection"—the stationing of American military personnel overseas. Thus shifts in the geographical origins of refugees can be attributed to factors other than host country immigration policies.

So far, there has been little evidence to link "push" factors, such as unemployment and environmental degradation, to immigrant flows. Such factors generally appear as causes of internal migration and south-to-south migration, rather than of immigration to the United States. For example, overpopulation in China generally leads to internal migration.

Immigration policy must respond to the increasing trend of transnationalism that has developed primarily around labor issues. Papademetriou identified two new groups of "international citizens": one with very high skills, the other with very low skills. Immigration policy treats only the first group as desirable, thus compelling the second group to immigrate illegally. The makers of immigration policy must recognize the effects of such "push" factors involving labor and must construct policies to accommodate the inequities.

Chavez and audience members next turned the discussion to public concern about the assimilation of immigrants into U.S. society and fears that this will pose a challenge to the prevalence of the English language. Bach argued that the English language is not threatened, pointing out that most second-generation immigrants speak English. Furthermore, reaching proficiency through vehicles such as English language classes can be a source of upward mobility for immigrants and community stability.

Bach and Papademetriou challenged the concept of the United States as a melting pot, and emphasized the need for new and creative solutions to address problems of increasing immigration, particularly of integrating large numbers of people into American society. The two panelists stressed the importance of U.S. political leaders rethinking and articulating foreign and domestic policy goals. Only then can they formulate policies to address the immigration issues facing the United States and the world.

THE ROOT CAUSES OF REFUGEE FLOWS

The second half of the symposium was devoted to "The Refugee Crisis: Root Causes and Policy Options."

Zolberg discussed the need for new policies in the face of massive escalations of refugee flows over the past 20 years. On one hand, the West traditionally has felt a sense of obligation to offer protection to the victims of conflict and humanitarian emergencies. On the other hand, the United States also has attempted to separate the issue of international migration from that of refugee flows in formulating policy. This approach consistently has proven to be impossible. Policy makers' inability both to separate these issues and to create a viable, overarching working definition of refugees complicates most attempts to implement policy.

Over the last 20 years, the number of refugees worldwide has increased dramatically—from approximately 5 million, a number with which receiving nations could cope, to nearly 20 million. Most refugees remain near their countries of origin, often in neighboring states with similar problems. The total number of displaced persons in the world today is approaching 50 million people, and violence, environmental degradation, rogue regimes and anarchy add to this figure.

Such worldwide increases in refugees have occurred for two principal reasons. First, the fragmentation of empires into distinct countries has led to attempts by subsequent national leaders to homogenize populations using violence. Empires, or other similar political systems, by their very nature, forced populations to live together in relative peace. Once these empires dissolved, various ethnic groups attempted to gain ascendancy over other groups within the newly formed nation. The resulting internecine conflicts almost certainly created refugee flows. The collapse of the Soviet Union and the ongoing bitter struggle in the former Yugoslavia are telling examples of this course, which is rooted further in earlier histories of a number of European states: England, France and Spain provide examples of "religious cleansing," the precursor to the current tragedy of Bosnia's "ethnic cleansing."

The proliferation of new states around the edges of Europe in the 19th and 20th centuries set the stage for today's conflicts. Empires do not homogenize their populations but, rather, rule from above. They successfully freeze situations of conflict while doing little to persuade warring groups to cohabit peacefully.

Second, revolutionary upheaval contributes to increased refugee glows. The American, French, Russian and Chinese revolutions each produced their share of refugees and exiles. Later, during the Cold War, both the former Soviet Union and the United States contributed to these numbers by sponsoring clients and maintaining confrontations. Although the Cold War has long since ended, the weapons that proliferated remain to produce refugee situations. In fact, the weapons produced through super-power proxy wars are one of the most serious factors of refugee-creating conflicts.

The international community is now forced to confront these problems with institutions that were never intended to handle so many displaced persons. Furthermore, developing nations, which currently contain the majority of the world's refugees and displaced persons, seek membership in the United Nations, thereby imposing problems specific to the developing world on the entire international community. Similarly, the United Nations High Commissioner for Refugees (UNHCR), initially designed to cope with the demands of state-less persons after the Second World War, now possesses inadequate resources and an ill-equipped structure to attend to the numbers of refugees the world faces. Due to domestic pressures and financial constraints, the international community also displays a reluctance to redesign institutions, such as UNHCR, further complicating the refugee situation.

Although generous in their praise of UNHCR's efforts, participants and members of the symposium audience agreed on the pressing need for institutional change. UNHCR and other such international relief organizations do not and cannot, due to financial constraints, go beyond their mandate—to provide only relief. The international community must look beyond providing relief and granting asylum and instead address the root causes of the crisis and adequately confront the crisis that has arisen in the last 20 years. Ultimately, the group agreed that UNHCR requires increased funding and assistance and a formal recognition of its expanded role.

Speaking as a policy maker, Zimmerman stated that situations such as Bosnia, Haiti and Somalia are among the top in the hierarchy of troubling foreign policy issues facing the Clinton administration. Zimmerman agreed that the 40 to 50 million displaced persons in the world today present a severe problem to the world community. But while the administration is committed to coordinating lasting solutions to each of these conflict areas, Zimmerman argued that the two most important causes of refugees and displaced persons— economic problems and over-population—are not easy for the United States to confront alone.

Among the political aspects of the refugee crisis that involve principally the Department of State are persecution; human rights violations, such as those in Burma, Mozambique and Iraq; and the revival of intensely nationalist sentiments, such as in the former Yugoslavia. As stated earlier, nationalist sentiment remains a primary factor feeding into overall causes of displacement.

In fact, many nationalistic governments have replaced previously communist regimes, particularly because of the severe and forceful doctrines previously used to homogenize their populations.

The United States, like other nations, allocates limited resources to combat the refugee issue. Most of these resources are invested in relief, leaving little to be applied toward prevention of the root causes of displacement. Given the global scale of the refugee problem, the international community must approach it from a new theoretical direction. Zimmerman posited these options: First, the international community must deny the sovereignty of dictatorships that deprive their citizens of basic rights; and second, many more resources must be committed to deal with this devastating problem. Thus far, few countries have been prepared to commit the level of resources necessary to make even a dent in the refugee issue. Given its present commitment of resources, the United States is able only to deal with effects, not causes; the opportunity to immigrate to the United States is useful but does not, by any means, solve the problem. Zimmerman suggested that an improved record of removing dictators and a stronger emphasis on sustainable development are two possible tactics.

Participants and members of the symposium audience discussed many causes of the current crisis. Ethnic strife as a component of nationalism and the scourge of ethnic cleansing consistently entered the debate as primary factors leading to population displacement. Human rights violations and persecution by so-called "gangster governments" also play a significant role. In addition, exponential population increases and rising numbers of internally displaced persons present a significant challenge for human rights workers. For many recently formed states, internal societal divisions that include multiple languages and a multiplicity of cultures also threaten the maintenance of stability.

Symposium participants debated the issue of economic refugees, referring specifically to Haitian refugees. Given the previous acceptance of Haitians as economic refugees into the United States, participants questioned whether this group may not, indeed, legitimately claim refugee status, especially after the events of October 1993. Zimmerman disagreed, arguing the uniqueness of the Haitian case: In the months following the coup that overthrew President Jean-Bertrand Aristide, he said, few Haitians met the criteria for refugee status. In light of more recent events in Haiti, however, U.S. policy may soon change.

While the group did not attempt to reach consensus on the issue of identifying lasting solutions, they did propose several potential and partial solutions to the crisis. One solution that received audience support was to place punitive conditions on states that violate the basic rights of their citizens. The group did concede, however, that such a solution, although having certain diplomatic impact, is extremely difficult to implement.

Zimmerman stressed that ultimately, the international community must thoroughly consider the effect humanitarian intervention would have on the sovereignty of a particular state.

CONCLUSION

Stronger and more responsible leadership is needed both domestically and internationally. Such leadership requires formulating constructive and lasting policies, addressing the current refugee crisis and articulating these policies to the people they affect. For a better approach to immigration, U.S. policy makers must state their goals clearly and reformulate their methods. International leadership requires a revised philosophy on how to deal with population displacement. Such methods would confront the root causes of displacement rather than concentrating on providing relief for those who are already its victims. Ethnic strife, the disintegration of large states, population explosion, environmental degradation and governments' disregard of human rights all contribute to the current refugee and immigrant crisis, which can be resolved only through intelligence and farsighted leadership.

Editor's Note: This article has been edited for publication.

Responses of Industrial Countries to Asylum-Seekers

Charles B. Keely and Sharon Stanton Russell

Since the mid-1980s, governments of industrial countries have viewed burgeoning requests for political asylum with increasing skepticism, and their representatives have met in many forums to discuss ways to control the flow of asylum-seekers. Increasingly, they have stressed the security dimensions of what have been viewed as primary humanitarian issues. Furthermore, states have entered into regional-level discussions about initiatives to achieve the objectives of controlled and orderly movement. Their discussions, which raise fundamental issues about the effects of migration on states and societies in Europe and North America, pose a challenge to the role of multilateral agencies like the U.N. High Commissioner for Refugees (UNHCR) with their more global perspectives and narrow mandates. This article examines industrial states' recent exchanges and probable future policies in response to growing numbers of asylum applications during the last decade.

In Europe, North America and Australia, applications for asylum rose from 90,444 in 1983 to about 825,000 in 1992. Over three million applications have been made in Europe since 1983. The applicants came uninvited and unscreened. Governments skepticism about claims of political persecution was reflected in the fact that in 1991, a typical year, the acceptance rate for asylum applicants in Europe was 5 percent. Western European governments estimated that 70 percent of the 420,000 applicants in 1990 arrived without documents, many from countries that routinely issue them. Nevertheless, governments permitted many of the more than one million applicants rejected over the last decade to stay under ad hoc temporary statuses, such as "leave to stay for humanitarian reasons." The level of asylum applications made heavy demands on the asylum adjudication systems, which had large backlogs of unresolved cases. States viewed this situation as an invitation to those seeking away to penetrate industrial countries' labor markets. Care and maintenance of applicants and their families during the adjudication process siphoned off government funds and tested public tolerance. At the same time, governments, as well as human rights groups and public sentiment in many countries, emphasized

Journal of International Affairs, Winter 1994, 399–417.

that, despite the pressures and even possible abuse of asylum procedures, asylum itself must be maintained, and persecuted people ought not to be sacrificed to "public order."

DEMANDS ON ASYLUM SYSTEMS

In the mid-1980s, European states grew concerned about the growing number of asylum applications, the risk of terrorism and the use of Warsaw Pact states as a transit corridor for third world asylum-seekers to harass Western European states vulnerable because of their asylum systems. Applications continued to rise as communist governments unravelled in East Central Europe and the former Soviet Union. Instability in these regions was a growing concern for Western Europe. In North America, the migration picture had some similar dimensions. Canada was shaken by the arrival of a freighter from Germany with Sri Lankan asylum-seekers. Central Americans, Haitians and Cubans sought asylum in the United States.

As the numbers continued to increase, asylum, illegal migration, the remnants of guest worker programs and the fear of even greater asylum demands following the breakup of the Soviet Union all made migration a politically sensitive issue in Europe. Anti-immigrant political parties gained strength. Anti-foreigner incidents increased and provoked controversy. Questions were raised about Europe's capacity to absorb refugees and the wisdom of even trying to incorporate culturally very different people into ethnically based societies. Chancellor Helmut Kohl declared that Germany was not a country of immigration. French Interior Minister Charles Pasqua told Parliament: "France was once a country of immigrants, but it no longer wants to be one . . . [T]he goal we have set is zero immigration." The European press, intellectuals and the public discussed whether Muslims could be integrated into Western liberal democracies.

Economic unification in the European Community (E.C.—referred to as the European Union [E.U.] since November 1993) has complicated Western Europe's attempts to manage the demand for safe haven and settlement. Industrial countries' special relationships with refugees' countries of origin, based on colonial histories, geographical proximity and military alliances, make dealing with the arrival of asylum-seekers still more complex.

Requests by receiving countries that neighbors share the burden of reception and accommodation have fallen on deaf ears. Italy received little support in the face of boatloads of Albanian asylum-seekers. Calls by Austria and Germany to share the burden of refugees from the fighting in the former Yugoslavia have likewise evoked a limited response. These are only the latest weak responses to calls for burden-sharing agreements and mechanisms in the United Nations and European forums.

COST OF ASYLUM ADJUDICATION SYSTEMS

Asylum is expensive. Care for asylum applicants in industrial countries and adjudication of their claims are estimated to cost from $8 billion to $10 billion annually. This contrasts with a 1992 budget for the UNHCR of about $1.1 billion. Even adding in the separate U.N. Relief and Works Agency, which is responsible for Palestinian refugees, the bill for asylum adjudication in industrial countries is many times the amount U.N. agencies spend on refugees.

At the same time, hard times in Europe and North America have increased the burden of generous asylum policies. The economies of the two continents remain in the grip of sluggish growth that began in the early 1980s. Unemployment in Europe runs at about 10 percent and is forecast to climb even higher. The United States experienced no growth in the labor force outside the public sector between 1990 and 1992. Moreover, fears that the North American Free Trade Agreement (NAFTA) will cause unemployment have sharpened Americans' concerns.

Much of the U.S. debate and policy making has taken place amid charges by some political leaders and proponents of immigration restriction that immigration, in all its guises, is "out of control" and that "something has to be done." Public figures, like Governor Pete Wilson of California, are calling for rethinking immigration policy and improving border control. Haitian boat people and Chinese asylum-seekers arrived against this background.

An economic argument for permitting, much less welcoming, large-scale settlement by asylum-seekers would be difficult to make. The costs of adjudication and maintenance during prolonged asylum processing seem unjustified to the president and to congressional proponents of streamlining the asylum process, especially when so many applicants are eventually rejected.

GOVERNMENTS' RESPONSES

Rising asylum applications in Western Europe—from 65,000 in 1983 to 164,000 in 1985—forced governments to discuss the implications of these changes for Europe and for asylum as an institution. At the outset, the only forums for such contacts were the UNHCR Executive Committee's Subcommittee on Protection (meeting once a year) and The Ad Hoc Committee of Experts on the Legal Aspects of Territorial Asylum (CAHAR, following the acronym for its French title) within the Council of Europe (meeting twice a year). By 1991, more than 100 meetings on asylum took place in 30 different forums in that year alone.

While the public discussion swirled around immigrants in general and asylum-seekers in particular, governments talked to one another and took measures, primarily in their individual sovereign capacities, to alter their asylum procedures, which had given applicants the benefit of the doubt. High rejection rates led governments to conclude that many applicants were abusing their liberal asylum procedures. If asylum and public support for it were to be preserved, and order brought to the system, changes had to be made.

Many changes in domestic asylum law in both Europe and North America were designed to screen out manifestly unfounded applicants at the border. States also imposed regulations fining carriers that transported passengers with insufficient or false documents. Germany and Finland legalized fingerprinting to prevent the same people from filing multiple applications. Belgium, Switzerland, Austria and Finland introduced laws to screen out clearly unqualified applicants, and the United States introduced the Immigration Enforcement and Asylum Reform Act in July 1993 (but it was not acted on by the end of the 1993 session) with similar objectives. Germany altered its Basic Law in June 1993 to permit changes in asylum procedures.

Bilateral agreements were another mechanism, for dealing with unwanted flows of asylum-seekers. Germany now has agreements with neighboring states permitting rejection of applicants at the border if they have passed through a "safe country"—that is, a country that has an asylum process that meets international standards and is not itself a source of asylum-seekers. For example, Bonn returns asylum-seekers who travel through Poland to claim asylum in Germany. The German government supplies funds under its bilateral agreement to meet the additional costs Poland incurs. The intention is to send the message that safe haven may be found in Eastern Europe if one is fleeing danger and persecution. While there is a right to seek asylum, asylum-seekers have no right to choose the country in which it will be granted.

Governments admit that fewer asylum-seekers may settle in Western Europe. They argue, however, that many of those screened out through rapid procedures would also be excluded through more elaborate processing. They maintain that streamlining does not reduce access to asylum but rather makes asylum processing more efficient. Asylum is still available, but not necessarily in Western Europe. If would-be asylum claimants choose to stay home rather than receive safe haven in Poland or Hungary, this merely calls into question how genuine their asylum claims were in the first place.

Many critics argue that these moves have reduced genuinely persecuted people's access to safe haven. Many European countries now require that citizens of the former Yugoslavia (notably those from Bosnia and Kosovo) possess entry visas. Because diplomatic representation is scarce in the successor states of Yugoslavia, would-be applicants must travel to a neighboring country to apply for a visa. If they go first to Germany, then neither Britain nor Sweden will entertain their asylum requests because Germany is a safe country.

The United States also has made asylum consistently difficult to obtain for applicants from the Western Hemisphere. In 1980, the United States adopted a policy intended to screen people in refugee camps in an orderly way and transport them to the United States for permanent settlement. The ink on the legislation, signed in March 1980, was hardly dry when the Mariel boat lift from Cuba to the United States began in April. The Marielitos were the decade's first case of what was to become the major refugee issue of the 1980s for the United States—asylum claims by Central Americans and Caribbean Islanders. Successive U.S. presidents tried to avoid the transformation of orderly refugee resettlement into a massive asylum program.

The United States has followed an unofficial policy of not being a first asylum country for the Western Hemisphere. U.S. policies toward migration and asylum claims by or on behalf of Nicaraguans, Salvadorans, Guatemalans and Haitians support this interpretation. During the Reagan and Bush administrations, the acceptance rate for Central American asylum applicants was low, often in the single digits. For example, in 1981, President Reagan introduced a policy of interdicting Haitians on the high seas and providing quick adjudication on board ship or at the Guantanamo Naval Base in Cuba. In 1992, the Bush administration adopted a policy to return interdicted Haitians directly to Haiti without hearings. Haitians must apply within Haiti for asylum to the United States. President Clinton has continued this policy. The Supreme Court of the United States has permitted the practice to stand, holding that it does not violate treaty obligations. Large-scale migration from Haiti or Cuba remains a distinct worry for the State Department and the Immigration and Naturalization Service. While Cubans continue to be treated differently, because of U.S. opposition to the Castro regime and the political influence of the Cuban-American community, there has been no attempt to encourage or accommodate large-scale emigration even from Cuba.

The United States plans to accept about 122,000 refugees for resettlement from overseas in fiscal year 1994, most of them from the former Soviet Union or Vietnam. In contrast, most asylum applicants come from the Western Hemisphere, 62 percent in 1993. El Salvadorans and Nicaraguans are arriving in smaller numbers, only to be replaced by Guatemalans, who, in 1992, accounted for 44,000 (42 percent) of the 104,000 asylum applications received in the United States. The island nations of Haiti and Cuba present the greatest risk of mass, uncontrolled movement to the United States in the near future.

Canada adopted a law in December 1992 that tightened asylum adjudication and permitted Canadian authorities to return applicants to a safe country in which they had been turned down, or through which they had passed without requesting protection. The purpose is to reduce asylum shopping—asylum applicants going to a country with the easiest criteria or with procedures that permit a lengthy adjudication.

ECONOMIC INTEGRATION

In both Europe and North America, economic integration is complicating efforts to deal with asylum. The European Union's plans to do away with internal borders mean that every member country will be affected by the asylum policy, practice and capacity of every other member. Like many issues affecting national identity in the E.U. context, this has been controversial. Any immigration policy that *de jure* or *de facto* increases membership in a country increases the potential pool of E.U. internal migrants.

In North America, on the other hand, economic integration has not included the issue of free movement. The Canada-U.S. Free Trade Agreement and NAFTA contain migration provisions that simplify movement of non-immigrants for business purposes, but neither agreement gives citizens access to residence and work across an open border. Therefore, there is no question, as in Europe, of a direct link between integration and migration. However, economic links and Mexico's potential attractiveness to refugees as its economy grows tie together the interests of the North American partners more closely on issues related to asylum seeking, such as political and economic conditions in Central America and the Caribbean. Mexico is now a country of immigration, with large movements from Guatemala and El Salvador over its southern border, even while it remains a significant country of emigration. It is in the interests of Canada and the United States to discuss with Mexico the harmonization of asylum and refugee policy and practice. Furthermore, cooperation among the North American partners on asylum issues and, more generally, on migration policy, will add to NAFTA's success.

THE DRIVE TO HARMONIZE POLICIES

In response to rising applications for asylum, combined with economic integration and slow growth, industrial countries have sought to coordinate their asylum policies. "Harmonization" became the buzzword for attempts to agree upon and implement policies, undertaken jointly or collectively or, if pursued unilaterally, that nevertheless are compatible and similar in goals, content and style. As previously noted, over 100 meetings among developed countries of Europe and North America addressed this issue in 30 forums in 1991 alone. These diplomatic forums have been distinctively intergovernmental. Each government reserved for itself the competence to deal with the issue. Only in the case of the European Commission of the European Union with Maastricht Treaty has any multilateral body been given powers over migration, and even these are limited. States have the right and obligation to protect their borders, including deciding who may enter and under what conditions. The state is expected to protect its citizenry and culture from being overwhelmed by undue external influences, strengthening national integrity and continuity through protective educational and institutional means. Prevailing concepts of the nation include the right to preserve a culture and the way of life, and the state is expected to strengthen cultural integrity and continuity through education, cultural institutions and efforts to protect national cultures from "undue" external influences. The controversy over films and television production in the Uruguay Round of the General Agreement on Tariffs and Trade is an example of states' sensitivity to what they perceive as their obligations in such matters. State policies on education, language, cultural institutions and even integration services given to refugees on arrival merely underscore the widespread acceptance of the government's role in maintaining cultural integrity. The close relation of protecting borders to the traditional concept of an international community based on nation-states makes transfer of entry control to a multilateral agency controversial. States are reluctant to cede asylum decisions to the United Nations or any other multilateral body. Issues of citizenship and entry, of culture and language and of political values and structure, cut close to the core of nation-states' vital functions.

The proliferation of diplomatic forums reflects the lack of existing bodies with the right mix of members to deal with the many facets of migration. In Europe, for example, the E.C. member states had to address migration and asylum issues to achieve a single market, but the Twelve realized that they had to reach out collectively even to countries outside Europe to address other issues like East-West movement and cooperation among all industrial countries facing massive asylum claims. The end of Soviet hegemony in East Central Europe and the collapse of the Soviet Union itself continue to pose a threat of massive migration that would affect all of Western Europe, including nonmembers of the European Union, as well as the North Atlantic partners, Canada and the United States.

Even when migration and asylum issues were taken up in existing forums, discussion often occurred outside normal institutional frameworks in various ad hoc committees, informal groups and periodic meetings referred to as "processes." Migration issues did not fit easily into existing forums, and special arrangements were developed to formulate policies. Special-purpose, multilateral agencies (like UNHCR) had mandates that did not directly address important aspects of the bond presumed to underlie liberal democracies—national integrity, fundamental political values and legitimation of the state through self-government rooted in nationality (and often an ethnically based national identity).

Both Canada and the United States participated with European countries in forums that discussed asylum, including visa requirements, carrier sanctions and the choice of "safe" countries. Canada has sought the signature of the United States and some European countries to a Memorandum of Understanding specifying criteria for determining which country should decide on a application for asylum. The basic concept is that people who travel through a safe country but do not seek asylum will be returned there for asylum adjudication. In other words, if a person from Central America went to Canada through the United States and requested asylum only upon arriving in Canada, Canada would return the applicant to the United States to decide on the application. This is to prevent asylum shopping. The idea is similar to arrangements proposed in Europe's Dublin and Schengen agreements and the bilateral accords that Germany struck with Poland and Hungary, with Bonn paying the costs. Canada proposes to share some of the burden this more orderly system may impose on the United States by voluntarily adjudicating some cases during a phase-in period. Neither the United States nor Europe has embraced the Canadian proposal, probably for the same reason. Under its proposed memorandum, asylum-seekers would move only out of Canada, not into it.

These European and American discussions have involved a large expenditure of diplomatic resources and yielded precious little collective action. Broad agreements like Dublin and Schengen, to say nothing of grander schemes like a single market for migration in the European Union, have taken much time to conclude and remain to be implemented. To put things into perspective, there have been fewer than ten years of diplomatic effort. The discussion involves such fundamental principles as sovereignty, identify, security and social stability. It is no wonder that states and their citizens balk at solutions that challenge these basic values.

If one looks at these diplomatic efforts not in terms of substantive solutions but as a search for governance models, their richness and ingenuity is amazing, even if that creativity may sometimes make substantive results harder to achieve. The expansion of forums to discuss various aspects of migration and to accommodate different mixes of participants runs the risk of diffuse or uncoordinated actions or inaction. The Declaration of the Rhodes European Council of 1988 mandated the establishment of a group of national coordinators on the Freedom of Movement of Persons precisely in response to the proliferation of groups and subgroups dealing with asylum, refugee and migration issues.

On the other hand, that governments have even discussed issues that were heretofore in the realm of sovereign rights is a major change. In the past decade they have reached common understandings about the nature of the asylum issue and shared goals, and adopted unilateral policies that mirror or harmonize with those of their neighbors. Collective asylum policies may be incorporated into expanded mandates of existing organizations. Or asylum may be a new problem that requires new institutions for cooperative action. Alternatively, the current pattern of harmonizing individual state programs through discussion may persist.

REGIONAL INITIATIVES

In the course of meetings in Europe and in North America, negotiators have generally presumed asylum processes have an important regional character, and this has caused tension between states and UNHCR. While UNHCR has called for regional political efforts to resolve refugee-producing conflicts,

UNHCR has taken a dim view of states' efforts to organize regionally to agree on policy and programs.

Tensions between governments and UNHCR were evident in discussions about policies regarding the former Yugoslavia held in the framework of the Intergovernmental Consultations (IGC), an ad hoc mechanism involving 13 European governments, the United States, Canada and Australia. The IGC, funded by the member states, has an agreement with UNHCR to provide administrative services and UNHCR itself is a participant in the IGC. In the summer of 1992, a few member governments requested the assistance of the IGC secretariat in organizing a meeting limited to themselves (an action for which there were precedents on other issues) to discuss policies toward the former Yugoslavia that UNHCR considered to be at odds with its own policy line. The tension was over the proper role of states and a U.N. agency. Should a U.N. agency seek to block states from using a mechanism for which they directly pay when the agency objects to the orientation of the meeting? The matter is complex and arouses deep feelings. Regional efforts to share the burden of asylum in Europe, while supported by UNHCR in principle, can simultaneously challenge that agency, if it perceives that such efforts contradict or weaken global humanitarian standards for the protection of asylum-seekers and refugees. Sometimes governments wish to meet to discuss issues and share ideas without being held to certain positions. States emphatically refuse to concede their final sovereign responsibility for policy making to the United Nations or any other multilateral agency. This dispute concerns not just UNHCR's participation in the deliberations of IGC member states, but initiatives in policymaking, influence and the authority to make or veto decisions.

Neither the governments nor the publics of European countries universally support a goal of regional agreements on asylum. The difficulties in achieving ratification of the Dublin Convention are a case in point. The outcome of regional discussions to date has been to restrict access to European countries and, at least potentially, to threaten asylum as an option for the politically persecuted. Broadly speaking, within governments, foreign ministries are more open to multilateral institutions, even those with strong representation by developing countries that send migrants and asylum-seekers to Europe. Diplomats work in such an atmosphere and their willingness to accommodate their counterparts may overshadow the domestic implications of cooperation. When the issue involves refugee and asylum flows, not to some distant country but to an industrial country itself, policy influence shifts to officials responsible for home affairs, who tend to believe that states should continue to make the key decisions about migration. Until very recently in the development of the E.C./E.U., for example, migration and asylum issues were the almost exclusive concern of interior and justice ministers working out the procedures and policy to implement the single market. In the various European forums developed to discuss asylum, interior ministry representatives dominated or were highly visible members of delegations—not unusual for international meetings.

A major concern of European governments has been security; some fear that asylum programs may admit terrorists or that large-scale immigration, including refugees, may destabilize their countries. Recent diplomatic efforts such as the UNHCR meeting on asylum-seekers and refugees in May 1985, the Schengen Agreement in June 1985, and the Stockholm meeting in November of 1985, which included the leading European countries of asylum, were all intended to address security concerns and build domestic support for sustainable asylum programs.

While asylum remains a humanitarian issue, it has always contained an element of state self-interest. States act collectively when another state does not or cannot do what is normally expected of a sovereign state. Ever since states first developed intergovernmental agencies to deal with refugees, beginning in 1921 with the League of Nations, governments have cooperated on behalf of refugees outside their country of citizenship. Such actions do not necessarily require intervention on the territory of the state from which refugees have come. Rather, the international refugee regime is a collective effort to deal with the failure of individual states to protect their citizens, threatening other states with the influx of multitudes without documentation, protection or means of subsistence. Refugee programs and grants of asylum are not just humanitarian gestures by states. Beyond upholding human rights values, such collective programs, as well as state adherence to their obligations under international conventions, also have addressed a collective threat to the stability and operation of the nation-state system.

North American governments may also be according greater weight to security considerations in dealing with asylum and migration. A Clinton administration proposal to reorganize the U.S. State Department assigns responsibility for population and migration policy, along with refugee policy and programs, to the former Refugee Bureau under an assistant secretary reporting to a new undersecretary for Global Affairs, whose other responsibilities include the environment, human rights, terrorism and drugs. The Defense Department has created an office to develop training and doctrine on humanitarian responses by the military. The Central Intelligence Agency has established an office with a similar focus on humanitarian issues.

Meanwhile, strategic study think tanks and foundations in Europe and especially in North America are turning to "soft security" issues like population growth, migration, drugs and terrorism in their conferences and proposals. These developments indicate a trend toward defining migrants, refugees and asylum applicants as major security challenges. Asylum and refugee issues are no longer seen exclusively as humanitarian matters. The reputation and influence of the strategic analysis wing in academia, think tanks and the government increase the probability that security concerns will be asserted in future discussions.

In addition, trilateral and bilateral meetings in North America also suggest a trend toward regional state-led initiatives. This is not at all surprising in light of the United States' long-standing aversion to influence by multilateral agencies. Washington has not used UNHCR to assist or provide guidance on refugee and asylum issues on its own territory. The United States has always preferred to channel most development assistance directly through the U.S. Agency of International Development rather than through U.N. agencies. Consensus and regional cooperation arrived at through discussion still preserve the state initiative and freedom of action so prized by opponents of multilateralism.

It is easy to assert that these trends toward a regional and security-minded approach reveal double standards. Human rights supporters and others concerned with protection of refugees pressure governments not to give in to fear or prejudice. They consider asylum essential to the integrity of the liberal democratic values that states claim they are trying to protect by restricting access. Human rights supporters point out that acknowledgement of longstanding pluralism, even in so-called homogeneous societies, is one way to overcome hesitation and fear of foreigners in need of protection and help. UNHCR and the human rights communities emphasize the need to protect hard-won universal standards in refugee work. Current regional discussions, with their emphasis on control and reducing unfounded claims, seem to them to threaten asylum and UNHCR's refugee protection mandate.

The counterargument is that Western countries are *de facto* being asked to provide not safe haven but resettlement. Their critics often do not acknowledge that the asylum system is abused. The need to have public support for asylum or any other migration policy cannot be brushed aside by demands for greater moral leadership.

These philosophical and institutional trends already have borne fruit in both European and North American law, regulation and programs. First, as noted, many countries adopted triage procedures to remove manifestly unfounded applications for asylum. Second, they have simplified procedures to reduce time-consuming advisory opinions and other mechanisms that have contributed to long backlogs in adjudication. Third, many countries have adopted the safe country concept and now refuse entry at the border of a safe country or have entered into agreements to return asylum-seekers to safe countries. Finally, states are increasing resources for more staff and modern technology to process applications, to prevent multiple applications in different countries and to protect borders.

In contrast, most intergovernmental regional efforts have not gone beyond discussion. Collective initiatives may develop in the future, but they are likely to be confined to the European Union and other close economic unions.

States have harmonized policy, however, by adopting similar legislation and procedures, and by concluding bilateral agreements, especially those establishing programs between countries with common borders. If states act unilaterally in a similar fashion in their sovereign capacities, the outcome for the asylum applicants may be indistinguishable from a response under the authority of an international agency. Although states have not achieved a high level of joint action on asylum through multilateral agencies, even in the context of the European Union, discussions by participant states in the many forums on both sides of the Atlantic have led to common understandings and similar laws and regulations that have tightened up access to asylum procedures, reduced the number of reviews and increased information sharing among states.

Asylum applications declined in many countries following state initiatives on asylum procedures. Between February and October of 1992, Canada reported 25,500 applications for asylum. After passage of asylum legislation, applications fell to 13,000 over the same 9-month period in 1993. Applications fell in other countries that took "defensive" measures. Between 1991 and 1992, applications for asylum in Switzerland declined from 41,600 to 18,100; in the United Kingdom, from 57,700 to 24,600; in France, from 46,500 to 27,500; and in Austria, from 27,300 to 16,200. Such legislation, however, may prompt many who formerly used asylum procedures to enter illegally.

CONCLUSION

Attempts to harmonize asylum policy must consider the issue of sovereignty. Control of access at the border is assumed to be one of its essential elements. Yet the European Union has required modifying individual states' absolute claims to control of entry. In a similar manner, safe country agreements for determining which country should adjudicate an asylum application may add to a country's caseload, even if the applicant has already left the country and never applied for asylum while there. To be sure, a state may repudiate an agreement, and this can be used to argue that sovereignty is not being relinquished. In reality, the practice of sovereignty is modified if states pursue cooperation to regularize and manage what seems beyond their capacity to manage unilaterally.

While regional and security-oriented approaches are in tension with global and humanitarian orientation, it is misleading to present these alternatives as mutually exclusive. A regional approach can maintain universal standards in a particular regional context. Inefficient procedures that allow delays are not synonymous with protecting the right to seek asylum. A tension remains, however, concerning not only theory and doctrine but also budgets and control of multilateral agencies.

At this point, much of the debate over asylum policy gives the impression that these approaches are incompatible. "Global humanitarians" claim that a regional or security-oriented stance is an attempt to destroy the asylum system and endangers persecuted people. Those emphasizing the central role of states and security concerns condemn the former group's failure to acknowledge abuse of the system, waning public support and the legitimacy of concerns about security as unrealistic at best and, at worst, as a greater threat to the political viability of asylum than any tightening of access.

UNHCR will most likely continue to play a central role in refugee and asylum policy making and program implementation around the world. The office's past performance, its mandate and its reputation for nonpolitical, humanitarian policies remain strong sources of influence. States, however, will insist that ultimately they retain the right and responsibility to decide what constitutes a danger to their territories and citizens. States will continue to remind supporters of asylum that claims must be defensible and systems fair and efficient if support for asylum is to be maintained.

We suspect that asylum claims will fall off and that developed countries will seek alternatives to asylum that provide refuge within the developing world, including within safe areas of their own countries. Regional burden sharing and regional efforts to reach consensus about asylum and refugee policy and procedures will continue. Disputes will also continue about whether such efforts violate global standards. States are likely to abandon sovereignty in such matters, but neither are human rights supporters, intergovernmental agencies, concerned citizens or even governments themselves likely to forsake international standards that have developed over the past 70 years. Asylum systems in many countries will change, but that does not mean that they will be destroyed.

Editor's Note: This article has been edited for publication.

Immigration and Criminality in the U.S.A.

John Tanton and Wayne Lutton

Criminal activities committed by immigrant aliens in the U.S.A. have escalated dramatically. Aliens are crowding local, state and federal jails across the country. The U.S. Bureau of Prisons reports that more than 20 percent of federal inmates are non-U.S. citizens, from over 120 countries. Half were convicted on drug offenses and most are subject to deportation.

"If we think the 20 percent figure is high, what is worse is that seven out of eight [criminal] aliens are either released or given probation and never serve time in prison," explained Representative Lamar Smith (R-Texas), a member of the House Judiciary Subcommittee on Immigration, Refugees, and International Law.

For the U.S. population as a whole, the incarceration rate in federal and state prisons is 233 per 100,000 persons. Among illegal aliens, the incarceration rate is three times the U.S. average. Since 1980 there has been a 600 percent increase in alien inmates, principally for drug-related offenses. Over the past five years, an average of more than 72,000 aliens have been arrested annually on drug charges.

Under current immigration laws and procedures, frighteningly large numbers of newcomers see crime as their avenue to the American dream.

FOREIGN CRIME SYNDICATES TARGET U.S.

The FBI warns that international crime and terrorist organizations have placed America under siege. INS spokesman Gary Renick noted that crime bosses in such places as Columbia, Mexico, Nigeria, South Korea, Japan, and Hong Kong view the U.S. as an especially inviting "land of opportunity." According to the INS, organized criminals of each nationality seem to specialize: Colombians in cocaine; Mexicans in marijuana, alien smuggling, and auto theft; Nigerians in heroin, student-loan and credit-card fraud; Chinese in heroin, and alien smuggling; South Koreans in prostitution; Russians in drugs and insurance fraud; Jamaicans in cocaine.

The Journal of Social, Political and Economic Studies, Summer 1993, 217–234.

Since the mid-1980s, major crime operations have not only come to be directed by foreign nationals, but staffed by them as well, instead of employing American agents. An INS report titled, *The Newest Criminals: The Emergence of Non-Traditional Organized Ethnic Crime Groups and INS's Role in Combating Them,* says that many of the ethnic criminal organizations exist in their native countries and simply expand into the United States. Said David Leroy, chief of domestic intelligence for the U.S. Drug Enforcement Administration, "Ethnic gangs appear to be the *new* trend in crime."

Criminal activities in the U.S. run by Third World natives can be traced back to the Immigration Act of 1965 and failure to control immigration. The social effects of the 1965 Act were not felt immediately. Only after a "critical mass" of foreign colonists arrived here, did law enforcement agencies begin to learn about the presence of criminal elements among the new immigrants. As the *U.S. News and World Report* conceded, "it is startling the degree to which the clout of newer ethnic gangs is reflective of immigration trends."

ASIAN CRIMINAL ORGANIZATIONS

The Triads

The Triads date back to the 17th century, when Han Chinese founded secret societies to resist the foreign Manchu invaders and restore the Ming dynasty. By the end of the 19th century, many Triads had largely abandoned their political idealism and transformed themselves into sophisticated criminal enterprises. Leading politicians, including Dr. Sun Yat-sen and Chiang Kai-shek, found it expedient to trade favors with the powerful Triads, whose opportunities for profits improved after the Manchus were finally overthrown in 1911.

Triads have been active in Hong Kong since 1842. During World War II, they often cooperated with the Japanese. In time, they came to control the dockyards. After Mao-Tse-Tung seized power on the mainland in 1949, some Triads moved to Hong Kong and others to Macao (the Portuguese colony near Hong Kong that comes under the authority of Beijing in 1999) and Taiwan. Today, most Triads are based in Hong Kong and Taiwan, with branches operating in other parts of Asia, Europe, Canada, and the United States. According to the Royal Hong Kong Police Force, approximately 50 Triad societies are active there, with a combined membership of some 300,000. One society, the 14 K Triad, has nearly 40,000 members. The State of California Attorney General's Office reports that the Wo Hop To Triad, which is one of the most active Triads in California, has an active membership of 28,000.

Alien smuggling has become an important part of their work. *The Washington Post* reported on Feb. 9, 1993 that more than 60 international routes are used to illegally bring 100,000 Chinese nationals into the U.S. each year [and additional tens of thousands into Canada and Australia as well]. The individuals pay huge fees to the professional smugglers, often ranging from $25,000 to $50,000, for this "service." Those who are taxable to pay in advance settle the balance of their debt by becoming indentured to Triad-controlled businesses over here, especially garment sweatshops, prostitution rings, gambling operations, and drug dealing.

Writing in *The Christian Science Monitor,* December 24, 1991, Arm Scott Tyson revealed that, "The Chinese groups tend to specialize in certain kinds of crime in big cities. Fujianese criminals in New York tend to be involved in violent crime. Cantonese from China's Guangdong Province operate vice and extortion rackets in San Francisco, and Taiwanese crime groups are active in money laundering and white collar crime in Los Angeles and Houston."

The Triads' most important source of wealth derives from their control of the major supplies of heroin. The hilly area bordering Burma, Laos, and Thailand, known as the "Golden Triangle," is where over 70 percent of the world's opium is grown. As investigator Gerald Posner points out in his study of the *Triads, Warlords of Crime,* "Without heroin they are just another group of criminals. With heroin they have a potential for profit unmatched in the annals of organized crime."

The FBI reports that Asian youth gangs, notably Vietnamese "refugees" and their American-born offspring, employed as "street muscle" by the Triads, operate in the U.S. through Tongs. (The world "Tong," derived from "Town Hall," describes fronts that often publicly engage in charitable work in Chinese communities). These Asian syndicates pose special problems for law enforcement, since their members are bound to secrecy, and because the almost insurmountable barriers of language, dialect, and culture make prosecution difficult in the extreme including reading arrestees their Miranda rights, not just in the proper language, but in the correct dialect!

Federal officials say that New York City has become the central hub for Chinese criminal operations that extend to Boston, Philadelphia, Dallas, Houston, and Portland. San Francisco and Los Angeles are their West Coast headquarters.

The forthcoming transfer of control of Hong Kong to Communist China in 1997 has spurred a flight from the colony. Among those seeking refuge elsewhere are the Triads, whose destinations of preference are the United States, Canada, and Australia. Some Triad chiefs, known as "dragon heads," are suspected of trying to take advantage of the new visa category that permits immigration by individuals who promise to invest a million dollars in the U.S.

The Wah Ching

The Wah Ching is a one-time street gang that has evolved into a sophisticated organized crime group. With international ties to Hong Kong and Taiwan

Triads, its U.S. base of operations is San Francisco, with powerful factions working out of other California cities, including Monterey Park, Los Angeles, and Oakland.

Like the Triads, the Wah Ching is engaged in gambling, prostitution, extortion infiltration of businesses, and drug trafficking. They also own myriad legitimate businesses.

Membership in the Wah Ching is growing, thanks in large part to their active recruitment of Viet Ching gang members. "Viet Ching" are gangs made up of youths who are ethnic Chinese from Vietnam.

In his annual report to the legislature, *Organized Crime in California,* the state Attorney General details Wah Ching activities, including their growing involvement in *pai gow* gambling (*pai gow* is a Chinese high-stakes game played with domino tiles). Through the California-based Productions Entertainment Company, they also play a major role in the Chinese entertainment industry, which includes arranging concert tours to the U.S. of Oriental actors, as well as distributing Chinese video cassettes in this country. Overseas tours are controlled by the San Yee On Triad of Hong Kong. Triads control the worldwide distribution of Chinese videos originating in Hong Kong and Taiwan.

The Yakuza

The Yakuza are the Japanese crime syndicates. According to Japan's National Police Agency, they have well over 100,000 members divided among 3,300 "families" and federations. Four years ago, their annual income was estimated to exceed $10 billion. Among Asian criminals today, they rank second only to the Chinese Triads in power.

In the United States, as elsewhere, they are involved in drug smuggling, gunrunning (to Japan), extortion, money laundering, pornography, and prostitution. The California Attorney General warns that they are reinvesting the proceeds from their criminal activities in legitimate businesses throughout this country. The Securities and Exchange Commission, in July 1991, revealed that President George Bush's brother, Prescott, acted as a consultant for companies controlled by Yakuza godfather Susumu Ishii that were interested in buying small American firms (see *Business Week,* July 8, 1991, p. 29).

Over twenty years ago, Yakuza started "casing" the site of Hawaii. As David Kaplan and Alec Dubro observe in their book, *Yakuza: Japan's Criminal Underworld,* "Given the dollar value of Yakuza-related enterprises, Hawaii is becoming dependent on Yakuza investment . . . The money is now part of the economic structure of the islands. "It is in Hawaii, perhaps, that the future can best be seen, where a panoply of Eastern and Western gangsters cooperate."

CARIBBEAN CRIMINALS

Jamaican Posses

According to *U.S. News & World Report,* Jamaican criminals are "probably the most active after the Asians among the newer ethnic gangs." Known as *posses,* they got their start smuggling marijuana into the U.S. They moved into cocaine after discovering the huge profits to be made dealing that product. In many American cities, Jamaicans now dominate the crack market. As Al Lamberti of the Broward (Florida) Sheriff's Department pointed out, "They're moving American blacks off the street corners. And they're ready to use whatever violence is necessary to do the job." James Scott of the Miami-Dade police added, "We've worked with all sorts of ethnic groups involved in the drug trade—Cubans, Colombians, American blacks. But none of these have the weaponry the Jamaicans do."

Over thirty posses have been identified by law enforcement agencies. Some of the bigger gangs, such as the "Spangler" and "Shower" posses, are now involved in the international gunrunning trade.

Many of these Jamaican gangsters are adherents of the Rastafarian religious cult and have been enormously successful, particularly in Brooklyn. Newcomer criminals from Panama have mimicked Rastafarian hair locks and dress as a way of breaking into their drug operations.

Haitians

North America is now home to a Haitian population equalling over one-sixth of Haiti's 6.3 million people. A loosely structured network of Haitian criminals is engaged in drug dealing, car thefts, and armed robbers. A major source of income is prostitution.

In late 1990, as reported in the *Montreal Gazette,* the Montreal, Quebec police broke a notorious cross-border gang that operated in Canada and the United States. Hundreds of Haitians were arrested who had forced into prostitution young Canadian and U.S. women, a number of whom were taken from foster homes. They were subjected to unspeakable treatment. A spokesman for the Haitian community complained that "by targeting a single gang, police risk fueling racist feelings."

It is noteworthy that many of the Haitians who have engaged in crime originally came to the U.S. as refugees, or were recruited by the Quebec Immigration Ministry when it sought to bring in more French-speaking people. On both sides of the border, many Haitian neighborhoods have become violent, crime-ridden slums. French language newspapers have coined a new word to describe the transformation: *se bronxifier*—to become like the Bronx.

Cubans

In the Spring of 1980, Fidel Castro opened the Cuban port of Mariel to those wishing to leave. Among the 125,000 who took advantage of this opportunity to migrate to the United States were thousands of criminals, sex offenders, and mental patients. Police officials and fellow refugees place the number of undesirables at 40,000. The Marielitos brought no records with them. U.S. authorities could not even verify their names.

The Cubans who arrived here in the 1980 boatlift differ dramatically from the first waves of refugees who came over between 1959–1962. The Marielitos were younger, less educated, poorer, included fewer families, and had fewer U.S. ties.

From Miami, Marielito crime has spread across America. According to a report prepared by the Las Vegas Police Department, "a national conspiracy exists" among Cuban "refugee" criminals. They have specialized in such crimes as airline ticket fraud, credit card fraud, and drug dealing.

Local police officials from around the country complain that the federal government has done little to aid them in combatting refugee-related crime. For reasons that remain unclear, the Federal Bureau of Investigation does not collect information on refugee crime. As a spokesman for the FBI, Manuel Marquez, said, "It's just not our problem."

Few of the Marielitos who have committed felonies in the United States have been expelled, as federal law mandates. Over the past twelve years, the government has engaged in largely fruitless negotiations with the Cuban dictator, but only a few felons actually have been returned. Castro has made it clear that he doesn't want them back. And, ethnic lobbyists and civil rights activists have created further impediments to deporting anybody to Cuba. In the meantime, Cuban criminals detained at U.S. prisons staged destructive uprisings in 1987 and 1991.

The results of a poll conducted by Mason-Dixon Opinion Research should come as no surprise: 77 percent of the non-Hispanic whites and 72 percent of the non-Hispanic blacks said the quality of life in Florida has been hurt by emigration from Cuba. Only 1 percent said they believe Florida has been helped by Cuban emigration.

OTHER NEWER ETHNIC GANGS

Russian Emigres

Insight magazine reports that, "among the 100,000 Soviet immigrants in the United States, most of whom are Jewish emigres, the so-called 'Russian mafia' has shown a penchant for get-rich schemes and a ready willingness to use extreme violence to Jack up their operations."

According to the President's Commission on Organized Crime, Soviet authorities took advantage of special emigration rights granted to Jews and, over the past twenty years, "included a significant number of criminals who were forced to leave Russia." The Presidential Commission suggested that by means of Jewish emigration, "The Soviet Union attempted to empty their prisons and rid their society of undesirables, much as Fidel Castro did several years later during the Mariel boatlift."

Federal authorities estimate that at least a dozen Russian gangs operate out the greater New York area, with the Brighton Beach section of Brooklyn serving as their headquarters. Other groups are based in Los Angeles, San Francisco, Portland, Dallas, Miami, Chicago, Cleveland, Boston, and Philadelphia.

Their activities include extortion, loan-sharking, counterfeiting, arson, insurance fraud, burglary, murder-for-hire, and cocaine and heroin dealing. Cooperating with the Italian Mafia, they have become increasingly involved in the bootleg gasoline trade. Distributors deliver gasoline to service stations, but fail to pass on the federal excise taxes collected. In November, 1991, a leading Russian emigre gangster, Oleg Yasko, was convicted in California for skimming 40 cents in unpaid taxes on each gallon of gasoline his company delivered to other wholesalers and retail service sections.

In July 1991, federal authorities broke one of the biggest cases of medical fraud in history, when they arrested the twelve leaders of Michael and David Smushkevichs' emigre ring. Michael traveled around the world with passports from the Soviet Union, Israel, and Mexico. The Smushkevichs used mobile medical clinics to attract patients with promises of free tests, and then billed some 14,000 insurance companies for over $1 billion in phony claims. "It ranks right up with the Drexel Burnham insider stock trading case," said David Smith, head of the Postal Inspection Service in Los Angeles.

The Los Angeles Times reports that "ill-gotten gains in this country are being shipped back home [to Russia] to some of the estimated 5,000 crime syndicates there so they can get an upper hand economically as the once-communist economies move to a free market." Displaced former members of the KGB are suspected of being involved.

The U.S. Justice Department considers the Russian gangs to be an "emerging crime problem." On April 14, 1992, the newly formed federal task force on Russian emigre crime held its first meeting in Los Angeles. Like other ethnic criminal organizations, Russian gangs have evolved through three major stages: extortion of their own people; expansion into other crimes; and movement into legitimate businesses.

Israelis

Organized crime in Israel reached a peak in the mid-1970s. Vigorous police work encouraged the Israeli crime element to emigrate. Many moved to the United States. In the Northeast, Florida, and on the West Coast, Israeli gangs, "comprised mostly of Sephardic Jews born in Arab countries, are increasingly active in the U.S. heroin trade," according to *U.S. News & World Report*.

Los Angeles County sheriff Sherman Block told *The Jerusalem Post* that the potent Israeli mafia has spread across America, graduating from extorting money from poor and elderly Jews—many of them former concentration camp inmates—to major drug dealing and fraud schemes against the wealthy. A veteran Drug Enforcement Administrator agent testified, "We have seen Israelis buying heroin in Pakistan, Turkey, and Thailand. We are now seeing their ability to interact with other criminal groups, including La Cosa Nostra [and] the Chinese." Peter Moses and Carl Pelleck reported in the *New York Post* that while the Israelis currently deal mainly in heroin, they are now moving into cocaine.

Nigerians

Nigerian citizens, many of whom enter on student visas, are part of an international crime syndicate headquartered in Washington, D.C. and now active across the country. They specialize in huge drug deals and major fraud schemes, and are among the most violent of criminals.

The Nigerians have obtained a growing share of the American heroin trade. Much of the contraband enters the U.S. through Customs via Canada into New York and Michigan. In 1990, one of the biggest heroin bust recorded in the Midwest involved Ojo Adighibe, a Nigerian living in Grand Rapids, Michigan, who had heroin stashed in typewriters shipped to his stateside address from his homeland.

Law enforcement authorities admit that Nigerians are difficult to deal with. They tend to organize locally into small "cells" of five to twelve members, each headed by a boss. Members often are relatives or members of the same tribe—frequently Ibo or Yoruba. They like to cooperate with each other. If apprehended, few will inform on their fellow cell members.

Furthermore, federal authorities do not keep track of foreign "students" to see that they remain registered in school and are attending classes. Nigerian students recruited by criminal gangs will often remain in school, but reduce their course load. Others stop attending altogether. Student visas are issues for up to five years and there is no mechanism in place to monitor the holder's compliance with the law.

Nigerians are among the foremost perpetrators of credit card fraud. A California police report on the 'Nigerian mafia' discloses that they are responsible for over $1 billion in credit card losses every year. An "African church" in Los Angeles fronts as a training school, where Nigerian immigrants are taught the niceties of this trade. One method used to obtain credit card information illegally is to take employment in hospitals, hotels, post offices, and the mail rooms of corporations and apartments. There they can acquire names, addresses, and social security numbers, which are then used to apply for credit card issuers and giving them a new address. Phony letters of credit are also employed to gain access to our financial network.

One ring was broken by Houston, Texas postal authorities in August 1991. Nigerian Ikembe Azikiwe offered letter carriers $3,000 for each MasterCard or Visa 'Goldcard' they turned over, and 50 percent of the value of any large commercial checks they were able to steal. Azikikwe boasted that a friend of his, engaged in the same work in Chicago, was able to steal enough in one week to pay cash for a new Mercedes. The U.S. Postal Inspection Service, in its *Law Enforcement Report,* Fall 1991, pointed out that, "attempted bribery of postal employees is being conducted on relatively large scale basis by criminal elements within the Nigerian community."

Even when they are arrested, many Nigerians, like other felons, are released on bond and then fail to show up for trial. Lawyers representing bonding companies sometimes make up false death certificates, reporting that their client has died and asking for bond release.

THE IMPACT ON THREE MAJOR STATES

The impact of the new alien crime wave is being felt nationwide, but is acute in states with large alien populations. And the dollar costs do not adequately reflect the burden on society of additional crime. The administration of justice—including bilingual interpreters and court-appointed attorneys—is bogged down by the necessity of dealing with foreign-born criminals.

California

Michael D. Antonovich of the Board of Supervisors, Los Angeles County, recently stated that "The hard evidence is that criminal aliens are committing serious crimes." Furthermore, according to a California state Senate report issued on March 23, 1993, "State and local governments in California spend more than $500 million a year to arrest, try and imprison illegal aliens who commit serious crimes,

The legal costs of dealing with all types of crimes by illegal aliens could run as high as $1.5 billion, according to an estimate included in the report.

"The California Attorney General reports that approximately 16,000 illegal alien felons are incarcerated in state prisons. Every year it costs California taxpayers $350 million to keep these criminal aliens behind bars."

A study commissioned by the San Diego Association of Governments found that one in four jail inmates acknowledged being in this country illegally.

Judges estimate that up to 35 percent of the felony cases in Superior Court involve illegals. A 1990 check in felony disposition court discovered that 41 percent of the defendants had immigration "holds"—on completion of sentence, they would be released to the INS for detention.

As a test, Orange County Superior Court Judge David O. Carter invited the INS (Immigration and Naturalization Service) into his courtroom to help identify criminal aliens and develop deportation cases against them. Judge Carter informed the House Judiciary Committee that;

> the results are staggering . . . My criminal calendar is 36 percent illegal felons. These statistics would be much higher except the INS does not place holds on illegal felons who have stated the amnesty processor come from countries where the United States is an adversary and has no extradition authority. Vietnam, Cambodia, Iran and Cuba are some of the most obvious countries which will not accept extradited felons.

Orange Police Chief Merrill Duncan disclosed during a press conference in April 1992 that the 12 percent increase in crime from the previous year in that city is the result of a "tremendous influx of illegal aliens." He added that, "most crime suspects are illegals."

New York

Twelve percent of the nearly 58,000 inmates in New York's state correctional system are foreign born (either illegal aliens or legally admitted aliens who have committed crimes). The Governor's office report it costs taxpayers $27,000 per alien, per year, to house these criminals, or about $183 million annually. Nearly half of the foreign-born inmates in New York come from Caribbean nations.

On April 27, 1992, the state of New York filed a suit against the Federal Government, demanding that it start taking custody of thousands of illegal aliens currently incarcerated in state prisons. The suit charges that the Federal Government is responsible for taking charge of these inmates and launching deportation proceedings against them. But too often, the U.S. Justice Department fails to do that. Once convicts serve their terms, the state is forced to simply release them onto the street, where they are often arrested for new crimes.

Texas

In the Texas state prison system, only 4.3 percent of the inmates are foreign-born. But this is because, as *The Dallas Morning News* pointed out in its February 2, 1992 issue, "the state in effect uses municipal and county jails to house some of its prisoners. In the largest jail on the Texas-Mexico border, the county facility at El Paso, the percentage of criminal aliens ranges from 10 to 15 percent of the inmate population. Of the federal inmates in Texas, 36 percent are foreign-born." How extensively aliens are involved in crime throughout the state is difficult to determine, since many jurisdictions, such as Dallas, keep no statistics on the nationality of criminals.

STREET GANGS

As "refugee" communities have sprung up across the nation, new efficiently-based youth gangs have emerged. They are heavily involved in the drug trade and are responsible for a growing portion of the violence that wracks America's metropolitan areas.

This gang culture belies the media-created image of immigrants as "model citizens." For example, in California, as reported by *The New York Times,* "the simmering ethnic stew pot that is Los Angeles seems to favor youth gang activity. Gangs of almost every nationality flourish: Samoan, Filipino, Salvadoran, Mexican, Korean, Vietnamese. Experts estimate there are about 600 gangs . . ." Law enforcement officials put the current number of members for these gangs at over 100,000. In nearby Long Beach, a war between Cambodian and Hispanic gangs has been raging for over two years.

Gang activity is no longer limited to the traditional areas of immigrant settlement. As new immigrants have migrated to the Midwest, America's heartland has come to experience the ethnic 'violence that plagues the East and West Coasts, Florida, and the Southwest. In Chicago, the police are doing battle against not only black and Hispanic gangs, but Assyrians, Chinese, Cambodians, Vietnamese, Filipinos, and Greeks.

Symptomatic of the trend, St. Paul, Minnesota law enforcement officials have called for tough measures to combat Asian teen crime in the wake of a rash of major burglaries, including gun shops. Special programs to divert Asian youth from lives of crime have been authorized by the state legislature in an effort to manage the problem.

The western Michigan communities of Holland and Grand Rapids are experiencing a rise in violence attributable to young Asian males. A confidential police memo circulated in 1991 identified several gangs operating locally and regionally, such as "38 Crew," "Oriental Posse," "Crips With an Attitude," and "BBC" (Born Before Christ). Police admit that they have been reluctant to discuss the problem openly. The area has seen a huge increase in its Asian population, "many of them church-sponsored immigrants," the *Grand Rapids Press* reported.

As bad as the situation is now, the problems created in the U.S. by our new immigrant street gangs are bound to become much worse in the future if corrective measures are not quickly enacted and strictly enforced.

CROSS-BORDER AUTO THEFT

Along our border with Mexico, auto theft has become a multi-million dollar growth industry. Thieves in California and Texas communities, including some Mexican law enforcement officers, charge several hundred dollars to steal cars and zip across the border to Mexico. Teens are favored as drivers, since they face little more than a mild rebuke if they are arrested.

High-priced luxury cars and off-road vehicles, such as Jeeps and Broncos, are prized. The cars are shipped from Mexico to buyers in Latin America, Europe, and the Middle East. Before the Persian Gulf war, many vehicles were bound for Kuwait.

Because U.S. Customs does not check identification of outgoing cars, it is relatively easy for thieves to cross the Mexican border headed south. "It's almost a license to steal," Lt. Bob Samples of the Los Angeles Police Department remarked.

THE WAR ON DRUGS

The celebrated U.S. "War on Drugs" has been three-pronged: trying to eradicate drugs where they are grown and manufactured, called "going to the source;" a nationwide education effort to discourage drug use by youngsters; stepped up law enforcement. Thus far, the campaign has not been marked by much success. Despite generous increases in foreign aid to countries where cocaine, heroin, and marijuana are produced, production has soared. This is hardly surprising, given that profits generated by the drug trade are far greater than those deriving from other cash crops.

When faced with issues that require decisive action, Americans have come to rely on "education" as the preferred, safe response. While the "Just Say No!" campaign may have heightened public awareness, among those elements of the U.S. population most inclined to use drugs, such education has proved to be a remarkable failure. Drug use is actually growing.

Law enforcement agencies nationwide have been overwhelmed by drug-related crime. Courts are backlogged for years, to the extent that even with special "drug courts," other pressing cases are delayed for months and even years. Many serious crimes are being plea-bargained away by local prosecutors, and others are not even taken into court. America's jails and prisons are overflowing with inmates convicted of drug-related offenses.

No matter how much apologists for America's promiscuous immigration policy may wish to obfuscate the issue, one cannot separate the illegal drug and immigration problems from one another. Back in 1986, then Attorney General Edwin Meese informed Congress that, "The reality is that immigration is contributing to the drug problem." He pointed out that drug smugglers "get lost in the crowd" of aliens crossing the border and that traffickers regularly use aliens to transport drugs into the U.S.

The international dimension of the drug trade in America highlights the failure of past policies to protect the nation's interests. Federal officials concede that foreign nationals not only are responsible for producing virtually all of the drugs consumed in the U.S., but are in charge of nearly all of the distribution.

Cocaine, and its inexpensive, smokeable derivative, "crack," is produced in the Andes, refined in Columbia and Mexico, and distributed worldwide by Colombian drug lords who cooperate with other foreign nationals, including Panamanians, Nicaraguans, Mexicans, Jamaicans, Dominicans, Haitians, Nigerians, Indians, Pakistanis, and Asians.

Florida remains a major hub for their North American operations. The drug trade has pumped billions of dollars into the Sunshine State's economy. But as Florida, which sits astride the major air and trade routes from South America, has come under increasing surveillance by law enforcement, our porous border with Mexico has become the path favored by foreign suppliers. As one Colombian drug dealer told a Miami-based colleague, "Come to California. It's the promised land."

All along the border, from California through Texas, small communities have sprung up that serve as staging areas for the US-bound shipments. Mexican burros smuggle drugs across the border. As Tom McDermott of the U.S. Customs Service explained, "There are a lot of advantages" to using Mexican routes. "They can stage loads in Mexico with little or no risk, and they have a nice interstate highway system to get to their markets."

The drug trade generates billions of dollars in profits, with an increasing portion being reinvested in the U.S. and used to purchase real estate and legitimate businesses.

Although it is viewed as a "friendly" country by many Americans, Mexico remains among the top sources of heroin and marijuana, and the major supply route for cocaine. Mexico City routinely promises to cooperate with U.S.-sponsored anti-drug efforts. William van Raab, customs chief under President Reagan, is among those who charge that official complicity in the international drug trade reaches high levels of the Mexican government (c.f., Elaine Shannon in *Desperados: Latin Drug Lords, U.S. Lawmen, and the War America Can't Win*. The White House and State Department have been reluctant to highlight the role played by ranking Mexican political figures in the drug commerce.

Cocaine and marijuana are only two of the most popular drugs being smuggled into the U.S. Heroin continues to generate billions of dollars of profit annually. Since President Nixon declared his own "war on drugs" in 1971, the number of heroin addicts in this country has increased by several hundred thousand. In a number of metropolitan areas, nearly three-quarters of urban crime is committed by heroin users. The millions of dollars spent on anti-heroin education have done little to discourage heroin usage. Only the deadly disease AIDS has actually reduced the number of junkies. Dealers have now developed a smokeable version of heroin, which they have already introduced to America.

Like cocaine, the burgeoning heroin trade is dominated by aliens. *The New York Times* reported, "As the Mafia's role declines, the multi-billion-dollar heroin trade is increasingly being conducted by criminal organizations that together sound like a United Nations of drug smugglers, including Chinese, Thais, Pakistanis, Indian, Iranians, Afghans, Nigerians, and Israelis." Robert Stutman, a special agent for the FBI, noted that "these groups are posing a major challenge to law enforcement. We now are dealing with languages and cultures that we have no real depth in."

Until the federal government is willing to secure our borders, there is little hope that the "war on drugs" can be won.

CONCLUSION

The alien-related crime that plagues the United States is one of the consequences of its failure to enact and enforce sensible immigration controls. The problem posed by alien criminals is not new. Since the early days of the Republic, foreign criminal elements have viewed this as a "land of opportunity."

In past years, American legislators passed laws to try to keep criminals out. But its current leaders lack the same will. Few communities in America have gone untouched by alien-related crime. As Prof. James O'Kane of Drew University observes in his new book, *The Crooked Ladder:* (Transaction, 1992):

> Ethnic organized crime among current minority newcomers is flourishing and ever-expanding, with no end in sight. . . . Police and organized crime task forces scarcely know what to do about these new groups and have their hands full merely trying to describe these activities, let alone control them. With respect to certain groups (e.g. Chinese, Japanese, Vietnamese, and Soviet Jews), police even lack undercover agents who speak the same language as the newcomer criminals.
>
> The prognosis for the elimination of ethnic organized crime is indeed grim. Compounding this reality is an equally depressing one: many of the former lower-income ethnic criminals have not necessarily become law-abiding citizens. Many simply have "moved up to white collar crime, and as such, have blended with their dominant groups in American life . . . We constantly delude ourselves that ethnic organized crime is "on the way out."

Editor's Note: This article has been edited for publication.